# AN INTRODUCTION TO THE REFORMED TRADITION:
## A WAY OF BEING THE CHRISTIAN COMMUNITY

# AN INTRODUCTION
# TO
# THE REFORMED TRADITION

## *A Way of Being the Christian Community*

Revised Edition

## JOHN H. LEITH

John Knox Press
ATLANTA

Library of Congress Cataloging in Publication Data

Leith, John H.
  An introduction to the reformed tradition.

  Includes bibliographical references and indexes.
  1.  Theology, Reformed Church.  I.  Title.
BX9422.2.L45     1981      230'.5      81–5968
ISBN 0–8042–0479–9                     AACR2

© copyright 1977 and 1981 John Knox Press
10 9 8 7 6 5 4 3 2
Revised edition, 1981
Printed in the United States of America
John Knox Press
Atlanta, Georgia 30365

To the Congregation of
The First Presbyterian Church, Auburn, Alabama
Who in a Remarkable Way Embodied
the Reformed Tradition

# *Preface*

This study of the Reformed tradition is motivated by gratitude for a heritage that has nurtured and shaped the writer's own life and by the conviction that the tradition provides resources, clues, and inspiration for life in the last quarter of the twentieth century. Ancient traditions that have been tested by time and that carry with them the wisdom of the race provide depth and perspective in a day when life is frequently rootless, shallow, and even banal. Yet traditions can provide this depth only when gratitude for them is balanced by critical judgment of them. No one tradition exhausts the meaning of Christian faith, and every tradition has its share of false starts, mistaken judgments, and betrayals of its own best convictions. The Reformed tradition has been one of the authentic and powerful ways in which Christian people have lived out their faith. It has much to offer contemporary human beings as they attempt to be Christian in the grand and awful days in which we are living, but only if it is appropriated by a living community that unites appreciation with critical acumen.

The church has never found it easy to balance gratitude with critical judgment. Gratitude easily becomes nostalgia for the past, and critical judgment slips into contempt. Prior to the Second World War churchmen were very much aware of the past. At least this was particularly true of American Presbyterianism. The great need was an openness to the new demands of the present and the future. Today in a highly pluralistic, secular society that exaggerates its unique and transitional nature few need to be reminded of the claims of the future. History is not a primary concern of modern people. Openness to the future is no longer the issue.

There is evidence, however, that an open future without the guidance of a tradition is so formidable a challenge that many cope with it by resorting to such *ersatz*, strange traditions as the revival of astrology, divination, shamanism, and magic even on college campuses. Hence there is a need for a presentation of the Reformed tradition that is appreciative yet critical and that is comprehensive but manageable in scope for the churchman.

It is hoped that this study will be a help to those who are beginning their theological education. It is also hoped that it will be of value to leaders in local churches who want to draw on the riches of their own tradition as they seek to be Reformed churchmen in the twentieth century. This particular study proposes to be an introduction to the Reformed tradition, not a history of Reformed churches or a comprehensive statement of Reformed faith and practice. It presupposes the many books that render these services, in particular such works as John T. McNeill's *The History and Character of Calvinism.*

The Reformed tradition cannot be precisely defined. Here it is broadly understood to be that pattern of Protestant Christianity which has its roots in the sixteenth-century Reformation in Switzerland and Strasbourg. The tradition is well established theologically by the authoritative achievements of Calvin's *Institutes of the Christian Religion* in the sixteenth century and Karl Barth's *Church Dogmatics* in the twentieth. Other aspects of the tradition do not have such definitive statements. No one creed, liturgy, or polity can be defined as typically Reformed. This study does not claim to exhaust the Reformed tradition. It does claim to be an authentic presentation. Care has been taken to base the study upon primary materials in theology, liturgy, and polity that belong to central, not peripheral, strands of the tradition. Hence it is hoped that while much has been omitted, everything that has been included is genuinely Reformed. Furthermore, the study has focused upon English-speaking Presbyterians and especially upon the tradition in the United States. It is hoped that this will make the book more useful for American Presbyterians, but unfortunately this focus will not do justice to others who have an equal right to the tradition.

Many persons have contributed to whatever virtues this book may have. Teachers, colleagues, students, and institutions have all played their part. Erskine College and Columbia Theological Seminary were important in my early theological training. Appreciation must be expressed particularly for my Yale University teachers, Professors Roland H. Bainton and Albert C. Outler. My colleagues Mathias Rissi, James L. Mays, John Bright, Charles Swezey, Paul Lehmann, and E. T. Thompson have helped me on specific points. Professor Roland M. Frye of the University of Pennsylvania has in many friendly conversations enlarged my appreciation of the Reformed tradition. He has also reviewed the chapter on the Reformed tradition and culture. Professor Alec C. Cheyne of New College, University of Edinburgh, has enhanced my knowledge of the Reformed tradition through his friendship and has made helpful suggestions for portions of the manuscript. I. John Hesselink, President of Western Theological Seminary, has not only supplied the photograph of Karl Barth and Emil Brunner, but he has also provided helpful advice about the Dutch Reformed tradition. Union Theological Seminary in Virginia, under the leadership of President Fred R. Stair, Jr., has been an indispensable source of support and help. Neely D. McCarter, Dean of the Faculty, has given every proper encouragement. The Union Theological Seminary Library deserves a specific word of gratitude, and John Trotti, the Librarian, and Martha Aycock, the Reference Librarian, deserve special mention. The Advanced Religious Studies Foundation of Texas made possible the study by a generous grant. New College and the University of Edinburgh graciously provided during my 1974 sabbatic leave the comforts of Abden House and the privileges of a visiting professor. John McIntyre, Acting Principal of the University, and D.W.D. Shaw, Dean of New College, were gracious hosts in Edinburgh, that old and engaging center of the Reformed and Presbyterian traditions. Richmond Smith, Secretary of the Department of Theology of the World Alliance of Reformed Churches, provided the membership statistics of the Alliance churches and welcomed me to his office in Geneva. The theological concern and commitment of Richard Ray, editor of the John Knox Press, have been important factors from the beginning. The first draft of the manuscript was typed by Mary D. Herndon of the seminary staff; and the draft delivered to John Knox Press was edited and typed by my wife, Ann White Leith. Joan Crawford of John Knox Press worked faithfully on the manuscript.

Traditions are learned first of all from the living community, not from books. So it is most appropriate to dedicate this book to the congregation of the First Presbyterian Church, Auburn, Alabama, where the writer was pastor during the years 1948–

1959. Included also in this dedication are Greenville Presbyterian Church (South Carolina Presbytery), where the writer was baptized and where he worshiped his first twenty-one years, and the other congregations that he served in the ministry of the Word: Silver Creek Presbyterian Church, Lindale, Georgia; the congregation that gathered on Sunday afternoons (1943) in Spring Hill, Alabama, subsequently becoming Spring Hill Presbyterian Church; and the Second Presbyterian Church, Nashville, Tennessee.

This new edition provides an opportunity to make revisions and additions in the light of several recent studies and of suggestions by reviewers and friends including Ford Lewis Battles, James I. McCord, John Kromminga, Howard Hageman, John Hesselink, Edward Dowey, and David Willis. When once printed books are not easily altered. Hence, they have to stand as they were written. In this case I still affirm what I wrote five to six years ago.

I am grateful for and encouraged by the use to which this book has been put in the general life of the church, in church school classes, and in officer training, as well as in the academic setting of universities and seminaries.

John H. Leith
November 1980

# Contents

# AN INTRODUCTION TO THE REFORMED TRADITION:
## A WAY OF BEING THE CHRISTIAN COMMUNITY

# I

# TRADITIONING
# THE FAITH

Tradition and the gospel are indissolubly united. Each is indispensable to the other and to the life of the Christian community. The gospel is God's will "for us men, and for our salvation"[1] as it has been worked out and disclosed in God's revelation of himself, especially in that segment of history culminating in Jesus Christ and in the giving of the Holy Spirit at Pentecost. Tradition is the authoritative delivery of this gospel from believer to believer, from community to community, from generation to generation. Thus tradition has two uses. It may refer to the *act* of passing on, and it may refer to *what* is passed on. The New Testament speaks of the "faith which was once for all delivered to the saints." (Jude 1:3) This delivery is fundamentally God's handing over of Jesus Christ (cf. Romans 8:31–32) "to share our existence and to effect our salvation."[2] It is secondarily the human act of authoritatively delivering this gospel to all people through the succeeding centuries. This secondary traditioning of the faith, this handing on of the gospel in an authoritative and living way, is essential to the life of the Christian community. Emil Brunner has put it very well.

> Tradition is necessarily involved with the unique revelation of God in the historical facts concerning Jesus Christ. This unique historical event, in which the disclosure of salvation is contained, must be conveyed to later generations in order that they may share in its saving benefits. *Paradosis, traditio* belongs, therefore, to the very nature of the Gospel; to preach the Gospel means necessarily and always to transmit an account of what has happened for man's salvation. Without tradition, no Gospel.[3]

## The Tradition and the Traditions

*(a) The living tradition.* The traditioning of the faith is always the transmission of a living, growing reality, not of an impersonal

thing. The transmission of the faith does of course include many impersonal things which are important for the living community. Significant among them are buildings, sacramental vessels, organizational structures, literature, endowments, and even the Bible itself. Just as a son may inherit his father's bank account, so a new generation of Christians may inherit not only buildings and endowments but even an accumulation of the means of grace. Faith itself, however, cannot be handed on as an impersonal thing any more than a father can hand on his courage in the same way he bequeaths his bank account. Even buildings have to be remodeled, structures have to be revised, and literature has to be enlarged. The Christian community is a living community, and its life has to be traditioned in a living way. This is to say the tradition is always alive, open to its own time and the future, never fixed.

The Bible, as an object that can be mechanically handed on, appears to contradict this emphasis on the living character of the tradition. For this reason it must be noted here that the Bible is the concretion, the putting into writing, of the tradition in a particular time and place. The Bible is the original witness to and interpretation of God's revelation and work "for us men and for our salvation" in Jesus Christ. In this sense the Bible is the church's memory reduced to writing by the prophets and the apostles who were the original witnesses of and believers in God's revelation and work that constituted his people. The inspiration of the Scriptures is the divine inspiration of this original witness and interpretation, and it is the inspiration of the Holy Spirit in the hearing of the Word of God in Scripture today. The Bible as the forward and backward looking testimony to Jesus Christ sets the boundaries and is the unique authorization for all Christian theology and life. Yet it cannot be handed on in a mechanical way or impersonally assimilated. It is properly read and heard only in the living tradition of the church, under the living inspiration of the Holy Spirit by persons who are very much alive, that is who respond by faith.

The high place that Protestantism has always given the Bible obscures the importance of the living tradition even for the Bible itself. Consequently, it is crucial to emphasize that the Bible was written within the living Christian community and tradition; and when it is properly understood, it is read and heard within this same living community and tradition. The importance of the living tradition becomes clear if we can imagine some holocaust blotting out all traces of the Christian community so that no knowledge of it remains. Then if we can further imagine someone's walking amid the ruins of some western city and stumbling upon a sealed box containing the Bible, let us now estimate the possibility of the Bible alone without a living community, without a living interpreter, giving rise to a new Christian community. The chances would be very small or nonexistent.[4]

The importance of a living tradition for the transmission of any faith or any perspective that must be personally assimilated is true for many areas of life. Émile Bréhier in his important history of philosophy has noted that

> philosophical thought is not one of those stable realities which, once discovered, continues to exist like a technical invention. Philosophical thought is constantly in question, constantly in danger of being lost in formulas which, by fixing it, betray it. The spiritual life exists only in the undertaking, and not in the possession of a supposed acquired truth.[5]

This is a precise description of the significance of the living tradition, rooted in past centuries but alive to the future, for the transmission of faith commitments, styles of life, and perspectives on the universe and its meaning. A living tradition is indispensable to the transmission of human qualities and of communal faith and ways of living. The church has continued through the centuries by telling the story and inviting the hearer into a lively community.

*(b) The human tradition.* The act of traditioning, of handing on the gospel, is also a very *human* as well as a *living* act. The confusion of local customs with the gospel, the sanctification of parochial prejudices are all a part of it. The tradition is filled with false starts and wrong turns. Yet in the darkest times Jesus Christ has been presented, and by the power of the Holy Spirit the Christian community has survived. Moreover, the traditions of the church have exhibited an amazing power to purge, to reform, and to redirect themselves in the light of the original tradition as attested in Scripture.

*(c) Tradition as the work of the Holy Spirit.* The traditioning of the faith is not only a living and human act; it is also a work of the Holy Spirit. Albert Outler has stated this with clarity and insight.

This divine 'tradition,' or *paradosis,* was a divine act in human history—and it is renewed and made contemporary in the ongoing course of history by the act of God's Holy Spirit, whom Jesus 'handed over' to his disciples in the last hour on the cross (παρεξωκεν το πνευμα John 13:30). The Holy Spirit—'sent by the Father in my name' (John 14:25)—re-creates the original act of tradition *(traditum)* by an act of 'traditioning' *(actus tradendi),* so that the tradition of Jesus Christ becomes a living force in later lives and in faith based on response to a contemporary witness. It is this *actus tradendi* which changes a man's historical knowledge of Jesus Christ —far away and long ago—into vital faith in Jesus Christ—'*my* Lord and *my* God!'[6]

The traditioning of the faith as a human phenomenon is not to be simply identified with the work of the Holy Spirit. In fact, the recognition of the work of the Holy Spirit in the tradition is finally an act of faith. Amid all the paraphernalia of traditioning, some good, some bad, some indifferent, there is still the reality of the church and of the Holy Spirit. This is the Christian confession even in the darkest hour of the church. If the doctrine of infallibility has any meaning for Protestants, it is precisely at this point. No Protestant can believe that any human being or any institution is ever wise enough or good enough to be at any point exempt from mistakes. Protestant Christians may and do believe that in the providence and mercy of God the Christian community is preserved from making a final and fatal mistake.

*(d) Jesus Christ as the tradition.* Jesus Christ is the *tradition,* and the human act of traditioning what God did "for us men, and for our salvation" in Jesus Christ is always subordinate to him. For Protestants and for the Reformed community, this subordination has been expressed in the supreme authority that has been ascribed in the life of the church to the Holy Spirit speaking through Scripture. The early reformers set the Bible over against all human tradition. Their protest against the aberrations of the human traditions at times seemed to suggest that tradition had no significance at all. The Bible alone became the religion of Protestants, or so it seemed. Yet the Bible was never alone. Calvin himself spoke in highest terms of the authority of the Bible, but he always read and heard the Bible in terms of the traditions. He revised his liturgy according to the practices of the ancient church, and he worked out his polity with a great appreciation of the way polity had developed in the early church. He wrote his

*Institutes* in the framework of the Apostles' Creed, and he studied Scripture and did his theological work with the help of countless interpreters and theologians of the preceding centuries. Calvin did not worship the Bible or the church and its traditions but the God who had visited his people in Jesus Christ.

Protestants have always been tempted to believe that they could somehow omit all the centuries of Christian history and read the Bible without either the help or hindrances of those who have gone before. In actual fact those who have refused to read the Bible in the light of the church traditions have always read it in the light of the traditions of their own history and culture. Karl Barth, the great Reformed theologian of the twentieth century, has written,

> In actual fact, there has never been a Biblicist who for all his grandiloquent appeal directly to Scripture against the fathers and tradition has proved himself so independent of the spirit and philosophy of his age and especially of his favourite religious ideas that in his teaching he has actually allowed the Bible and the Bible alone to speak reliably by means or in spite of his anti-traditionalism.[7]

Barth goes on to affirm that Reformed theology along with Roman Catholicism has had its church fathers or teachers of the church, but these fathers or teachers of the faith are clearly subordinate to the authority of Scripture. In the early church, Athanasius and Augustine are teachers of the church for Protestants and Roman Catholics. Barth also has a place for the medieval theologians Thomas, Anselm, and Bonaventura. The authority of a father of the church is real but relative to that of other fellow pupils. Only some teachers are "teachers of the church" or "church fathers."

> Not every Church witness who at some point and period is an example and stimulus to certain members of the Church is for that reason a father, to whom the Church can and must trust itself, in the sense that the line held by him is the right one for it. This real guidance of the Church, as it was exercised by Luther and Calvin, is a rare thing.[8]

Yet even in the case of Luther and Calvin the function of a "teacher of the church" is to point to Scripture and Jesus Christ. Enthusiasm for a "teacher of the church" must not crowd out the worship of God that makes the church the church. " 'Of course, I stand in the Reformed tradition,' " Barth declared, " 'but I believe, as Calvin did, that there is only one Master in the church and in the world. Consequently, I try to be obedient to Christ and not to Calvin.' "[9] Jeanne d'Albret (1528–1572), the remarkable leader of the French Reformed Church, was truly Reformed when she wrote her cousin, Cardinal d'Armagnac, "I follow Beza, Calvin, and others only in so far as they follow Scripture."

*(e) The traditions.* From the very beginning, the Christian traditions have been diverse. There is no one uniform act of traditioning in the New Testament. The handing on of the gospel by Peter was different from the way the gospel was handed on by John and by Paul. The consensus of the ancient catholic church was real, but it did not obscure its diversities: Jewish Christianity, Hellenistic Christianity, the special versions elaborated by the Nestorians, the Monophysites, the Montanists, the Donatists, and many others. Some of these small and isolated traditions continue to exist today as the Coptic, Syrian, Armenian, and Nestorian Christians, all with small communities in the United States.

The major division between Eastern and Western Christianity was present very early and was clearly official in 1054. Eastern Christendom, divided into autocephalous, national churches, has remained strange and foreign to Christians of western Europe. Only recently have western Christians begun to understand and to appreciate the unfamiliar Christian practices of the Eastern churches. Western Christendom itself was split in the sixteenth century with the major division between western Catholicism that centered in Rome and Protestantism. Protestantism fragmented at a rapid rate. In part, the fragmentation of Protestantism was due to geographical isolation and the emergence of powerful nation-states. In part, it was due to the Protestant conviction, which accepted the risk of division as preferable to any institution or authority with power to dictate how Christian communities were to read the Bible. The emphasis upon the Holy Spirit's speaking through Scripture as the final authority and upon the obligation of all believers as priests before God to take responsibility for their own faith was a source of Protestant strength and also of divisiveness.

Particular Christian traditions are all subordinate to the tradition, the revelation of God in Jesus Christ, who is Lord of the Christian community in all its manifestations. Furthermore, the particular traditions with their parochial and partial perspectives cannot be properly isolated from the fullness of the one, holy, catholic, and apostolic church that no particular tradition fully embodies. This is the meaning of ecumenical, catholic Christianity. The Reformed community and tradition must therefore always be understood in the larger context of the Christian community and in the context of other traditions that in their various ways bear witness to God's grace in Jesus Christ. The Reformed tradition shares a common faith and a common tradition with all those who believe that the God who created the heavens and the earth has visited his people in a decisive and definitive way in Jesus Christ. The Apostles' Creed, the Nicene Creed, and the Chalcedonian Definition are the primary theological statements of this universal Christian tradition. The Reformed tradition and community is also a part of the Protestant community. As such, it shares with other Protestants the basic affirmations of Martin Luther's great writings of 1520: (1) The final authority of the Holy Spirit's speaking through Scripture, (2) Justification by grace through faith, (3) The priesthood of all believers, (4) The sanctity of the common life, (5) The radical rejection of magic in Christian belief and practice.[11] These emphases give to Protestant Christianity a particular character and style. Within the Protestant community the Reformed community is distinguished from the Lutherans, the Anglicans, and the more radical Protestants (e.g., the Mennonites). The uniqueness of the Reformed tradition will be explicated in this book; but as has been indicated in the preface, this cannot be simply done, for the Reformed tradition has its own diversities created by the influence of theologians, cultures, histories, and experiences with particular Christian and non-Christian neighbors.

Reformed (and Presbyterian) Christians can therefore identify themselves as (1) Christian, (2) Protestant, (3) Reformed, and (4) belonging to a particular denomination in a particular national setting. The order in this process of definition has some importance. The particular situation may make one term in the total identification more important at one time than another. It also ought to be clear that *Christian* is not only the most comprehensive but the most important identification. Furthermore, the awareness that Jesus Christ is Lord of all of our traditions, even of our definitions of basic Christianity, is the first article of the faith. A clear distinction must be made between the *tradition* (Jesus Christ and the gospel of God's salvation in him) and the traditions, and this distinction must never be violated.

## A Secular and Pluralistic Society

The Christian community began its existence as a small, politically insignificant group subject to police action whenever it upset the established order. By the third century, however, the Christian community was rightly seen as a threat to the pretensions of the Roman Empire. Emperor worship was the peg on which Romans could hang their faith that the meaning of life was to be found in the rationally ordered society of Rome.[12] The Christian conviction that Jesus Christ alone is Lord was subversive of any absolutist claims of the state and of any claims of salvation by its order. The state therefore took the Christian community with great seriousness and sought to eliminate it in the third-century persecutions. Constantine, the emperor, became a Christian, however; and the Christian community received official toleration and then imperial favors. Under the emperor Theodosius, the empire became officially Christian. Thus there came into being Christendom, a community, a dominion, that is officially Christian in all its members.[13] Local congregations became parish churches. A parish church defined the local congregation in terms of geography, one church in a geographical area. This church was responsible for all the people in that area, and they in turn were officially related to it. Thus in the thirteenth century, medieval Europe was a Christian society. This does not mean that everyone was Christian but that the society was Christian in its symbols, in its official allegiances, and in its organization.

The mainstream of the Protestant Reformation did not reject the idea of Christendom or of the parish church. Calvin thought, as did the Westminster Assembly a century later, that the parish was the best arrangement for local congregations. Calvin knew that Christendom was an illusion; but instead of rejecting the idea, he sought with great vigor to make it a reality, to see that church and community were at least coextensive in Geneva.

Christendom and the parish church were made obsolete by three movements. The first, the secularization of society from the thirteenth century onward, gradually removed many areas of life from the dominion of the church and the theologian. By the twentieth century in much of the West the state was officially secular; and most human enterprises, such as science, education, and the care of the sick, were autonomous—that is, controlled by principles and regulations that arose within the specific enterprise itself.[14] The second movement was the fragmentation of Protestantism and the emergence of the denominational pattern of church life in the seventeenth and eighteenth centuries.[15] The third movement was the development of religious freedom.[16] The combination of the denominational pattern and religious freedom meant that the old concept of one community, one church was over. The settlement of America and the challenge of the frontier provided the optimum condition for the development of voluntary churches in a free and secular society. Sociologists speak of this type of society as pluralistic; that is, a society which tolerates in the same community many different religious practices and life-styles.

The emergence of a secular and pluralistic society has been slow, and the time schedule has varied in different cultures. In the southern part of the United States, Protestantdom, if not Christendom, existed certainly until and sometimes after the Second World War. This society was in intent, if not in public law, Christian. The public schools were in considerable measure Protestant schools. Many sanctions, public and hidden, supported what was regarded as a Christian life-style. Moreover, young people grew up in the same communities with their parents, grandparents, and relatives. Community supports undergirded the transmission of the faith of the parents to the children. This support has now disintegrated. The Christian community increasingly exists today as a highly voluntary society (no pressures, legal, psychological, or social, compel people to be Christian) in a free, pluralistic, secular, mobile, industrial, urban society.

The consequence of this development is that people are freer to be or not to be Christian than they have been in many places in the West since the fifth century. The supports and sanctions of the community do not undergird the traditioning of the faith from parent to child, from generation to generation. The breakdown of the old order, the high mobility of society, the pervasiveness of the mass media make it possible for people to choose their own traditions to an extent that was never possible before.

This freedom provides exhilarating possibilities for human development. It ought to be received with gratitude. It also is the occasion for the overtaxing of human capacities for responsible decisions. Hence, the proper response to this new freedom is a certain awe because the decisions made in it are fateful for persons, the church, and the social order.

The freedoms of a pluralistic and secular society provide to the church the possibility of being its own true self in a way that more coercive societies sometimes do not. This is the new opportunity. But this new society lays upon the church new responsibilities. In Protestantdom, the faith was taught by many agencies of the community. The regular worship of God was supported by community practice. A relatively Christian style of life, at least what was conceived to be a Christian style of life, was supported by community sanctions. This is no longer the case. A free, pluralistic, secular, and mobile society expects more of young people, young married couples, and older people in both forming and maintaining their lives than perhaps any society in human history. Hence, the church must discover new ways to tradition Christian faith and life. It must learn anew to give real support to young people as they struggle with growing up and with setting the direction of life. It must learn to protect and nurture the Christian family against the forces in society that destroy it. To use an old phrase, the church must be in our time the *mother* of the faithful in a way that it did not have to be in a "Christian" or "Protestant" society.

The faith and life of the Christian community must now be traditioned, authoritatively handed on, in a society that provides people the freedom and means to choose their own traditions. In this society, many will be traditionless. Others will be the victims not simply of alien traditions but of traditions that are personally and socially destructive. Hence, in this day, the church must become critically aware of the nature of traditions and of the problems of traditioning faith and a way of life in a free, pluralistic, secular, and mobile society.

A secular and pluralistic society that offers freedom of traditions and memories is the occasion for Christian evangelism and invitation. Christian faith and commitment is life in a tradition. To be a Christian is to have Abraham, Isaac, and Jacob; Isaiah, Jeremiah, and Amos; Paul, Peter, and John; Augustine, Calvin, and Barth as one's fathers in the faith. The "story of one's life" is told not primarily in terms of biological heritage but in terms of traditions and memories that can in some measure be freely chosen.[17] Spiritual lineages are subject to change as genetical lines are not. Many Reformed Christians whose biological ancestors were natives of northern Europe know that Augustine, an African, and Paul and Abraham, ancient Semites, are their fathers in the faith and that Geneva and Jerusalem are their ancestral cities. The people of God have always been a society based not on blood but on historical experiences, as John Bright has well said.

> The existence of Israel as a people thus rested in the memory of a common experience as handed down ultimately by those who participated in it, who were the nucleus of Israel. Although we cannot control the details of the Biblical narrative, it is unquestionably based in history. There is no reason whatever to doubt that Hebrew slaves had escaped in a remarkable manner from Egypt (and under the leadership of Moses!) and that they interpreted their deliverance as the gracious intervention of Yahweh, the "new" God in whose name Moses had come to them. There is also no objective reason to doubt that these same people then moved to Sinai, where they entered into covenant with Yahweh to be his people. With that, a new society was founded where none had been before, a society based not in blood, but in historical experience and moral decision.[18]

Whenever a person becomes a member of a new community, the history of that community is appropriated as the individual's own history and memory. This has been said with classic simplicity by H. Richard Niebuhr.

> So immigrants do not become true members of the American community until they have learned to call the Pilgrims and the men of 1776 their fathers and to regard the torment of the Civil War as somehow their own. Where common memory is lacking, where men do not share in the same past there can be no real community, and where community is to be formed common memory must be created; hence the insistence on the teaching of history in modern national communities. But by the aid of such provincial memories only partial pasts can be appropriated and only limited human communities can be formed. To Christians the revelatory moment is not only something they can all remember as having happened in their common past, be they Hebrews or Greeks, slaves or free, Europeans or Africans or Americans or Asiatics, medieval men or modern. It becomes an occasion for appropriating as their own the

past of all human groups. Through Jesus Christ Christians of all races recognize the Hebrews as their fathers; they build into their lives as Englishmen or as Americans, as Italians or Germans, the memories of Abraham's loyalty, of Moses' heroic leadership, of prophetic denunciations and comfortings. All that has happened to the strange and wandering people of God becomes a part of their own past. But Jesus Christ is not only the Jew who suffered for the sins of Jews and so for our own sins; he is also the member of the Roman world-community through whom the Roman past is made our own. The history of empire through which his life and death must be understood is the history of our empire. Beyond all that, he is the man through whom the whole of human history becomes our history. Now there is nothing that is alien to us. All the struggles, searchings after light, all the wanderings of all the peoples, all the sins of men in all places become parts of our past through him. We must remember them all as having happened in and to our community. Through Christ we become immigrants into the empire of God which extends over all the world and learn to remember the history of that empire, that is of men in all times and places, as our history.[19]

In the older society of Christendom or Protestantdom the traditions and memories that constitute the Christian community could be taken for granted. This is no longer true. Evangelism as incorporation into the Christian community will now have to give more attention to memories and traditions and to their maintenance in a secular and pluralistic culture.

## The Open Tradition

Tradition is not a "good" word in common speech. For many it means old-fashioned, out of date, rigid and fixed, or past-oriented. Good reasons are in part responsible for the various negative connotations of the word. The negative impressions are rooted in the fact that traditions may die at some fixed point. Having died, they can only be repeated in a legalistic way by their adherents. When traditions die and become fixed, they may be discarded; or they may become oppressive burdens upon those who continue to live by them. The negative impression of tradition also has its source in traditionalists for whom the past is so good that the future has no possibilities of its own.

Tradition in itself is a good word. More than that, it is virtually an indispensable word. Human beings are distinguished from animals by a cultural memory, by a capacity for tradition. Animals have no traditions and no cultures. By tradition people are saved from the tyranny of the moment, and by it they gain some transcendence over time. A traditionless person is tossed about by every wind that blows at a particular moment and is bereft of perspective by which to judge the future. Tradition properly enables one to live out of the resources of the past with an openness to the future. In fact, appeal to tradition has been historically one way of opening up the future to change, even to revolution.[20]

Tradition, as has been indicated, is a human act. In the church, traditions have taken wrong turns, have turned in on themselves, and have become prematurely fixed. Contemporary fundamentalism and some types of liberalism represent the fixation of conservative and liberal traditions in the nineteenth century. There have always been liberal and conservative components of the Christian traditions. The problem arises not in the liberal and conservative components of the traditions themselves but with the fixation of the traditions in a particular time and place so that those who come after can only repeat what has been fixed in another time and place. The tradition, whether liberal or conservative, is no longer alive but dead and fit only for sterile repetition.

Traditions also have a way of isolating themselves and living according to their own internal principles. Sometimes this internalizing of tradition is a means of self-protection in the context of a hostile society. This has been the tactic of some traditions in Enlightenment cultures or in totalitarian societies in the twentieth century. Pietistic Christianity protected itself in this way from societies it could not control and from the intellectual upheavals of the nineteenth century. Yet too great an internalization of a tradition, even when necessary, always erodes its vitality. Traditions have been strongest when they have lived not only by their own internal principles but also in dialogue with the total culture.

The discarding of traditions, however, is no adequate answer to the problem of dead and aborted traditions or of traditions that are turned in upon themselves. This is abundantly clear in much contemporary church life. Since 1955,[21] theology and churchmanship have been plagued by lust for novelty and narcissistic delight in being original.[22] The result has been faddism. In a single decade it has been possible for one person to have passed through the civil rights movement, the theology of the secular, the theology of hope, black theology, political theology, the women's liberation movement, and the theology of play. In addition, there has been the Jesus movement. Some have gone from movement to movement with no place to call home. All of these movements have their positive contributions to make to the life of the church and have their rightful claim to the attention of all. Yet these movements and thematic theologies became nonproductive of constructive achievement when they monopolized the attention and energies of their adherents and thus lost perspective and the capacity for critical self-criticism. Two basic criticisms that can be made of most of the theological and social enthusiasms of the 1960s are lack of gratitude for what is given by the past and lack of capacity for critical self-judgment. The same complaints can be made concerning rootless churchmanship that has also been tossed about by every new form of worship, or experimental ministry, or management system.

The great asset of a tradition is its provision of a rich resource of accumulated wisdom that gives perspective to the present moment. Its wisdom has been tested and tried in the crucible of life, not once or twice, but many times over. Out of the wisdom and stability of living tradition, it is possible to carry on dialogue or debate with all that is contemporary and new without being tossed about by every new wind that blows. Tradition provides criteria that enable one to test the spirits. Furthermore, traditions preserve resources from the past that otherwise would be lost when they are most needed. Many elements of the Christian tradition only seem to die, and they have an amazing capacity for "resurrections from the dead." The theology of Schleiermacher was "dead" in the 1930s but alive in the 1950s. Tradition "saves" many valuable components of the Christian experience that are prematurely dismissed as dead but which are sources of light in new situations. Thus traditions give both perspective and depth to the Christian community.

Inordinate love of the past, the repetition of dead traditions as laws for contemporary life, the refusal to change are clearly destructive ways of life. Yet change in itself is not necessarily good. The future is not automatically an open door to inevitable progress. The wisdom of the past has not been outdated because it is the integrity that has been wrested out of actual human experi-

ence. Human nature is still human nature. The temptation of the
liberal spirit to reject all traditions uncritically deprives the
church of a great resource for facing the future. A more productive procedure is to test the traditions and in particular the ones
by which we live; all traditions must continually be critically reviewed and open to self-reformation. They must live and develop
not only in terms of their own internal principles but also in
dialogue, even debate and confrontation, with other traditions,
movements, and events. One of the great achievements of the
ecumenical movement has been the catholicizing of the theological enterprise. Good theologians read their own theological tradition in the context of the theology of the whole church. The
church must also learn not only from those who love her but from
those who reject her as, for example, Marxists in our time.

The living and open tradition of the church has its liberal and
conservative components. It has assimilated in a living way the
wisdom of the past, and it is open to the future. The living
tradition of the church is the indispensable link between the
believing community today and the events, witness, and interpretation that are its origin. A historian of doctrine has put it very
well. Tradition is the living faith of dead people. Traditionalism
is the dead faith of living people. For this reason tradition is a
source of the church's vitality and traditionalism the occasion of
its death.

God's salvation of men and women in Jesus Christ has been
handed on in many diverse ways. Some ways have been good,
some have been bad, and some have been indifferent. Every
generation must therefore test the tradition or traditions to see
how clearly they represent God's grace and action in Jesus Christ
to the life of faith and obedience today. Therefore, all traditions
must be received with gratitude and with critical judgment.

The Reformed tradition does not claim to be the only Christian tradition. It does claim to be *one* way the one, holy, catholic,
apostolic church has lived, handing on its faith and life to every
new generation. It does claim to be an authentic form of the
Christian community that has its special strength and also its
weaknesses and problems. It intends to be the people of God in
all their fullness. On the basis of this claim, it asks for both
acceptance and criticism.

# II

## THE REFORMED CHURCHES

The Scots Confession of 1560, declaring that the church began with Adam, thus dispelled any notion that the Protestant reformers were involved in a new enterprise.[1] They thought of themselves as engaged in the reformation of the people of God according to God's Word. No Protestant, Anglican, Reformed, or Lutheran would have dated the origin of the church from the sixteenth century. According to the popular rhetoric of the market place, when a Lutheran was asked where his church was before Luther, he replied with the question, where was your face before you washed it?[2] The Protestant Reformation was a reform, not a beginning anew.

The word Protestant has a negative sound to modern ears, but its original use was positive. A "protestation" was presented to the Second Diet of Spires (1529) contending that the new diet could not overturn the freedom that had been given the Zwinglians and Lutherans by the First Diet of Spires (1526). The protestation had a positive emphasis. It declared,

> "The Ministers shall preach the Holy Gospel according to the interpretation of the writings accepted by the Holy Christian Church. This raises the question: What is the true and Holy Church? There is no small diversity of opinion at this point. There is, we affirm, no sure preaching or doctrine but that which abides by the Word of God. According to God's command, no other doctrine should be preached. Each text of the holy and divine scriptures should be elucidated and explained by other texts. This Holy Book is in all things necessary for the Christian; it shines clearly in its own light, and is found to enlighten the darkness. We are determined by God's grace and aid to abide by God's Word alone, the Holy Gospel contained in the biblical books of the Old and New Testaments. This Word alone should be preached, and nothing that is contrary to it. It is the only Truth. It is the sure rule of all Christian doctrine and conduct. It can never fail us or deceive us. Whoso builds and abides on this foundation shall stand against all the gates of hell,

while all merely human additions and vanities set up against it must fall before the presence of God."[3]

The Reformation was above all a positive proclamation of the Christian gospel. It never depended negatively upon its opposition, for it was first of all a protest in the sense of making a solemn declaration. This positive character of the Reformation generally was pre-eminently true of the Reformation in Switzerland.

## The Beginnings

The Lutheran Reformation had its origin in the personal struggles of Martin Luther, who was tormented by the question, how can a sinful man stand in the presence of a righteous God?[4] Luther was aware of the holiness of God and of the sinfulness of man as few persons have ever been. He knew that no effort of his, whether in the monastery or in the confessional, could ever obligate God to him. The evangelical experience that God's favor and forgiveness are never earned but freely given was for him decisive. The wonder of the Divine Love that forgave the sinner was the heart of his experience and of his faith. The sale of indulgences and the sales ditty "As soon as the coin in the coffer rings, the soul from purgatory springs" were for him blasphemy. The Ninety-five Theses of October 31, 1517, dealt with a wide range of corrupt practices in the church, but the heart of it was the proclamation of God's forgiving love. "The true treasure of the church is the most holy gospel of the glory and grace of God." (Thesis 62) Luther's great writings of 1520 likewise elaborated the meaning of his evangelical experience. Luther's experience of the grace of God was no unique, eccentric experience but one that illuminated the experiences of multitudes who had been burdened by the prevalent religion of work-righteousness that oppressed people with the necessity of winning God's favor. The consequence of Luther's Ninety-five Theses, debates, writings, and preaching was a great revival of Christian faith that became the Lutheran Reformation.

## The Reformation in Switzerland

The Reformation in Switzerland was not directly dependent on the work of Martin Luther, though Luther's work in many ways influenced and shaped its development.[5] Here the Reformation grew out of the Christian humanism that was pervasive in the area. Erasmus had settled in Basel; and around him there were gathered many who were interested in the new learning, including in particular Thomas Wyttenbach. The new stirrings in religion were the work of no one person, and they were related to the Christian humanism that had been developing for years.[6]

Huldrich Zwingli, however, is rightly known as the first Swiss reformer; for it was his powerful personality, his skill as a churchman and preacher, that precipitated the Reformation. Zwingli was born January 1, 1484, two months after Luther. He received a humanist education, and as a priest he took a charge in Glarus near his childhood home in the Alps. The Alps were his home, and their imprint was stamped indelibly on his personality. After a charge at Einsiedeln he was called to the Great Minster in Zurich. He began his Zurich ministry on January 1, 1519, with the resolve that he would preach through the book of Matthew, expounding it from the pulpit page by page. For twelve years Zwingli adhered to this method, preaching through much of the Old and New Testaments. Calvin followed this same procedure in Geneva. In the application of Scripture to the life of the church the Swiss reformers were more radical than Luther. Luther wanted to eliminate from the life of the church everything condemned by Scripture, but the Swiss insisted that every Christian practice should have positive warrant in Scripture. As Zwingli himself wrote, "Eventually I came to the point where led by the Word and Spirit of God I saw the need . . . to learn the doctrine of God direct from his own Word."[7] Zwingli had experienced no personal struggles of soul comparable to Luther's, and the Reformation in Zurich began in good humanist fashion as a return to the sources of the faith in the Bible. The church would be cleansed and reformed by the study and preaching of Scripture.

The radical emphasis of the Swiss Reformation on reform according to the Word of God is the basic source of the designation "reformed." In a general sense all Protestant churches are reformed, and this designation was commonly used in the sixteenth century as a synonym for protestant and evangelical. It came to be applied specifically to the Swiss Reformation because the Swiss reformers were more stringent in applying the Biblical principle to the life of the church. Authority in the church had to have specific and positive Biblical warrant. Queen Elizabeth in a letter once referred to non-Lutheran churches as "more reformed." The Lutheran and Reformed controversies in the latter part of the sixteenth century, particularly over the sacraments and worship, emphasized the more radical character of the Swiss reform and probably contributed to the differentiation.[8] Also, Calvin's personality never was as significant for his followers as Luther the person seems to have been for the Lutheran tradition, though the Lutherans of the sixteenth century frequently expressed resentment against those who call "the dear, holy Gospel Lutheran."

Zwingli's teaching and preaching of the Word of God quickly began to transform the life and the practice of the church. The ensuing controversy, especially in the context of what was happening elsewhere, particularly in Germany, demanded some resolution or settlement. The Great Council of Zurich called disputations in 1523 which were decided in Zwingli's favor, thus insuring the continuance of his program. Images were destroyed. The Mass was declared not a sacrifice but the remembrance of a sacrifice. The worship of the church was reformed by Zwingli in the direction of a simple preaching service. A visit by Hinne Rode, a scholar from the Netherlands, introduced Zwingli to the work of Cornelius Hoen, who had interpreted "This is my body" (1 Corinthians 11:24) in the sense of "This signifies my body."[9] This insight helped Zwingli to formulate his own doctrine. For Zwingli, the Lord's Supper was a memorial of what Jesus Christ had done and an occasion for the believers to affirm their faith. The presence of Christ was spiritual, not physical. By 1525 the Lord's Supper was celebrated in Zurich according to these principles. It is probably impossible today to realize the spiritual excitement of the congregation when for the first time believers passed the bread and wine among themselves, using plain wooden plates and cups. Zwingli's teaching on the Lord's Supper was the occasion of the split between Martin Luther and Zwingli at the Marburg Colloquy in 1529. The two reformers agreed on all other major doctrines, fourteen out of fifteen articles adopted by the Colloquy. The difference, however, was rooted in the different Christian experiences of Zwingli and Luther and in Zwingli's humanist background, which was different from Luther's more traditional and conservative background.

Zwingli's leadership was to be brief. He was killed in battle against the Catholic cantons in October 1531. The Reformation that he had begun, however, could not be contained. The leadership passed to Heinrich Bullinger (1504–1575) in Zurich. He, along with leaders such as Oecolampadius (1482–1531), an outstanding scholar at Basel, and Berthold Haller (1492–1536) in Bern, carried on the tradition that Zwingli had established with skill and with piety.

The Reformation began in Geneva under the leadership of the fiery Frenchman William Farel (1489–1565). Farel was a product of the Christian humanist movement in France, which had its center around Jacques Lefèvre (1450–1536). Also, Farel had been in contact with German-speaking reformers of Zurich and Basel. The great work of reform in Geneva would be done, however, by another Frenchman, John Calvin (1509–1564). Calvin, too, began as a French humanist.[10] The authority of the Bible had figured significantly in his conversion to Protestantism, and he sought to cleanse the church by returning to its source in revelation. He can best be described as a churchman. He was a scholar, an exegete, a theologian, a preacher, a pastor. Probably more than any other Reformer, he *combined* all of these functions in his person and his work. He published the most influential statement of the Protestant faith, the *Institutes of the Christian Religion.* He reformed worship, and he initiated and sponsored the development of the Genevan Psalter, a work that would be completed by the poets Marot and Theodore Beza and the musicians Bourgeois and Goudimel. The Psalter would be one of the influential books of history. He reorganized the church, and his ecclesiastical *Ordinances* would influence polity for centuries. His commentaries and sermons qualify him as one of the great interpreters of Christian history. His vision of the Christian community and his leadership in the reformation of the city of Geneva guarantee his place in political and social history. Yet it is in his letters—eleven volumes of them in the *Corpus Reformatorum*—that the full range of the man is revealed in his pastoral concern for the Reformed movement throughout Europe. Under Calvin's leadership Geneva became the center of great influence in the development of Reformed churches through Europe. While the Reformed movement always maintained its local freedoms and varieties and while Geneva must not be thought of as the only center, the city was surely the most influential. Calvin died in 1564, and the leadership of the Genevan church passed to Theodore Beza (1519–1605), who like Calvin exercised an influence on Reformed churches throughout Europe.

The Waldensians, located chiefly in the Alps on the French-Italian border, owe their beginning to Peter Waldo, who in 1174 took seriously the words of Jesus, "If thou wilt be perfect, go sell that thou hast, and give to the poor." William Farel visited them on one of his preaching missions. They felt a strong affinity with the Protestant Reformation, partly due to their strong Biblical emphasis, and they identified themselves with the Reformed tradition.

## *Europe*

The Reformed churches in France had their origin in the Christian humanism of the first half of the sixteenth century.[11] From the 1540s on, the movement was directed in large measure from Geneva, which was free from the political control of France. A Protestant church was organized in Paris in 1555 and soon thereafter in many other cities. A national polity was worked out in 1559 which included a consistory (session), colloquy (presbytery), provincial synod, and national synod. No one church could have primacy over any other. For the first time presbyterianism was worked out on a national basis. A confession of faith was also adopted. The nucleus of this confession had been written by Reformed ministers in Paris in 1557. It was then revised by Calvin and probably by other ministers in Geneva. Further revisions were made by the assembly that adopted it in 1559. It was reaffirmed with minor revisions by the French synod that met in La Rochelle in 1571. It is highly regarded as an excellent statement of the Reformed faith.

The growth of the Reformed church in France was handicapped by the wars of religion. The Reformed believers were a minority and in political opposition to the king. Henry of Navarre, a Protestant who gave up his religion to become king, was crowned in 1594. Under his leadership the Reformed community gained freedom, though not without restrictions, with the Edict of Nantes in 1598. The revocation of this edict in 1685 led to a dispersion of the Huguenots (French Reformed), many of them coming to the United States. It is estimated that more than 300,000 fled France. The church maintained itself under the leadership of Antoine Court and Paul Rabaut during this period of persecution. An edict of liberation was secured in 1787.

The reform movement in the Netherlands began long before Martin Luther in such movements as the Brethren of the Common Life.[12] These movements were Augustinian in theology and emphasized Biblical studies as well as the devotional life. Lutheran writings were condemned as early as 1520; and two followers of Luther, Henry Voes and John Esch, were burned in 1523. Reformed influences date from the contact of Rode and Zwingli (1523), and by the late fifties the Reformed type of Protestantism was firmly entrenched. In 1561, Guy de Brès wrote a confession " 'for the faithful who are everywhere scattered through the Netherlands.' "[13] This confession, adopted by a synod at Antwerp in 1566, became known as the Belgic Confession; and with some modifications it became the confession of Dutch Reformed Protestantism along with the Heidelberg Catechism and the Canons of Dort. A presbyterial system of church government based on the French model was adopted for a national church by the synod that met in Emden in 1571. The development of the Reformed community paralleled the fight for Dutch independence. The alignment of the Reformed community with the battle for freedom against the Spanish was a source of strength for the Reformed. William the Silent, the patriot leader in the struggle for freedom, became a member of the Reformed community in 1573.

The Dutch Church was the source of diligent and able theological work and became a very influential center of Reformed thought in the late sixteenth and seventeenth centuries. It also became the scene of the best known theological debate in early Reformed history. Arminius (1560–1609), who had his roots in the Dutch tradition as well as in the Reformed theology of Geneva, sought to modify Calvin's doctrine of predestination, particularly against the exaggerated form of the doctrine as advocated by Gomarus, a Dutchman, and Theodore Beza, Calvin's successor in Geneva.[14] Arminius was especially concerned to refute any doctrine of irresistible grace, though he always insisted that no person can turn to God at all except by the grace of God. The bitter controversy that ensued was settled at the Synod of Dort in 1619. The synod took a middle road between the hyper-Calvinists and the disciples of Arminius. It reaffirmed the Calvinist doctrine of total depravity, unconditional election, limited atonement, irresistible grace, and the perseverance of the saints. The names of the doctrines were given in the heat of controversy and are not wholly accurate as to what the synod affirmed. Limited atonement meant that the atonement, while it was adequate for all, was efficacious only for the elect.[15] Irresistible grace could better have been formulated as invincible grace. Total depravity did not mean that man was totally evil but that he was crippled by sin and that at the crucial point of turning to God he was totally unable to do so apart from God's grace. While the Synod of Dort has sometimes become a symbol of extreme Calvinism, it actually sought to arrive at a consensus of the sixteenth-century Reformed community.[16]

Reformed churches were late in establishing permanent communities in the Rhineland and Germany.[17] The Reformation in Strasbourg under the leadership of Martin Bucer was friendly to the Swiss reformers. Calvin himself had served as pastor of the French church there (1538–1541). However, Martin Bucer was forced to leave Strasbourg for England during the Augsburg Interim (1548). After the Peace of Augsburg (1555), Lutheranism was firmly established. Hesse under the leadership of Philip had also been open to Reformed influences. Here Francis Lambert wrote one of the earliest Reformation polities (1526) that probably influenced later Reformed polities. Luther and Zwingli had their debate over the Lord's Supper at the University of Marburg. But again Reformed influences were excluded after the Peace of Augsburg.

The Reformed church became established in the Palatinate under the leadership of Otto Henry and his successor, the Elector Frederick III (1559–1576). Frederick affirmed the Augsburg Confession as the Peace of Augsburg required, but he also invited Reformed theologians to the Palatinate. Among them were Zacharias Ursinus and Kaspar Olevianus, who wrote as a confession for the territory the Heidelberg Catechism. Ursinus and Olevianus brought to this task a background not only in Swiss Reformed theology but also in the mild Melanchthonian Lutheranism. A distinguished faculty was gathered at the University of Heidelberg: Ursinus; Bouquin; Zanchi, a Reformed theologian who had fled Strasbourg; Erastus, a Zwinglian who believed that excommunication was a function of the state and whose name became attached to the theory that the church is subordinate to the state, a more radical notion than he espoused; and Tremellius, a Jewish-Christian scholar. After Frederick, Lutheranism was re-established and the Reformed theologians left; but the reign of Frederick's son, John Casimir (1583–1592) brought back the Reformed community. Under the leadership of David Pareus, a student of Ursinus, Heidelberg once again attracted Reformed students.

Other Reformed communities were established in Nassau and Wesel, in Brandenburg, and in scattered communities throughout German territory. Beginning with the Prussian Union of 1817, Reformed and Lutheran churches entered into confederations composed of Reformed and Lutheran territorial churches and some union churches of the two confessions. This arrangement has continued to the present time.

Reformed influence reached Poland during Calvin's lifetime. King Sigismund was one of Calvin's correspondents. John à Lasco (1499–1560), the great Polish reformer, served influential churches in London and Emden. His *Whole Form and Method of Church Service in the Church of the Strangers,* designed for the London congregation, was widely influential. He returned in 1556 to Poland to organize the Reformation churches there, but in this he did not succeed. The Counter-Reformation of the Roman Catholic Church was in the end too effective, and only a small Reformed community survived.

In Bohemia the Protestant Reformation built upon the work of the reformer John Huss (1369–1415). Most of the Hussites became Lutheran, but Reformed influences were present from the 1540s. In spite of great political handicaps that have persisted to the present time, a Reformed community still survives in what is today the nation of Czechoslovakia.

In Hungary, Lutheranism was punishable by death in 1523, an evidence of its early influence there. The association of Lutheranism with German political masters handicapped growth. Reformed theology suffered no such handicap and was easily adopted here as elsewhere by nationalist forces. Stephen Bocskay, a patriot who delivered his people from the Turks and the Holy Roman Empire, was a Calvinist; and his work is memorialized in the Reformation monument in Geneva. The Hungarian Reformed community developed a polity that included superintendents or bishops with jurisdictional status but not with any special status of order.[18]

## Great Britain

The medieval church was an easy prey when the Protestant movement reached Scotland in the 1520s.[19] A law forbidding the importation of Lutheran books was passed in 1525. Patrick Hamilton, a student of Luther, was burned in St. Andrews in 1528. The Reformed type of Protestantism was brought to Scotland by George Wishart (1513?–1546), who had studied in Switzerland and who had accepted the First Helvetic Confession. The decisive break came in 1560 under the leadership of John Knox when the Scottish Parliament adopted the Scots Confession of 1560. The Scots Confession is clearly reformed. *The First Book of Discipline,* proposed as a program of reform but not adopted in 1560, was significantly influenced by Calvin's polity and was easily open to Presbyterian development. While the General Assembly and the Session were elements of polity from the beginning, fully developed Presbyterianism was the work of Andrew Melville, who had studied in Geneva and who returned to Scotland in 1574. Reformed theology consistently dominated the history of the Church of Scotland, but presbyterianism and episcopacy struggled for ascendancy during the late sixteenth and early seventeenth centuries. Presbyterianism was vigorously reasserted in 1638 under the leadership of Alexander Henderson. After the Commonwealth period, episcopacy was again the pattern of church life until the settlement in 1689. Since then the Church of Scotland has been consistently Presbyterian.

The history of the Reformed tradition in Scotland has been enlivened and marred by numerous controversies and divisions. (See chart in Appendix.) It has, however, exerted very great influence upon the whole of Christendom, as well as upon the world-wide Reformed community. It combined learning with piety better than perhaps any other community. Its universities have been the source of solid and effective, if not creative, scholarship. Emigrants have established the Scottish brand of the Reformed community throughout the English-speaking world. Its missionaries have left their imprint especially in what is today called the Third World.

In England, Reformed influences were powerfully present during the reign of Edward VI (1547–1553). Martin Bucer, the Strasbourg reformer, spent his last years in England. John à Lasco was pastor of the Church of the Strangers in London. John

Calvin corresponded with Cranmer, the archbishop of Canterbury; Edward, the king; and Somerset, the lord protector. *The Prayer Book,* which Cranmer produced, shows evidence of Reformed influence.[20] The Thirty-Nine Articles are Reformed in statements on predestination and the Lord's Supper and were included by the historian Philip Schaff as a Reformed confession.[21] During the reign of Mary, many English Protestants took refuge in Zurich and Geneva. Under Elizabeth the influence of John Calvin and Henrich Bullinger of Zurich cannot be overestimated, though the status of Richard Hooker's *Of the Laws of Ecclesiastical Polity* (1594ff.) is sufficient evidence that the Reformed tradition did not dominate the church. The Church of England was comprehensive, and Reformed theology lived with the worship of the *Book of Common Prayer,* with episcopal polity, and with divergent theologies such as Arminianism. The Puritan movement accommodated Reformed theology to its special concern for the nurturing of the religious life and sought to gain recognition for presbyterian and congregational polities.

Puritanism for two decades (1640–1659) had an opportunity to establish a new church order, but the experiment of the saints failed. Henceforth, the Church of England would be episcopal; and Reformed theological influences, which to this point had been powerful if not dominant, would fade. The Reformed community survived in England in the life of the dissenting churches; that is, the Baptists, Congregationalists, and Presbyterians. In Wales a Presbyterian church (Calvinistic Methodist Church of Wales, now the Presbyterian Church of Wales) came into being during the awakening of the eighteenth century somewhat independent of earlier Reformed traditions.

The Reformed tradition in Ireland dates from the Plantation of Ulster, which began in 1606, except in so far as this tradition had been found in the episcopal Church of Ireland.[22] (Archbishop Usher of Dublin was Augustinian, if not Calvinist; and Cartwright and Travers, ardent Presbyterian Calvinists, had served in Ireland.) The English government which had been endeavoring to "domesticate" the Irish in the seventeenth century sought to accomplish this purpose by planting Scottish and English communities in the war-devastated areas of northern Ireland. This opportunity to begin anew was very attractive to lowland Scots whose life had been hard and primitive but who were under the influence of the Protestant Reformation in Scotland. Many of them migrated to the neighboring counties of northern Ireland, Down and Antrim, and others came to the plantations or with the military. Hardness of life had not dulled the shrewdness of mind nor energy of person that made the lowland Scots great settlers of a rugged country and later the great pioneers, Indian fighters, and settlers of the American back country. Moreover, they brought with them their Presbyterian church government and their Reformed theology which would be a source of identity for them for years to come. The settlement in Ireland was also enriched by the coming of French Huguenots and English Puritans along with the lowland Scots. The settlers soon achieved new prosperity in Ireland, but they were subjected to political, economic, and religious disabilities by the English government in addition to the calamities that befall farmers such as drought. Hence the Ulster Scots began the great migration to America where they have been identified as Scotch-Irish. Beginning in 1717, the emigration of Presbyterians from northern Ireland became a torrent, by conservative estimate at least 250,000 coming by 1776.[23]

A presbytery was established in Ulster in 1642, and by 1659 it had developed into five presbyteries. In 1681 the Presbytery of Laggan licensed Francis Makemie to respond to a call from the colony on the eastern shore of Virginia. Makemie would subsequently become the leading influence in the establishment of the first presbytery in America.

In 1921 Northern Ireland was separated from the rest of Ireland. The Presbyterian Church in Ireland has the largest membership of any church in Northern Ireland. Here the problem of religious pluralism in a single community has not yet been settled, as recent controversy has demonstrated.

It is significant to note that Reformed churches in sixteenth- and seventeenth-century Europe were usually associated with minorities and in opposition to the old political and social patterns of society. This fact contributed to the development of political democracy in the churches and to an openness to social and economic change. The vigor of the Reformed churches in these minority and opposition situations also indicates an affinity in the Reformed ethos for this role. From the beginning the Reformed churches have been overwhelmingly "middle class."

Here again there has been mutual interaction. Middle-class culture has shaped Reformed churches, and Reformed churches have helped create middle-class cultures.

## The United States and Canada

The early settlement of what is now the United States was rooted in religious convictions for which the Reformed tradition was an important source. For English Puritans the New World offered opportunities for the glorification of God, freedom to establish Christian communities that would be models for the decaying society of Europe, and the salvation of the natives. There were other motives, of course, but the significant role of religious and theological motives cannot be gainsaid. Richard Hakluyt, Puritan preacher and advocate of colonization, wrote in *Discourse of Western Planting* that English sovereigns " ' . . . are not onely chardged to mayneteyne and patronize the faithe of Christe, but also to inlarge and advaunce the same. Neither oughte this to be their laste worke but rather the principall and chefe of all others.' "[24] Louis B. Wright, a distinguished authority on English and early American history, comments that Hakluyt's *The Principal Navigations* "quickly found a place beside Foxe's *Book of Martyrs* and the King James version of the Bible, as reading deemed necessary to all good Englishmen."[25] Wright also concludes:

> To the twentieth century, the motives and purposes of the religious groups who so powerfully affected the expansion of English-speaking peoples may seem narrow and hypocritical. But that interpretation ignores the spirit of the times which produced the movements that we have been discussing. Self-interest there certainly was. But to doubt the sincerity of these people is to misunderstand the age in which they lived. Once more let me emphasize that they were conscious of being a part of a great undertaking, of being the instruments of God's will, and, if profits accrued to them, it was a clear indication of the favor of the Almighty. The Hebraic, Old Testament faith of the men and women of the seventeenth century and of their spiritual descendants in later periods was often harsh and conducive to bigotry. But it had sinews and strength.
> Today we smile in a superior fashion at the naïvete of their religion and the way it was used as the handmaiden of self-interest. But we ought to ask ourselves what we have put in its place. . . . Although no worshiper of the past would wish a return of seventeenth-century Puritanism, . . . many Americans have felt that the

lack of a positive national faith and goal has been one of our greatest shortcomings. Historically, we must be aware that a nation without a zeal for something besides its own ease and comfort is doomed.[26]

Sydney Ahlstrom, a distinguished church historian, estimates that at the time of the American Revolution three fourths of the American people were heirs of the Reformed tradition.[27] "The exploration and settlement of those parts of the New World in which the United States took its rise were profoundly shaped by the Reformed and Puritan impulse, and . . . this impulse, through its successive transmutations, remained the dominant factor in the ideology of the Protestant Establishment."[28] Another student of American life has written, "It is safe to assume . . . that the influence of puritanism, in the broad Calvinistic sense, was a major force in the late colonial period, and that it contributed uniquely and profoundly to the making of the American mind when the American mind was in the making."[29] Ahlstrom dates the Puritan era from the death of Mary Tudor in 1558 to the election of John F. Kennedy in 1960.[30] There is no question that the Reformed tradition, inclusive of Puritanism and of Calvinism, has been buffeted as have most religious traditions. Some critics contend that Ahlstrom exaggerates its influence in American history. Yet it is also possible that Ahlstrom's conclusion that the Puritan era ended in 1960 is premature.

The first Reformed settlement in America was carried out by French Huguenots as part of a settlement in Brazil. Here the first Reformed worship service in the New World was conducted by Pierre Richier in 1557.[31] Later the Huguenots also participated in the settlement at Port Royal (Parris Island, S. C.) in 1562.[32] These settlements did not survive. Calvinists were also among the settlers in Virginia. Alexander Whitaker, a conforming Puritan and the son of an ardent Calvinist theologian, William Whitaker, is known as the Apostle of Virginia (1611–1617). Puritan activity in the colony was restricted from 1643 on, and the Puritan element in the Church of England in Virginia migrated or died out, though the low-church character of Virginia Episcopalianism is a legacy from this influence.

The settlement of Plymouth (1620) by separatist Puritans and of Massachusetts (1628) by conforming Puritans constituted the first permanent Reformed settlements.[33] The Cambridge Synod of 1646–1648 established the direction of New England Puritanism. The Westminster Confession was adopted with modifications. (Three New England ministers had been invited but did not attend the Assembly.) The synod also produced the Cambridge Platform that established with official care and detail the congregational pattern of the church's life. The Massachusetts Puritans had quickly become Congregationalists, but they retained some elements of a connectional church. The Puritan tradition thus became one of the most important elements in shaping American life and culture. The Congregationalists have produced many of the ablest theologians and preachers that the Reformed tradition has to its credit in America. Congregational churches united with Christian churches in 1931 to form a general council of Congregational-Christian churches, and with the Evangelical and Reformed churches to form the United Church of Christ in 1957. The Congregationalists, perhaps because of their theological freedom and congregational autonomy, were subject to erosion from the theological left by the Unitarians in the early nineteenth century and various liberal movements in the twentieth. Yet this congregational freedom contributed to theological creativity and social activism.

American Baptists have their most important   historical sources in English Puritanism, and many have maintained a Calvinist theology. Roger Williams, a Puritan settler in Massachusetts, was exiled to become one of the founders of the American Baptist tradition. The London Confession which appeared in 1677 and was approved by London congregations of Particular Baptists was a modification of the Westminster Confession. It was adopted by the Philadelphia Baptist Convention in 1742. Calvinism has been an important influence in American Baptist theology and practice along with Arminian theologies and traditional Baptist emphases.[34]

The Reformed tradition was also brought to America by the Dutch Reformed, who began immigrating to New York (then New Amsterdam) in 1624.[35] Jonas Michaelius, the first minister, arrived in 1628 and began holding services of worship. Even though the territory became English by conquest in 1664, the Dutch Reformed community continued to thrive. The Dutch brought with them the theological achievements of seventeenth-century Dutch Calvinism, including their confessional documents, the Belgic Confession, the Heidelberg Catechism, and the Canons of the Synod of Dort.

The Reformed Church in America, organized in 1792 in independence of the Dutch church, also grew rapidly from Dutch immigration that accelerated in 1847 and settled mostly in the Mid-West, particularly around Holland, Michigan, and Pella, Iowa. Some of this later group formed the Christian Reformed Church, which originated in small secessions from the Reformed Church in America. Today the Christian Reformed Church continues a tradition of conservative but stalwart Calvinism. (The Dutch settlers had seceded from the state church in the Netherlands in 1834, united with the Reformed Dutch Church, now the Reformed Church in America, in 1850, and some seceded again in 1851 to form the Christian Reformed Church.)

The Scots and Scotch-Irish were the third group to bring the Reformed tradition to America.[36] Scots had been sent to America by Cromwell in 1651 as indentured servants. Cotton Mather hoped they would establish colonies in the West as a barrier to the Indians. After 1714 large numbers of Ulster Scots began to migrate to America. Many of the first immigrants landed at Boston, but after some difficulties with New England Puritans a great number made their way to the Hudson valley. The majority entered through the Delaware River ports, spreading out to western Pennsylvania and to the South through the Valleys of Virginia and the piedmont regions of the Carolinas and Georgia. Smaller groups of Ulster Scots entered through Charleston, going from there to the "back country," and through other American ports. Having left the hard life in the lowlands of Scotland for Ireland where they achieved a measure of prosperity but were subjected to repressive economic, political, and religious practices, they came to America free to commit themselves to the establishment of a new way of life. They brought with them no deep attachment to old cultures, but they came with their shrewdness of mind, individualism, determination, and identity as Presbyterians. The most influential "Irish" vote in shaping American life has not been the Catholic Irish but the Scotch-Irish vote which long ago lost any ethnic identity.

Highland Scots also began to migrate in large numbers after the Battle of Culloden (1746). They established a strong Presbyterian settlement in the Cape Fear area of North Carolina. Other settlements were Altamaha valley of Georgia and the Mohawk and upper Hudson valleys of New York. Scots were also scattered in smaller numbers across the eastern seaboard. Immigrants from Scotland to colonial America numbered around 25,000 during the years 1763–1775. Prior to this time very few Scots migrated to America.[37]

The Scots and Scotch-Irish brought with them their Reformed theology and their zeal for presbyterian government. They were joined in the establishment of the Presbyterian Church by Presbyterian Puritans. The Presbyterian Church at Hempstead and later Jamaica, Long Island, was composed mostly of Puritans[38] and is probably the oldest continuing Presbyterian church in America, dating from 1644. Leadership in establishing the Presbyterian Church was assumed by Francis Makemie, who came from Ulster; but the first presbytery, organized in ca. 1706 under Makemie's leadership, included Scotch-Irish, Scots, and English Puritans. The first synod met in 1717, and in 1729 the newly formed church adopted the Westminster Confession and catechisms as its doctrinal standards. During the next seventy years the church was firmly established from the Middle Colonies to Georgia through the dedicated efforts of lay members and ministers. Organizational developments were not simple as the churches split between Old Side and New Side (1741–1758); but in 1788 a general assembly was established with four synods: New York and New Jersey, Philadelphia, Virginia, and the Carolinas, holding its first meeting in 1789. It is significant to note that the historical development, in contrast to Scotland, was from congregation to presbytery, to synod, to general assembly. The Reformed Presbyterians and the Secession churches, which had split from the Church of Scotland, also perpetuated themselves in America.

German-speaking refugees from the Palatinate, other parts of western Germany, and Switzerland in the early eighteenth century were the beginning of the German Reformed Church in America. In the early days there was a close relation with the Dutch Reformed Church, but in 1792 the German Reformed Church became independent of this connection.[39] The theological seminary at Mercersburg, Pennsylvania (after 1871, Lancaster), became the center of a theological revival known as the Mercersburg theology under the leadership of John Williamson

Nevin (1803–1886) and Philip Schaff (1819–1893). This theology was christocentric with a highly catholic doctrine of the church and a strong emphasis on the mystical presence of Christ in the Lord's Supper. It sought to revise the liturgy with greater emphasis on the liturgical principles of the past. It was a creative revival of the Reformed tradition, emphasizing elements in that tradition that had been neglected in American life. Charles Hodge of Princeton called it crypto-Lutheranism.

In 1934 the Reformed Church (German) in the United States united with the Evangelical Synod of North America, which had been established by German immigrants who blended Lutheran, Reformed, and pietist traditions. In 1957 the Evangelical and Reformed Church united with Congregational-Christian to become the United Church of Christ.

Other European groups such as the Huguenots and the Hungarian Reformed have also made their contribution to the Reformed tradition in America. The Huguenots have been absorbed in various churches. The Hungarian Reformed maintain their own identity as the Hungarian Reformed Church.

The Reformed tradition came to Canada largely through migration from Scotland and northern Ireland during the nineteenth century. The Presbyterians represented all the divisions that existed in Scotland, but in 1875 they united in one church. Congregationalists were much weaker in Canada than in the United States. In 1925 the Methodists, Congregationalists, and a majority of the Presbyterians united to form the United Church of Canada. Today the United Church reports 2,140,102 members and the Presbyterians 174,555.[40]

The temptation was always great, even for the Presbyterians and Puritans from England, Scotland, Ireland, and Wales, to perpetuate in America the forms and customs of the old church in the new land. The Old Side-New Side split in American Presbyterianism (1741–1758) was in part over the question of whether American Presbyterians would be responsive to the new situation or committed to the reproduction of the Scottish church. The New Side far outstripped the Old Side because it had accommodated itself to the new situation. The experiences of the Great Awakenings, denominational pluralism, and a voluntary church in a free society all left their imprint on the churches of the Reformed tradition in America. The pragmatic and experi-

mental bias of American culture also shaped theology and church
life. The traditions were alive, and they continued to grow in a
new situation without losing continuity with their history in another culture. A too-persistent endeavor to perpetuate the old in
a new situation and a too-eager enthusiasm for adopting the new
in place of the old alike proved sterile and nonproductive.

## Australia, New Zealand, and South Africa

The Reformed tradition in Europe was transplanted to Australia, New Zealand, and South Africa by emigration. The settlement of Australia occurred chiefly in the nineteenth century
when religious toleration had been achieved in Britain. Hence
the religious purposes that shaped the early settlement in the
United States were missing. The large migration of Scots and the
support of the Presbyterian churches in Scotland contributed to
the growth of the church. In the 1961 census, 9.3 per cent of the
population, or 976,518, declared themselves Presbyterian. In
1977 the Presbyterian, Methodist, and Congregational churches
formed the Uniting Church of Australia. A Presbyterian Church
also continues.

The Presbyterian Church was established in New Zealand
largely by Scottish immigration that began in 1839. The Free
Church of Scotland, which was established by the Disruption of
1843, was particularly active in the early settlement. The 1968
*World Christian Handbook* lists 566,174 New Zealanders as Presbyterians.

Cape Colony in South Africa was settled by the Dutch in 1652.
Huguenot settlers also brought with them their traditions. The
Dutch Reformed Church in South Africa has been influenced by
the social situation and the traditions of apartheid, but today it
exhibits new signs of theological life.[41] Alan Paton's *Cry the Beloved Country* was written out of the trauma of that situation and
is one of the finest statements of Christian theology in the form
of a novel.

## The Reformed Tradition and the Younger Churches

A historian of Protestant missions, Gustav Warneck, has given
public approbation to the charge that the Protestant reformers
were not interested in world missions.[42] Warneck was aware that
during Calvin's lifetime access to the non-Christian world was

largely controlled by the Catholic powers of Spain and Portugal and that Calvin had more than he could do in maintaining the church in Geneva and in Europe. There are three additional responses that ought to be made to Warneck's contention. First, Calvin's theology supports Christian missions. No theologian placed greater emphasis on the working out of the divine purposes in human history. Furthermore, Calvin explicitly believed that these purposes included the proclamation of the Gospel. "There is no people," Calvin wrote, "and no rank in the world that is excluded from salvation; because God wishes that the gospel should be proclaimed to all without exception. Now the preaching of the gospel gives life; and hence . . . God invites all equally to partake of salvation."[43] Secondly, Calvin himself approved of the attempt to establish a French colony on the coast of Brazil, composed largely of Reformed and including the intention of the Christianization of the natives.[44] To this end two ministers, Pierre Richier and Guillaume Chartier, and Jean de Léry, who had studied theology in Geneva, were sent to the colony. On March 21, 1557, Pastor Richier celebrated the Lord's Supper according to the Genevan rite. There is ample evidence that the conversion of the Indians was a prime purpose of the Reformed pastors. The first contacts with the Indians were very discouraging, but Pastor Richier wrote to Calvin, "Since . . . the Most High has given us this task, we expect this Edom to become a future possession for Christ."[45] The mission failed partly because its leader, Villegagnon, proved erratic and irresponsible; but it stands as a monument to the concern of the Reformed community, including Calvin, for missions.

Calvin and the Reformed leaders in Geneva, it should be noted in the third place, were most energetic in what more recently would have been called home missions.[46] No mission board has ever taken more seriously its responsibility for the establishment of churches, for sending of pastors to established churches, and for opening up new work, than the consistory of the church of Geneva under Calvin's leadership. In a day when communication was difficult, the Genevan consistory had remarkable intelligence as to what was happening in the cities and countryside of France, even of the Protestant community in all of Europe. Calvin's concern was for the preaching of the gospel, for church organization, for conversion. Indeed the concern of the

Reformed in Geneva was so intense and so effective that Robert Kingdon has likened it to that of social radicals in the twentieth century.

> Today's radicals are moved by the hope of a glorious future secured by economic action, not by prayer. They look to the capital of a world power as the source of their inspiration, rather than to an isolated mountain city. But the passion of their conviction, the charismatic role played by their leaders, their intolerance of deviation, and above all the nature of their organization—flexible but centralized—is much the same. Perhaps all of us can gain insight into contemporary Communist revolution by studying the ideological fury of the past. And perhaps those of us raised in the Reformed tradition could profit by recalling the agony in which our faith was born, and by searching afresh for the revolutionary implications it still should hold for human society.[47]

While the contention that the early reformers were not concerned for missions is not wholly fair, it is a fact that Protestant missions did not fully gain momentum until the nineteenth century. Again, it must not be forgotten that in the seventeenth century the Protestant communities of western Europe were hard pressed in maintaining their own existence, and they were devastated by the Thirty Years War. The popularity of deistic and enlightenment theologies likewise undercut missionary zeal. Yet throughout this period there were significant missionary undertakings. The work of David Brainerd and John Eliot among the Indians of New England was notable. In the East Indies, the Dutch India Company supported Reformed pastors in mission work.

The nineteenth century, according to Kenneth Scott Latourette, was the great century in the history of missions. It had its beginnings in the life and work of William Carey, who in 1792 made his famous address, "An Enquiry into the Obligations of Christians to Use Means for the Conversion of the Heathens." The Reformed tradition was well represented among the great leaders of this missionary movement: Moffat and Livingstone in Africa, Morrison in China, Paton in the Pacific Islands, Samuel Mills and Adoniram Judson of the hay-stack prayer meeting and the American Board of Commissioners for Foreign Missions, and Robert E. Speer and John Mackay of the twentieth-century missionary movement.

Kenneth Scott Latourette, in his definitive history of Christian mission, points to four characteristics of pre-nineteenth-century Protestant mission that also apply especially to the Reformed churches.[48] First, the interest of Protestants in extending their faith to non-Christians increased with each century. Secondly, Protestant churches established in North America by immigration were more active in propagating their faith than were any other Christian communities formed by migration. Thirdly, Protestants brought into being new instruments for the propagation of the faith such as the missionary societies and the support of missions by the laity in general. These new methods replaced the state and monastic orders. A fourth characteristic was an emphasis upon individual conversion rather than the conversion of a tribe, caste, community, or nation as a whole. These changes prepared the way for the great Protestant missionary movement of the nineteenth century, a movement that is without parallel in the history of the church for the marshalling of ordinary church members in the world-wide proclamation of the gospel.

The real evidence for Reformed mission is found in the numerous churches that exist on every continent as a result of this missionary movement. (See Appendix.) In these churches the Christian tradition that developed largely in western Europe and a Reformed tradition that developed largely in northern Europe and America must become indigenous in very different cultures. This is a long and difficult task, but there is evidence that the tradition lives with an openness to the future and to the new cultures in these new situations. The creed of the Batak Church is an example of an initial effort to state Christian theology in the idiom of a nonwestern culture. Other indications are the theological work of D. T. Niles in India, of Kazōh Kitamori in Japan, and the assimilation of African traditions in church life in Africa.[49] Among Reformed theologians who are working in this way are Allan Aubrey Boesak in South Africa, Ruben A. Alves in South America, and Choan-Seng Song in Asia.

## The Ecumenical Movement

In a famous letter to Archbishop Cranmer, John Calvin declared that the disunity of the church was to be ranked as one of the great evils of the time. ". . . the members of the Church being severed, the body lies bleeding. So much does this concern me, that, could I be of any service, I would not grudge to cross even ten seas, if need were, on account of it."[50] The denominational pattern of church life that was to develop in Protestantism could not have been imagined by Calvin. For the sake of Christian unity he was willing to tolerate not only inconvenience but doctrinal errors.[51] Yet it is also certain that for Calvin faithlessness is a greater sin than disunity.[52]

The Reformed churches from the beginning defined the church primarily in terms of the action of God in word and sacrament, not in terms of structures or even correct doctrine. This doctrine of the church enabled the Reformed communities to recognize the ministries, sacraments, and memberships of other churches. No major Christian community has been more ecumenical in this sense, or more open in recognition of other Christian ministries, sacraments, and memberships.

Reformed churches have during the past century developed a new sense of unity among themselves. The First General Council of the Alliance of the Reformed Churches throughout the World holding the Presbyterian Order (System) met in Edinburgh in 1877. The Council was the result of the work and leadership of James McCosh of the College of New Jersey (Princeton University), William Garden Blaikie of New College, Edinburgh, and G. D. Matthews, a minister of the United Presbyterian Church of Scotland and a pastor in New York and Quebec who was to be the first General Secretary of the Alliance. Marcel Pradervand who was Executive Secretary of the Alliance from 1949 to 1970 has recently written a history of the Alliance.[53] The First Council of Congregational Churches met in London in 1891. The Alliance and the Council came together at Nairobi, Kenya, in 1970 to form the World Alliance of Reformed Churches (Presbyterian and Congregational).

Numerous church unions have taken place between Reformed churches, as for example the United Presbyterian Church and Presbyterian Church in the U.S.A. united in 1958 to form the United Presbyterian Church in the U.S.A., the Evangelical and Reformed Church and the General Council of the Congregational Christian Churches united in 1957 to form the United Church of Christ, and the Presbyterian Church of England and the Congregational Union of England and Wales united in 1972 to form the United Reformed Church of England and Wales. Unions have also taken place between Reformed churches and churches of other traditions. In 1925 Presbyterians and Congregationalists united with Methodists to form the United Church of Canada. Reformed churches united with Methodists and Anglicans to form the Church of South India in 1947.

Reformed churches have been very active in councils of churches, and Reformed churchmen have provided outstanding leadership. Samuel McCrea Cavert, a Presbyterian, was General Secretary of the Federal Council of Churches from 1921 until 1950, and of the National Council of the Churches of Christ in the United States of America until 1954. Claire Randall, the present General Secretary of the National Council, is a Presbyterian. William A. Visser 't Hooft, a Reformed theologian of the Dutch church, was pre-eminent in the forming of the World Council of Churches, and he served as its first secretary from 1948 until 1966. He was succeeded by Eugene Carson Blake (1966–1972) who had been a prominent Presbyterian churchman in the United States and who was also a leader in the establishment of the Consultation on Church Union.[54]

*Appendix A:*

## MEMBERSHIP OF REFORMED CHURCHES
### (1972 Statistics)

There is no definitive list of Reformed Churches. No one has authority to set the boundaries. The following is the list of member churches of the World Alliance of Reformed Churches. Many Baptist churches would also qualify, and the Alliance is in discussion with Baptist churches.

Church statistics are unreliable but do give some indication of actual church strength. Church members may be defined as listed baptized membership, communicant members, state census designation or community membership, a more loose estimate. Communicant membership is always the smallest and most restricted figure.

### WORLD ALLIANCE OF REFORMED CHURCHES

AFRICA

Reformed Church in *Algeria:* 1,000–1,500 members; 6 congregations; 3 preaching stations; 8 ministers (1964)

Presbyterian Church in *Cameroon:* total community: 113,206; 70,221 communicant members; 799 congregations; 84 ministers; 1,833 elders (1968)

Presbyterian Church of West *Cameroon:* 90,855 members; 70,238 communicant members; 281 congregations; 1,464 preaching stations; 144 ministers; 2,252 elders (1970)

Synod of the Nile of the Evangelical Church *(Egypt):* 35,000 baptized members; 30,000 communicant members; census figure: 100,000; 200 congregations; 70 preaching stations; 187 ministers; 850 elders (1963)

Evangelical Church of *Equatorial Guinea:* 8,000 members; 2,588 communicant; 15 congregations; 68 preaching stations; 5 ministers; 70 elders (1964)

*Ethiopian* Evangelical Church-Bethel: 35,000 members; 20,000 communicant; 81 congregations; 65 preaching stations; 23 ministers; 410 elders (1969)

Evangelical Presbyterian Church *(Ghana):* total community 122,292; 40,372 communicant members; 400 congregations; 40 preaching stations; 75 ministers; 800 elders (1967)

Presbyterian Church of *Ghana:* total community 261,241; 52,478 communicant; 805 congregations; 158 ministers; 3,824 elders (1969)

Presbyterian Church of East Africa *(Kenya):* total community 70,000; 62,000 communicant; 40 congregations; 12 preaching stations; 36 ministers; 6,000 elders (1969)

Reformed Church of East Africa *(Kenya):* total community 5,472; 3,245 communicant members; 5 congregations; 58 preaching stations; 4 ministers; 65 elders (1971)

*Lesotho* Evangelical Church: total community 206,340; 64,500 communicant; 56 congregations; 470 preaching stations; 36 ministers; 2,896 elders (1969)

Presbytery of *Liberia* in West Africa: 1,136 communicants; 10 congregations; 10 ministers; 40 elders (1959)

Church of Jesus Christ in *Madagascar:* approx. 800,000 members; approx. 3,500 congregations; approx. 1,000 ministers (1970)

Church of Central Africa Presbyterian *(Malawi):* 266,695 communicant members; 219 congregations; 149 ministers; 8,000 elders (1971)

Evangelical Church in *Morocco:* 2,200 members; 10 congregations; 3 ministers; 37 elders (1971)

Presbyterian Church of *Mozambique:* total community 13,000; 10,125 communicant members; 15 congregations; 20 ministers (1964)

Presbyterian Church of *Nigeria:* total community 31,636; 17,142 communicants; 48 congregations; 3 preaching stations; 46 ministers; 961 elders (1970)

African Reformed Church in *Rhodesia:* 29,300 communicant members; 27 congregations; 580 preaching stations; 33 ministers (1970)

Evangelical Presbyterian Church in *Rwanda:* 19,615 baptized members; 22 congregations; 11 preaching stations; 16 ordained ministers; 316 elders (1971/72)

Bantu Presbyterian Church of *South Africa:* total community 59,298; 43,134 communicant members; 71 congregations; 960 preaching stations; 52 ministers; 1,712 elders (1970)

Nederduitse Gereformeerde Kerk *(South Africa):* total community 1,378,834; 635,233 communicant members; 1,067 congregations; 1,405 ministers (1972)

Nederduitse Gereformeerde Kerk in Afrika *(South Africa):* 423,584 baptized members; 132,930 communicants; 402 congregations; 330 ministers; 681 evangelists; 3,403 elders (1966)

Nederduitse Gereformeerde Sendingkerk in South Afrika: 95,253 communicant members; 196 congregations; 14 preaching stations; 130 ministers; 1,216 elders (1965)

Nederduitse Hervormde Kerk van Afrika *(South Africa):* total community 175,239; 105,062 communicant members; 226 congregations; 173 ministers; 3,971 elders (1969)

Presbyterian Church of *Southern Africa:* total community 83,000; 63,000 communicant members; 180 congregations; 480 preaching stations; 170 ministers; 2,800 elders (1970)

Tsonga Presbyterian Church *(South Africa):* 14,922 baptized members; 9,959 communicant members; 22 congregations; 281 preaching stations; 20 ministers; 730 elders (1966)

United Congregational Church of *Southern Africa:* 116,539 communicant members; 260 congregations; 180 ministers; 2,400 preaching stations (1970)

Presbyterian Church in the *Sudan:* 3,000 communicant members; 10 parishes; 20 preaching stations; 4 ordained ministers; 24 evangelists; 20 elders (1965)

Presbyterian Church in the Republic of *Zaire:* 138,724 baptized members; 941 congregations; 92 ministers; 1,176 elders (1965)

Reformed Church in *Zambia:* total community 23,201; 18,596 communicant members; 27 congregations; 75 preaching stations; 30 ordained ministers; 490 elders (1964)

United Church of *Zambia:* total community 31,000; approx. 25,000 communicant members; 75 ministers; 20 associate, seconded, etc.; 1,200 elders. (1971)

## LATIN AMERICA

Christian Reformed Church of *Brazil:* 2,000 communicant members; 6,000 baptized members; 7 congregations; 11 preaching stations; 5 ministers; 24 elders (1963)

Evangelical Reformed Church in *Brazil:* total membership 1,447; 654 communicant members; 4 congregations; 3 preaching stations; 8 ministers; 18 elders (1966)

Independent Presbyterian Church of *Brazil:* 130,000 communicant members; 348 churches; 546 congregations; 150 preaching stations; 283 ministers; 1,560 elders (1968/69)

Presbyterian Church of *Brazil:* 126,170 communicant members; total community 219,496; 817 congregations; 2,002 preaching stations; 574 ministers; 3,928 elders (1968)

Presbyterian Church of *Chile:* 7,000 baptized members; 3,000 communicant members; 25 congregations; 18 ministers (1964)

Presbyterian Church of *Colombia:* total community 8,500; 3,000 communicant members; 28 congregations; 20 preaching stations; 10 ministers; 142 elders (1969)

Presbyterian-Reformed Church in *Cuba:* total community 8,215; 1,913 communicants; 29 congregations; 23 preaching stations; 21 ministers; 305 elders (1969)

National Evangelical Presbyterian Church of *Guatemala:* 20,500 baptized members; 7,700 communicants; 64 congregations; 150 preaching stations; 45 ministers; 264 elders (1959)

*Guyana* Congregational Union: 7,000 communicant members; 37 congregations; 6 ministers (1966)

*Guyana* Presbyterian Church: 6,000 baptized members; 2,238 communicants; 41 congregations; 10 parishes; 5 preaching stations; 15 ministers; 62 elders (1964)

Presbyterian Church of *Guyana:* 3,250 communicant members; 25 congregations in 11 parishes; 9 ministers; 160 elders (1966)

United Church of *Jamaica and Grand Cayman:* Official census figure: 90,000; 15,000 communicant members; 160 congregations; 50 ministers (1969)

National Presbyterian Church of *Mexico:* official census figure: 84,815; 35,994 communicant members; 193 congregations; 817 preaching stations; 150 ministers; 665 elders (1968)

Associate Reformed Presbyterian Church of *Mexico:* total community 5,000; 2,500 communicant members; 20 congregations; 35 preaching stations; 13 ministers; 48 elders (1969)

Presbyterian Church in *Trinidad and Grenada:* total community 40,000; 6,000 communicant members; 33 congregations; 100 preaching stations; 22 ministers; 310 elders (1971)

Presbyterian Church of *Venezuela:* total community 3,000; 994 communicant members; 11 congregations; 4 preaching stations; 8 ministers; 55 elders (1971)

NORTH AMERICA

Presbyterian Church in *Canada:* 186,584 communicant members; 818,-558 official census figure; 1,083 congregations; 852 ministers; 12,078 elders (1970)

United Church of *Canada:* 1,033,533 communicant members; 3,664,008 official census figure; 2,424 congregations; 4,525 preaching places; 3,-503 ministers; 61,689 elders in 1969 (1970)

Associate Reformed Presbyterian Church *(USA):* total community 31,-237; 28,427 communicant members; 144 congregations; 147 ministers; 1,250 elders (1970)

Cumberland Presbyterian Church *(USA):* total membership: 92,636; 88,494 communicant members; 885 congregations; 710 ministers (1970/71)

Second Cumberland Presbyterian Church *(USA):* 6,955 official census figure; 6,355 communicant members; 139 congregations; 10 preaching stations; 130 ministers; 650 elders (1970/71)

Hungarian Reformed Church in America *(USA):* total community 11,600; 11,000 communicant members; 26 congregations; 5 preaching stations; 34 ministers; 346 elders (1970)

Presbyterian Church in the *U.S.:* 958,195 communicant members; 4,063 congregations; 145 preaching stations; 4,595 ministers; 35,181 elders (1970)

Reformed Church in America *(USA):* total community 379,506; 226,830 communicants; 928 congregations; 1,327 ministers; 6,200 elders (1970)

United Church of Christ *(USA):* 1,960,608 members; 6,727 congregations; 9,227 ministers (1970)

United Presbyterian Church in the *USA:* 3,095,791 communicant members; 8,662 congregations; 13,151 ministers; 90,962 elders (1970)

ASIA

Presbyterian Church of *Burma:* total community 11,430; 5,126 communicant members; 87 congregations; 6 preaching stations; 13 ministers; 85 elders (1970)

Presbytery of *Ceylon:* 1,000 families; i.e. approx. 4,000 baptized members; 15 congregations; 2 preaching stations; 8 ministers (1963)

Presbytery of Lanka *(Ceylon):* total community 800; 250 communicant members; 2 congregations; 5 preaching stations; 2 ministers; 25 elders (1971)

Church of Christ in *China:*

Hong Kong Council of the Church of Christ in China: official census figure 20,329 members; 31 congregations; 20 ministers (1970)

Church of *North India:* total community 569,546; 230,959 communicant members; 19 dioceses; each diocese has 100 or more congregations; 1,917 ministers; 1,118 evangelists, deacons, etc. (1970)

Indonesian Christian Church [Geredja Kristen Indonesia]: total community 70,000; 53 communicant members; 72 congregations; 89 ministers; 673 elders (1970)

Toradja Church [Geredja Toradja]: *(Indonesia)* 162,700 members; 347 congregations; 60 ministers; 20 evangelists; 300 local preachers (1971)

Christian *Javanese* Churches [Geredja Kristen Djawa]: 121,500 members; 174 congregations; 580 preachers; 136 ministers (1971)

Karo Batak Protestant Church [Geredja Batak Karo Protestan] *(Indonesia):* 72,492 members; 300 congregations; 30 ministers (1971)

Protestant Church in *Indonesia* [Geredja Protestan di Indonesia]:1,892,779 members; 2,550 congregations; 482 ministers (1971)

Christian Church of East Java [Geredja Kristen Djawa Wetan] *(Indonesia):* 126,000 members; 92 congregations; 152 preaching stations; 74 ministers (1971)

Pasundan Christian Church [Geredja Kristen Pasundan]: 18,890 members; 28 congregations; 21 ministers (1971)

Evangelical Church in Kalimantan [Geredja Kalimantan Evangelis] *(Indonesia):* 90,000 members; 301 congregations; 61 ministers (1971)

Protestant Christian Church of Bali [Geredja Kristen Protestan di Bali] *(Indonesia):* 5,000 members; 33 congregations, 11 ministers (1971)

Christian Evangelical Church in Irian Barat [Geredja Kristen Indjili di Irian Barat] *(Indonesia):* 360,000 members; 800 congregations; 77 ministers; 900 evangelists (1971)

The Sangir/Talaud Evangelical Church [Geredja Masehi Indjili Sangir/Talaud] *(Indonesia):* 170,000 members; 305 congregations; 84 ministers (1971)

Christian Church of Southwest Sulawesi [Geredja Kristen di Sulawesi Selatan] *(Indonesia):* 5,500 members; 25 congregations; 14 ministers (1971)

Christian Church of Sumba [Geredja Kristen Sumba] *(Indonesia):*43,121 members; 52 congregations; 50 ministers; 117 evangelists (1971)

Church of Christ in *Japan* [Nippon Kirisuto Kyokai]: total community

12,541; 5,346 communicant members; 123 congregations; 123 ministers; 411 elders (1970)

Korean Christian Church in *Japan:* 1,589 communicant members; 34 congregations; 18 preaching stations; 28 ministers; 37 elders (1964)

United Church of Christ in *Japan* [Nihon Kirisuto Kyodan]: total community 204,842; 134,325 communicant members; 1,643 congregations; 1,432 ministers (1970/71)

Presbyterian Church of *Korea:* total community 460,350; 132,585 communicant members; 1,148 congregations; 133 preaching stations; 1,204 ministers; 2,577 elders (1969)

Presbyterian Church in the Republic of *Korea:* total community 194,793; 379 congregations; 309 preaching stations; 459 ministers; 654 elders (1970)

United Presbyterian Church of *Pakistan:* 56,585 communicant members; 180 congregations; 12 preaching stations; 158 ministers; 1,260 elders (1966)

United Church of Christ in the *Philippines:* total community 239,159; 146,537 communicant members; 1,100 congregations; 438 ministers (1967)

The Presbyterian Church in *Singapore and Malaysia:* total community 9,908; 7,456 communicant members; 32 congregations; 21 preaching stations; 31 ministers; 91 elders (1971)

Presbyterian Church in *Taiwan:* total community 163,604; 69,463 communicant members; 461 congregations; 458 preaching stations; 350 ministers; 443 evangelists (1970)

Church of Christ in *Thailand:* communicant members 23,000; 152 congregations; 64 preaching stations; 52 ministers; 740 elders (1969)

NEAR EAST

Evangelical Presbyterian Church of *Iran:* 3,067 communicant members; 32 congregations; 4 preaching stations; 12 ministers; 2 lay preachers; 70 elders (1970)

Evangelical Synod of *Syria and Lebanon:* total community 20,000; 3,175 communicant members; 53 congregations; 8 preaching stations; 20 ministers (1971)

Union of Evangelical, Armenian Churches in the *Near East:* 17,000 communicant members; 30 congregations; 14 preaching stations; 28 ministers (1970)

AUSTRALASIA

Congregational Union of *Australia:* total community 76,588; 14,219 communicant members; 183 ministers; 234 congregations; 77 preaching stations (1970)

Presbyterian Church of *Australia:* total membership 1,043,570; 156,455 communicant members; 686 ministers; 740 congregations; 10,853 elders (1966)

Presbyterian Church of the *New Hebrides:* 8,616 communicant members; 39 congregations; 212 preaching stations; 45 ministers; 372 elders (1966)

Presbyterian Church of *New Zealand:* total community 582,493; 88,566 communicant members; 442 congregations; 1,195 preaching stations; 502 ministers; 6,906 elders (1971)

Congregational Union of *New Zealand:* 500 members; 9 congregations; 6 ministers; (1971)

Congregational Christian Church in *Samoa:* 19,000 members; 21 ministers; 244 congregations (1966)

EUROPE

Reformed Church of *Austria:* total community 17,927; communicant members 11,900; 10 congregations; 26 preaching stations; 12 ministers; 100 elders (1971)

Reformed Church of *Belgium:* 3,000 communicant members; official census figure: 12,000; 37 congregations; 11 preaching stations; 28 ministers; 223 elders (1971)

Protestant Church of *Belgium:* 15,800 members; 70 congregations (1966)

Evangelical Church of Czech Brethren *(Czechoslovakia):* total community 290,000; 81,110 communicant members; 272 congregations; 398 preaching stations; 320 ministers; 4,900 elders (1968)

Reformed Church of *Slovakia (CSSR):* 165,000 baptized members; 310 congregations; 86 preaching stations; 200 ministers; 3,450 elders (1969)

Church of the Brethren *(CSSR):* total community 10,000; 5,000 communicant members; 31 congregations; 184 preaching stations; 56 ministers (1971)

Reformed Synod of *Denmark:* 1,100 members; 3 congregations; 3 ministers; 21 elders (1969)

Reformed Church of Alsace and Lorraine *(France):* total community 50,368; 53 congregations; 55 preaching stations; 50 ministers; 320 elders (1970)

Reformed Church of *France:* 328,700 baptized members; census figure 375,000; 564 congregations; 650 ministers; 6,600 elders (1964)

Evangelical Reformed Church in Northwest *Germany:* total community 225,000; 125,000 communicant members; 131 congregations; 103 ministers; 850 elders (1970)

Reformierter Bund, *Germany:* approx. 2,000,000 members; approx. 600 congregations; approx. 1,000 ministers; approx. 5,000 elders (1972)

Congregational Church in *England* and *Wales (Great Britain):* 166,683 members; 2,280 congregations; 1,632 ministers (1971)

Presbyterian Church of *England:* 59,473 communicant members; 308 congregations; 23 preaching stations; 370 ministers; 4,803 elders (1970)

Congregational Union of *Ireland:* total community 2,735; 1,121 communicant members; 21 ministers; 24 congregations; 4 preaching stations (1970)

Presbyterian Church in *Ireland:* total community 395,513; 141,072 communicant members; official census figure: 432,066; 567 congregations; 33 preaching stations; 537 ministers; 5,917 elders (1970)

Church of *Scotland:* official census figure: 5,199,000; 1,154,211 communicant members; 2,097 congregations; 2,200 ministers; 49,807 elders (1970)

Congregational Union of *Scotland:* official census figure: 39,979; 24,671 communicant members; 118 congregations; 105 ministers (1971)

United Free Church of *Scotland:* total community 19,753; 17,248 communicant members; 100 congregations; 77 ministers; 1,022 elders (1970)

Presbyterian (Calvinistic Methodist) Church of *Wales:* total community 120,000; 108,064 communicant members; 1,329 congregations; 346 ministers; 6,328 elders. (1971)

*Greek* Evangelical Church: total community 6,500; 1,600 communicant members; 23 congregations; 8 preaching stations; 18 ministers; 70 elders (1971)

Reformed Church of *Hungary:* total community approx. 1,500,000; 1,200 congregations; 1,000 preaching stations; 1,358 ministers; approx. 18,000 elders (1969/71)

Waldensian Evangelical Church, *Italy:* total community 26,254; communicant members: 20,467; 76 congregations; 38 preaching stations; 82 ministers; 572 elders (1970–71)

*Netherlands* Reformed Church: total community 3,700,000; 1,000,000 communicant members; 2,000 congregations; 2,000 preaching stations; 2,000 ministers; approx. 20,000 elders (1969)

Remonstrant Brotherhood (*Netherlands*): 20,000 communicant members; official census figure: 40,000; 49 congregations; 50 ministers (1971)

Reformed Churches in the *Netherlands:* 465,954 communicant members; official (Gereformeerde Kerken in Nederland) census figure: 870,379; 827 congregations; 1,045 ministers (1970)

Reformed Evangelical Church of *Poland:* 4,900 baptized members; 9 congregations; 3 preaching stations; 6 ministers; 45 elders (1965)

Evangelical Presbyterian Church of *Portugal:* total community 3,500; 2,000 communicant members; 12 congregations; 19 preaching stations; 13 ministers; 45 elders (1970)

Reformed Church of *Romania:* 693,511 baptized members; 740 congregations; 738 ministers; 11,794 elders (1963)

*Spanish* Evangelical Church: 10,000 members; 54 congregations; 30 ministers (1964)

*Swedish* Mission Covenant Church: total community 139,863; 86,118 communicant members; 1,303 congregations; 709 preaching stations; 680 ministers (1971)

*Swiss* Federation of Protestant Churches: 2,888,122 baptized members; 1,191 congregations; 1,697 ministers (1964)

Reformed Church in Latvia *(U.S.S.R.)*: 450 baptized members; 1 minister; 6 elders (1960)

Reformed Church in Lithuania *(U.S.S.R.)*: 10,000 members; 5 congregations; 2 ministers (1970)

Reformed Church of Carpatho-Ukraine *(U.S.S.R.)*: 95,000 baptized members; 40,000 communicant members; 91 congregations; 46 ministers (1962)

Reformed Church in *Yugoslavia:* total community 26,716; 35 congregations; 23 preaching stations; 23 ministers; 533 elders (1970)

New Members of the World Alliance of Reformed Churches for which the statistics are not available:

AFRICA
Reformed Church of Equatorial Guinea
Presbyterian Church of Africa
Reformed Church in Africa *(Republic of South Africa)*
Protestant Church of Senegal
Church of Christ in Zaire, Presbyterian Community

LATIN AMERICA
Evangelical Congregational Church of Brazil
Waldensian Evangelical Church of the River Plate

ASIA
Indonesian Christian Church in Central Java
Indonesian Christian Church in West Java
Evangelical Christian Church in Bolaang-Mongondow
Christian Evangelical Church in Minahasa
Christian Evangelical Church in Timor
Protestant Church in the Moluccas
Protestant Church of Western Indonesia
Christian Evangelical Church in Irian Jaya
Evangelical Church of Iran
Presbytery of Lanka
National Evangelical Synod of Syria and Lebanon

EUROPE
National Church of Lippe (Federal Republic of Germany)
Reformierter Generalkonvent in der Deutsche Demokratische Republik
United Reformed Church

## REFORMED ECUMENICAL SYNOD

Organized in 1946, the synod seeks to unite "Catholicity in the church and firm loyalty to the whole counsel of God." Some churches are also members of the World Alliance. Statistics are from 1976 Handbook of the Reformed Ecumenical Synod.

AFRICA

Church of Central Africa Presbyterian (Malawi)
Total Members: 128,000
Number of Local Congregations: 77

The Benue Church of Christ in the Sudan (Ekan) (Nigeria)
Number of Local Congregations: 45

Church of Christ in the Sudan Among the TIV (Nigeria)
Total Members: Christian community: 201,329; Communicant members: 21,726
Number of Local Congregations: 58

African Reformed Church in Zimbabwe
Total Members: 26,823
Number of Local Congregations: 28

Church of Central Africa Presbyterian, Salisbury Synod (Zimbabwe)
Total Members: 8,216
Number of Local Congregations: 12

Church of England in South Africa
Total Members: About 35,000
Number of Local Congregations: 140+

Dutch Reformed Church in Africa (South Africa)
Total Members: 508,958 (adherents included)
Number of Congregations: 428

Dutch Reformed Church (South Africa)
Total Members: Confessing: 855,050; Adherents: 1,634,026

Dutch Reformed Mission Church (South Africa)
Total Members: 450,451
Number of Local Congregations: 230

Midlands Reformed Church (South Africa)
Total Number of Church Families: 5,346
Total Members: 27,461
Number of Local Congregations: 67

Reformed Church in Africa (South Africa)
Total Members: Communicant: 429; Baptized: 1,282
Number of Congregations: 10

Reformed Church in South Africa
Total Members: 110,613
Number of Local Congregations: 266

Reformed Church Among the Coloured (South Africa)
Total Members: 1,718
Number of Local Congregations: 7

Soutpansberg Reformed Church (South Africa)
Total Members: 4,960
Number of Local Congregations: 12

Evangeliese Gereformeerde Kerk in Afrika (NGK) (South West Africa)

Total Members: Communicant: 670; Baptized: 1,400
Number of Congregations: 3
Reformed Church in Zambia
Total Members: 40,000 (plus)
Number of Local Congregations: 35 (+ one in Zimbabwe)

ASIA

The Reformed Church in Japan
Total Members: 6,389
Number of Local Congregations: 88

Dutch Reformed Church in Sri Lanka
Total Members: Approximately 2,500
Number of Local Congregations: 9 (English speaking); 8 (Sinhala speaking); 3 (Tamil speaking)

EUROPE

National Union of Independent Reformed Evangelical Churches of France
Total Members: 11,308
Number of Local Congregations: 31

Christian Reformed Churches in the Netherlands
Total Members: 71,702
Communicants: 38,231
Number of Local Congregations: 174

The Reformed Churches in the Netherlands
Total Members: 884,468
Number of Local Congregations: 830

Evangelical Presbyterian Church (Northern Ireland)
Total Members: 800
Number of Local Congregations: 9

Reformed Presbyterian Church of Ireland (Covenanter) (Northern Ireland)
Total Members: 6,500
Number of Local Congregations: 37

Free Church of Scotland
Total Members: 22,000
Number of Local Congregations: 150

Reformed Presbyterian Church of Scotland
Total Members: 400
Number of Local Congregations: 5

NORTH AMERICA

Independent Presbyterian Church of Mexico
Total Attenders: 3,821
Number of Congregations: 9 fully organized; 71 unorganized; 46 consistory members

Associate Reformed Presbyterian Church (United States)
Total Members: 28,570
Number of Local Congregations: 153

Christian Reformed Church in North America
Total Members: 281,997
Number of Local Congregations: 695

Orthodox Presbyterian Church (United States)
Total Members: 15,227
Number of Local Congregations: 128

Reformed Presbyterian Church of North America (United States)
Total Members: 5,445
Number of Local Congregations: 69

SOUTH AMERICA

Reformed Church of Argentina
Total Members: 1,652
Number of Local Congregations: 9 independent 8 unorganized

Reformed Church in Brazil
Total Members: 1,600
Number of Local Congregations: 4

SOUTH PACIFIC

Presbyterian Church of Eastern Australia
Number of Local Congregations: 12

Reformed Churches of Australia
Total Members: 8,653
Number of Local Congregations: 36

Indonesian Christian Church of Central Java (GKI)
Total Members: 24,000 (incl. children)
Number of Local Congregations: 34

The Church of Toradja Mamasa (Indonesia)
Total Members: 53,923
Number of Local Congregations: 230

The Javanese Christian Churches (Indonesia)
Total Members: 130,000 (estimate)
Number of Local Congregations: 192 and 724 worship centres

Christian Church of Sumba (Indonesia)
Total Members: 46,000
Number of Congregations: 52

Reformed Churches of New Zealand
Total Members: 2,371
Number of Local Congregations: 14

Among Reformed churches that belong to neither the Alliance nor the Synod are the Presbyterian Church in America, Reformed Presbyterian Church Evangelical Synod.

*Appendix B:*

# DIAGRAM OF PRESBYTERIAN CHURCHES IN SCOTLAND

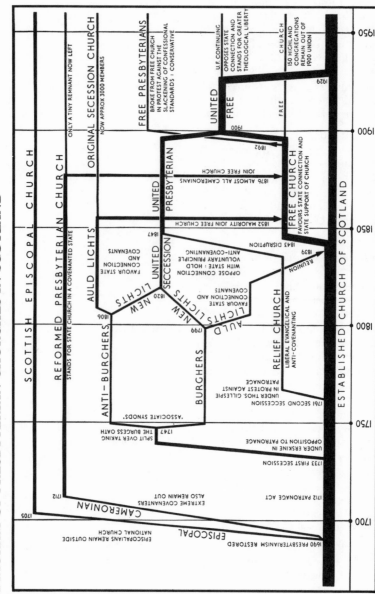

DIVISIONS AND REUNIONS OF THE SCOTTISH CHURCH 1690–1929 from *A Church History of Scotland* by J.H.S. Burleigh (London: Oxford University Press, 1960). p. 457. © Oxford University Press, 1960, used with permission.

*Appendix C:*

# DIAGRAM OF PRESBYTERIAN CHURCHES IN THE UNITED STATES

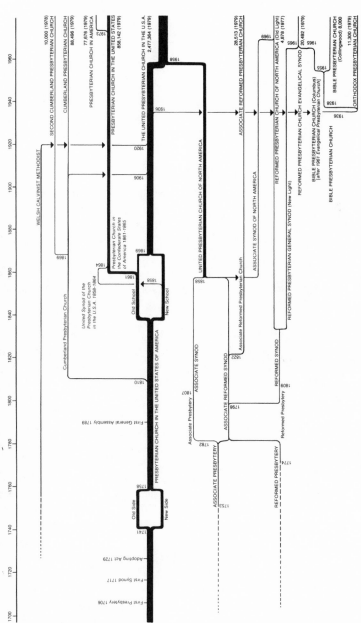

# III

# THE ETHOS OF THE REFORMED TRADITION

The faith of a people is written in theological books, structured in organizations, and expressed in worship. It is also embodied in style and manner of life. In fact, style of life always betrays basic theological and ethical convictions. "There is an intimate but seldom-seen connection between a person's thought and his style, which Alfred North Whitehead defined as the 'ultimate morality of the mind.' "[1] Hence it is appropriate to place at the beginning of a study of the Reformed tradition an analysis of those motifs that have given a particular style and manner to Reformed theology, worship, polity, culture, and life. Even though life-styles are never pure and are never subject to precise definition, certain themes can be specified and substantially verified. At least nine identifiable motifs have significantly shaped the Reformed style of being a Christian.

## The Majesty and the Praise of God

Popular estimates of the Reformed tradition have always identified it with the sovereignty of God and with predestination. This popular estimate has good basis in fact. While efforts to identify Calvinism with a central doctrine from which others are deduced have all failed, a case can be made that the central theme of Calvinist theology, which holds it all together, is the conviction that every human being has every moment to do with the *living* God.

The God with whom man has to do is the Creator of heaven and earth who maintains all things in their being and who governs them by his will. God is energy, force, and life. He is purpose, intention, and will. He is the Lord God, who "comes with might," "who has measured the waters in the hollow of his hand

and marked off the heavens with a span," and before whom "the nations are as nothing" and "are accounted by him as less than nothing." (Isaiah 40:10, 12, 17) This is the Creator God who works mightily in human history to accomplish his purposes. The chief end of man is to glorify God.

H. R. Niebuhr has brought out the peculiar characteristics of this motif by setting it over against another motif that has been widely influential in the Christian community, the vision of God. Thomas Aquinas gave classic statement to this understanding of the Christian life. "Man's ultimate felicity consists only in the contemplation of God."[2] The divine attribute that impressed Calvin, Niebuhr observed, was not the eternal perfection of goodness, beauty, and truth, but God's forceful reality and power.

> To call the vision man's greatest good is to make contemplation, however prepared for by activity and however issuing in action, the final end of life; to put the sovereignty of God in the first place is to make obedient activity superior to contemplation, however much of *theoria* is necessary to action. The principle of vision suggests that the perfection of the object seen is loved above all else; the principle of the kingdom indicates that the reality and power of the being commanding obedience are primarily regarded. The first term may also be interpreted to mean that the initiative lies with the one who seeks to see while the object is conceived as somehow at rest; and indeed Roman Catholicism has always been inclined toward a Christian or "other-worldly humanism" which believes that man's rational sight is almost, though never quite, sufficient to pierce through to the divine truth. The term "kingdom of God" puts all the emphasis on the divine initiative. The distinction must not be pressed so as to obscure the fundamental agreement between the Christianity of the vision and that of the kingdom. Whether we say *visio dei* or *regnum dei*, "God's first," in Thomas More's phrase. Whether end or beginning be stressed, God remains both end and beginning; whether Christ be called revealer or Lord, he is the mediator; whether one be Greek or Jew, in Christ he is a new creature. Yet it remains true that the differences between the two types of Christianity have been important in the past and are likely to be so in the future, though in no other way than as complementary views of a reality which refuses to be imprisoned even in the forms of a reason that has been enlightened by revelation.[3]

The consequences of this emphasis on the majesty of God are very vivid in the religious life that flows from it. As Troeltsch points out, the tone of the Christian life is not tied to "the level of self-preservation in the state of grace," and therefore "a constant preoccupation with personal moods and feelings is entirely unnecessary."[4]

> To Calvin the chief point is not the self-centered personal salvation of the creature, and the universality of the Divine Will of Love, but it is the Glory of God, which is equally exalted in the holy activity of the elect and in the futile rage of the reprobate.[5]

The glory of God and his purposes in the world are more important than the salvation of one's own soul. Personal salvation can be a very selfish act. Berdyaev paints a horrible picture of those who trample over their neighbors in the crush to get through the gates of heaven.[6] Those Calvinists who asked candidates for the ministry if they were willing to be damned for the glory of God were trying to root out the last element of self-seeking in religion. Human beings are religious, the Calvinist asserts, not to satisfy their needs or to give meaning to their lives but because God has created them and called them to his service. Karl Barth puts it this way.

> It seems to me that if we want to keep the order of the New Testament we must say: God has ordained and chosen them into his temporal and eternal service, and, consequently, into everlasting life. The notion of service should not be missing. In the New Testament, they did not come to the Church merely so that they might be saved and happy, but that they might have the signal privilege of serving the Lord.[7]

Calvin's own life illustrates this point. He thought he was best equipped by nature and inclination to be a scholar. Yet he gave himself with no self-pity to the demands of church organization, to the challenges of civil and ecclesiastical politics, and to the pastoral care not only of Geneva but also of Reformed Protestantism. When Farel invoked the judgment of God and Bucer reminded him of Jonah, Calvin did not hesitate to accept unpleasant responsibilities. His letter to Farel on his return to Geneva in 1541 reveals the personal dimensions of his theology.

> As to my intended course of proceeding, this is my present feeling: had I the choice at my own disposal, nothing would be less agreeable to me than to follow your advice. But when I remember that I am not my own, I offer up my heart, presented as a sacrifice to the Lord. Therefore there is no ground for your apprehension that you will only get fine words. Our friends are in earnest, and promise

sincerely. And for myself, I protest that I have no other desire than that, setting aside all consideration of me, they may look only to what is most for the glory of God and the advantage of the Church. Although I am not very ingenious, I would not want pretexts by which I might adroitly slip away, so that I should easily excuse myself in the sight of men, and shew that it was no fault of mine. I am well aware, however, that it is God with whom I have to do, from whose sight such crafty imaginations cannot be withheld. Therefore I submit my will and my affections, subdued and held-fast, to the obedience of God.[8]

The emphasis on the majesty and lordship of God has always been a theme of Reformed theology, but there have been variations in the experience. The increasing knowledge and awareness of the physical environment of human existence, as well as changes in the expected forms of Christian experience, led to theological changes. In the time of the Enlightenment and of the Great Awakening, Jonathan Edwards gave expression to the way in which the beauty of God had grasped him, which is different from the experience of Calvin.

"The first instance that I remember of that sort of inward, sweet delight in God and divine things that I have lived much in since, was on reading those words, 1 Tim. i:17. *Now unto the King eternal, immortal, invisible, the only wise God, be honor and glory forever and ever, Amen. . . .*"

"After this my sense of divine things gradually increased, and became more and more lively, and had more of that inward sweetness. The appearance of every thing was altered; there seemed to be, as it were, a calm, sweet cast, or appearance of divine glory, in almost every thing. God's excellency, his wisdom, his purity and love, seemed to appear in every thing; in the sun, and moon, and stars; in the clouds and blue sky; in the grass, flowers, trees; in the water, and all nature; which used greatly to fix my mind. . . . And scarce any thing, among all the works of nature, was so sweet to me as thunder and lightning; formerly, nothing had been so terrible to me. Before, I used to be uncommonly terrified with thunder, and to be struck with terror when I saw a thunder storm rising; but now, on the contrary, it rejoiced me. I felt God, so to speak, at the first appearance of a thunder storm; and used to take the opportunity, at such times, to fix myself in order to view the clouds and see the lightnings play, and hear the majestic and awful voice of God's thunder, which oftentimes was exceedingly entertaining, leading me to sweet contemplations of my great and glorious God."[9]

This emphasis upon God the Creator and Lord gave depth to life. Man does not live on the surface of universal history. Human life is not the simple product of history and of natural forces. Personhood is rooted in the will and the intention of God. God thought of every person before he was called into being and gave to him his individuality, his identity, and his name. Human existence is rooted in eternity, and its end is the praise of God. Hence the Christian lives in the quiet confidence that God is greater than all the battalions of earth and that life is at God's disposal. *The Book of Common Prayer* expresses the dialectic of the Christian life, as Calvin understood it, with remarkable clarity. "In the time of prosperity, fill our hearts with thankfulness, and in the day of trouble, suffer not our trust in thee to fail."[10]

## The Polemic Against Idolatry

More than a century ago Alexander Schweizer observed that Calvinism is distinguished from Lutheranism by its emphasis on the majesty of God and by its assault on all forms of paganism in the medieval church, whereas Lutheranism had been primarily concerned with "judaistic" lapses into salvation by works.[11] Reformed theology has resisted every effort to get control of God, to fasten the infinite and indeterminate God to the finite and the determinate whether it be images, or the bread and wine of the sacraments, or the structures of the church. God is free, and God acts and speaks when and where he chooses.[12]

Calvin never seriously contemplated the possibility of unbelief or no-faith. The human options were exhausted by faith in the living God and idolatry. "God himself is the sole and proper witness of himself."[13] Man's responsibility is to listen to the word of God and to correct what he thinks he has heard by continuing to listen. The human starting point is not one's own existence but the will of the creator or lord. Therefore every effort to domesticate God, to shape God according to man's own understanding of what he should be, to fasten God to some finite and determinate object and thus to control him must be firmly repudiated.

The practical consequence of this polemic against idolatry was an iconoclasm that held in question every human achievement and that refused final loyalty to any human being or to any human endeavor. As Richard Niebuhr has put it, "The converse of dependence on God is independence of everything less than God."[14] This iconoclasm was not merely negative, but it positively contributed to the strength of many human endeavors. In his perceptive biography of John Knox, Lord Eustace Percy has written that the best servants of the state are those whose highest loyalty was not to the state but to God.[15] The Reformed polemic against idolatry prevents human endeavors from overreaching themselves, claiming too much for themselves, and thus destroying themselves. Only God is great enough to answer to man's highest and total loyalty without destroying the truly human. Every lesser loyalty when made absolute is abortive and destructive.

## The Working Out of the Divine Purposes in History

God the creator and governor is lord of history and nature. Paul Lehmann's use of the metaphor "politician" to refer to God is surely in line with early Reformed theology.[16] God is working his purpose out in human history. He calls his people to be the instruments of his purpose. His purposes are not simply the salvation of souls but also the establishment of a holy community and the glorification of his name through all the earth.

John Calvin stands out in the history of the church as one who was more vividly aware than almost any other of the mighty working of God in human history and of God's call to his people for service in the world. Christopher Dawson, a Roman Catholic historian of culture, has written:

> For behind Western democracy there lies the spiritual world of Calvinism and the Free Churches, which is, as I have said, completely different in its political and social outlook from the world of Lutheranism, and which has had a far greater influence and closer connexion with what we know as Western civilization without further qualification.
>
> This divergence was only fully manifested in the course of centuries, but it was not simply a result of historical circumstance. It had its root in the very origins of the two confessions and in the personality of their founders. At first sight this may seem difficult to maintain. For there is in the teaching of Calvin the same pessimism with regard to human nature and human will, the same other-worldliness and the same exaltation of divine power and even arbitrariness that is to be found in Luther. Nevertheless, all these conceptions were transformed by the intense spirit of moral activism which characterized Calvin and Calvinism. The genius of Calvin was that of an organizer and legislator, severe, logical, and inflexible in purpose, and consequently it was he and not Luther who inspired Protestantism with the will to dominate the world and to change

society and culture. Hence though Calvinism has always been regarded as the antithesis of Catholicism to a far greater extent than
Lutheranism, it stands much nearer to Catholicism in its conception
of the relation of Church and State and in its assertion of the
independence and supremacy of the spiritual power. In this respect
it carries on the traditions of medieval Catholicism and of the
Gregorian movement of reform to an even greater degree than did
the Catholicism of the Counter-Reformation itself.

In an age when the Papacy was dependent on the Hapsburg
monarchies and when Catholics accepted the theories of passive
obedience and the divine right of kings, the Calvinists asserted the
Divine Right of Presbytery and declared that "the Church was the
foundation of the world" and that it was the duty of kings to "throw
down their crowns before her and lick the dust off her feet." But
these theocratic claims were not hierarchic and impersonal as in the
medieval Church, they were based on an intense individualism
deriving from the certainty of election and the duty of the individual
Christian to co-operate in realizing the divine purpose against a
sinful and hostile world. Thus Calvinism is at once aristocratic and
democratic; aristocratic in as much as the "saints" were an elect
minority chosen from the mass of fallen humanity and infinitely
superior to the children of this world; but democratic in that each
was directly responsible to God who is no respecter of persons.
Calvinism is, in fact, a democracy of saints, elect of God, but also
in a sense self-chosen, since it is the conscience of the individual
which is the ultimate witness of his election.[17]

Calvin's intention in Geneva was not simply the salvation of
souls but a Geneva that was reformed by the Word of God. John
Knox in a well known statement exclaimed, "In other places, I
confess Christ to be truly preached; but manners and religion to
be so sincerely reformed, I have not yet seen in any other
place."[18]

In Scotland and in England the Reformed community sought
to build the New Jerusalem. The Puritans who came to New
England were not simply seeking freedom to worship God as they
liked. They were going on an errand into the wilderness to establish a Christian society and to demonstrate to the decadent society of Europe the possibilities of a Christian community.[19]
H. Richard Niebuhr has persuasively argued that this awareness
of the powerful activity of God working itself out under the rubrics of the sovereignty of God, the kingdom of Christ, and finally
as the coming kingdom is the most characteristic motif of the
Christian movement in America.[20]

The Calvinist saint was responsible for his world. He was a

soldier of the Lord in conquest of the world, the flesh, and the devil. He was God's elect instrument to fulfill his purposes. Michael Walzer in his study of radical politics writes that it did not enter into the thought of Machiavelli or Luther or Bodin "that specially designated and organized bands of men might play a creative part in the political world, destroying the established order and reconstructing society according to the Word of God or the plans of their fellows." Walzer argues that

> it was the Calvinists who first switched the emphasis of political thought from the prince to the saint . . . and then constructed a theoretical justification for independent political action. What Calvinists said of the saint, other men would later say of the citizen: the same sense of civic virtue, of discipline and duty, lies behind the two names. . . .
> The saints saw themselves as divine *instruments* and theirs was the politics of wreckers, architects, and builders—hard at work upon the political world. . . . They treated every obstacle as another example of the devil's resourcefulness and they summoned all their energy, imagination, and craft to overcome it.[21]

Calvin, it must be clearly understood, did not think of himself as a "change agent" but as a servant of God. The kingdom of God, not a human Utopia; the glory of God, not humanitarianism, was his goal, though he did insist that love of neighbor is the truest test of orthodoxy and doctrine. Yet Calvin set in motion movements that did change society because he united his own theology and its peculiar emphases with an awareness of the modern world. Fred Graham has put it very well:

> What he did was stand more surely than any other thinker of his time within this new world. . . . He approved of the city and its activities. He was not instinctively disgusted with business and trade, as were medieval churchmen . . . . And he had the sure instinct to perceive the place of religion within this new age, and to curb the worse instincts of the age by the Word of God and godly discipline. . . . Neither Calvin, nor Huguenot, nor Puritan of Old or New England thought for a moment that riches were good or business holy. But they had decided to live in this world, and did their utmost to leash it to the Word of God.[22]

Roland Bainton, an astute church historian, has summarized the Calvinist outlook.

> The early Calvinist at any rate did not eat his heart out and consume his energies in concern as to his salvation. This point significantly sets off Calvinism alike from Catholicism and Lutheranism. . . .

Their commission was to establish a theocracy in the sense of a Holy Commonwealth, a community in which every member should make the glory of God his sole concern. It was not a community ruled by the Church nor by the clergy nor even in accord with the Bible in any literalist sense, because God is greater than a book even though it contains His Word. The holy community should exhibit that parallelism of church and state which had been the ideal of the Middle Ages and of Luther, but had never been realized and never can be save in a highly select community where the laity and the clergy, the Town Council and the ministers, are all equally imbued with the same high purpose. Calvin came nearer to realizing it than anyone else in the sixteenth century.[23]

The holy community was never realized, however remarkable in any relative judgment some achievements were. Human freedom and proclivity to sin made any achievement partial and precarious. Pietism, the definition of Christian life in terms of personal piety, and evangelism, conceived as plucking individual souls from the burning, were sometimes substitutes for the primal vision. In more recent years a pluralistic, secular, mobile society has rightly magnified human freedom in regard to faith and life-style and has made the possibility of the holy community even more remote. Yet the vision lives on in the conviction that the very existence of the Christian community in the larger community does shape history. Moreover, the Christian movement today still has the essential weapons of Calvin's warfare; namely, the power of the preached word, the strength of a Christian personality, and the testimony of the Christian community's life. These, when undergirded by the power of the Holy Spirit, are not inconsiderable. Furthermore, Reformed Christians in the tradition of the prophets have always believed that God used the Cyruses of the world to do his will.

Abraham Kuyper (1837–1920), a Dutch Calvinist, gave a distinctive formulation to the vision of the holy community in terms of the principle of sphere-sovereignty. This concept continues to be used in fruitful ways, especially by Dutch Calvinists. Kuyper believed intensely that all of life is lived under the sovereignty of God but that different spheres such as the state, the church, marriage, and education have an independence of each other. Sphere-sovereignty stands in contrast to sphere-subsidiarity in which one sphere, state or science for example, would be subsidiary to the church. Thus the sovereignty of God can be realized in a total society without some spheres of the society being subjected to the tyranny of other spheres in hierarchical subordination.[24]

## Ethics, a Life of Holiness

John Calvin insisted that Christians should approve their Christianity by a life of holiness. While an exposition of the ten commandments was characteristic of most catechisms, the Reformed gave very detailed attention to this exposition in their catechisms and systematic theologies. The polity that American Presbyterianism adopted in 1788 had in its preface the declaration that "truth is in order to goodness."[25] The end of the Christian life, according to Calvin, is a life conformed to the will of God. Therefore, any theology or worship which does not edify must be re-examined.

The Christian life is, on the one hand, justification by grace through faith and, on the other, sanctification. To put it in other words, salvation is both forgiveness and renewal, both God's grace as mercy and God's grace as power. The proper unity of these two aspects of the one experience of salvation is the art of the Christian life and is never easy to achieve. Some are tempted to overemphasize the experience of forgiveness. The awareness, so vivid to Luther, that we have to be forgiven our best deeds as well as our worst can lead to an indifference to the various levels of goodness and various degrees of sin. Yet on the human level these differences between forgiven sinners are very significant. Moreover, it is cheap grace that presumes upon forgiveness and refuses to strive to be perfect as the Father in heaven is perfect. Others overemphasize sanctification. They forget that salvation is by grace and not by merit, that man sins in his best as well as in his worst deed. The Christian life becomes obedience to laws. John Calvin, as Reinhold Niebuhr observed, put these two aspects of salvation together theologically as well as and perhaps better than any other in church history.[26] The Westminster Larger Catechism likewise exercised great care in answer to the question, "Wherein do justification and sanctification differ?"

> Although sanctification be inseparably joined with justification, yet they differ, in that, God in justification, imputeth the righteousness of Christ; in sanctification, his Spirit infuseth grace, and enableth to the exercise thereof; in the former, sin is pardoned; in the other,

it is subdued; the one doth equally free all believers from the revenging wrath of God, and that perfectly in this life, that they never fall into condemnation; the other is neither equal in all, nor in this life perfect in any, but growing up to perfection.[27]

This is a remarkably balanced statement. In practical life, however, Calvin and the Reformed tradition often failed to maintain the tension and overemphasized sanctification. One result has been legalism, which in the end always lacks grace. Another result has been self-righteousness, especially when sin is reduced to sensuality, which is more manageable than pride or apathy, especially in old age. A third consequence has been obscurantism when the will of God is prematurely identified with some human pattern of conduct. The proper balancing of forgiveness and holiness in Christian life is not simple.

The Reformed community's mistakes have been admittedly on the side of sanctification. This fact must not, however, obscure the strength of the tradition that has insisted that the Christian is not only a forgiven person but an ethical person. This emphasis is reflected in the theology, worship, and polity of the church. It is especially true of the ethos of the church's life. The elect person is called to a life of service and obedience. The forgiven person is summoned to live by the law of God after having heard the comforting words of the liturgy and the declaration of forgiveness. The first use of the law for Calvin was not to bring sinners to repentance or to restrain public behavior but to stimulate and to guide the Christian.[28] Whatever else the Reformed Christians may be, they are concerned about ethics, about the law, about morality.[29]

## The Life of the Mind as the Service of God

Zwingli had received a first-rate humanist education in preparation for the priesthood. John Calvin also was a humanist and a scholar before he became a reformer. The humanist tradition of the sixteenth century left an indelible imprint upon the whole future of the Reformed tradition.[30] Wherever the Reformed community went, it established schools alongside the churches not only to teach the Bible or to teach reading and other skills to study the Bible but also to teach the whole range of liberal arts in order to liberate the human spirit. Furthermore, Reformed theology has always been careful in the historical study of the sources of the faith, especially of the Bible and of the intention of Jesus Christ for the Christian and the church.

The Academy at Geneva was in many ways the crowning achievement of Calvin's work there. Its roots were in the *Institutes* and the church ordinances. In the *Institutes* Calvin wrote that those who have "tasted the liberal arts penetrate with their aid far more deeply into the secrets of the divine wisdom."[31] In the *Ordinances* he declared,

> The office proper to doctors is the instruction of the faithful in true doctrine, in order that the purity of the Gospel be not corrupted either by ignorance or by evil opinions. As things are disposed today, we always include under this title aids and instructions for maintaining the doctrine of God and defending the Church from injury by the fault of pastors and ministers. So to use a more intelligible word, we will call this the order of the schools. . . .
>
> But because it is only possible to profit from such lectures if first one is instructed in the languages and humanities, and also because it is necessary to raise offspring for time to come, in order not to leave the Church deserted to our children, a college should be instituted for instructing children to prepare them for the ministry as well as for civil government.[32]

Thus from the beginning the Reformed sponsored learning as Christian duty. They placed value upon the skills of language, reading, writing, and speaking. They also prized clarity, logic, and precision in mental procedure. They valued the ability to analyze a problem and to formulate an answer. The sermon was an intellectual exercise and a mental discipline that had a significant cultural impact. Yet the Reformed were not intellectualistic. Calvin had warned against curiosity and speculation. The learning that was joined to piety had a strong pragmatic and utilitarian quality.

The life of the mind as the service of God had special reference to the church. Calvin made knowledge as well as personal commitment a condition for admission to the communion table.[33] He was convinced that Christians should know what they believed and why they believed it. In his letter to Somerset on the reform of the church in England, he left no doubt about the importance of catechetical instruction.

> Believe me, Monseigneur, the Church of God will never preserve itself without a Catechism, for it is like the seed to keep the good grain from dying out, and causing it to multiply from age to age.

And therefore, if you desire to build an edifice which shall be of long duration, and which shall not soon fall into decay, make provision for the children being instructed in a good Catechism, which may shew them briefly, and in language level to their tender age, wherein true Christianity consists. This Catechism will serve two purposes, to wit, as an introduction to the whole people, so that every one may profit from what shall be preached, and also to enable them to discern when any presumptuous person puts forward strange doctrine. Indeed, I do not say that it may not be well, and even necessary, to bind down the pastors and curates to a certain written form, as well for the sake of supplementing the ignorance and deficiencies of some, as the better to manifest the conformity and agreement between all the churches; thirdly, to take away all ground of pretence for bringing in any eccentricity or new-fangled doctrine on the part of those who only seek to indulge an idle fancy . . . .[34]

Catechetical instruction simply focused a general passion for knowledge. Solidly written books and pamphlets, learned sermons delivered in plain style without the ostentation of learning were indispensable marks of Reformed churchmanship. As Calvin put it, "the tongue without the mind must be highly displeasing to God."[35]

## *Preaching*

The Reformation, writes James Nichols, was the greatest revival of preaching in church history.[36] There is good basis for this judgment. The Reformation began in Zurich as Zwingli undertook to preach through the book of Matthew. Preaching was at the very center of the Reformation in Geneva with sermons scheduled for different hours on Sunday and on most of the days of the week.

In his famous letter to Somerset, Calvin stressed preaching as well as catechetical education. There was too little preaching in England, Calvin feared, and the greater part of that, he chided, was read from a written text.

Preaching ought not to be lifeless but lively, to teach, to exhort, to reprove. . . . You are also aware, Monseigneur, how he [Paul] speaks of the lively power and energy with which they ought to speak, who would approve themselves as good and faithful ministers of God, who must not make a parade of rhetoric, only to gain esteem for themselves; but that the Spirit of God ought to sound forth by their voice, so as to work with mighty energy.[37]

Even if Calvin himself spent little time on the preparation of particular sermons but drew resources out of his general theological work, and even if he frequently repeated what he had said or written previously, preaching was still a most important part of his life's work. It was the means of grace above all others by which he expected God to transform Geneva. To this end he preached more than 3000 sermons in his fifty-five-year lifetime.[38]

The Reformed community sometimes dared to speak of preaching as the word of God. Bullinger declared in the Second Helvetic Confession, "Wherefore when this Word of God is now preached in the church by preachers lawfully called, we believe that the very Word of God is preached, and received of the faithful."[39] Yet the Reformed were careful not to bind the Spirit of God to the word in preaching, as they believed the Lutherans did. As Bullinger wrote in the *Decades,* a book of sermons:

> Whom he meaneth to bestow knowledge and faith on, to them he sendeth teachers, by the word of God to preach true faith unto them. Not because it lieth in man's power, will, or ministry, to give faith; nor because the outward word spoken by man's mouth is able of itself to bring faith: but the voice of man, and the preaching of God's word, do teach us what true faith is, or what God doth will and command us to believe. For God himself alone, by sending his Holy Spirit into the hearts and minds of men, doth open our hearts, persuade our minds, and cause us with all our heart to believe that which we by his word and teaching have learned to believe.[40]

Calvin sometimes used language that seems to bind the Spirit to the preaching of the word. The minister, he said, is the very mouth of God.[41] Yet he, like Bullinger, knew that preaching is the word of God only in a subordinate sense; and he insisted, as few have, in his exposition of the doctrine of predestination that the Spirit is not bound to preaching. God is still sovereign. Yet this did not diminish Calvin's estimate of preaching as the usual means of God's grace and power. Calvin's position is very well summarized in this statement from the *Institutes.*

> For first, the Lord teaches and instructs us by his Word. Secondly, he confirms it by the sacraments. Finally, he illumines our minds by the light of his Holy Spirit and opens our hearts for the Word and sacraments to enter in, which would otherwise only strike our ears and appear before our eyes, but not at all affect us within.[42]

Puritanism was also a preaching movement. The Puritan, like Calvin, had great confidence in the power of the written and spoken word. He worked to arrive at a style that was appropriate to the preaching of the word of God. This style, as expounded by the Calvinist theologian William Perkins and as written into the *Westminster Directory of Worship,* was plain; but it was not ineffective or unimaginative. It was designed to be understood and to move the hearer, which, the evidence indicates, it did in a remarkable way. The reaction against the ornate, witty, rhetorical style of the orthodox Anglican became a mark of the Puritan's conversion.[43] The preaching style of the Puritan was plain and powerful and in the tradition of Calvin. Its influence lingered long in Britain and in the United States, where it was tempered by the frontier revival.

Preaching has also been the great theme of the two best-known Reformed theologians of the twentieth century, Emil Brunner and Karl Barth. Each thought of himself as a preacher, and each wrote his theology for preachers. Brunner preached to large congregations in the Fraumünster in Zurich, and Barth took delight in preaching in the jails.

The Reformed community has always had great confidence, perhaps too great confidence, in written and spoken words and, in particular, in the power of preaching, when blessed by the Holy Spirit, to change human life and to create a godly public opinion. The demand for simplicity, directness, authenticity, and sincerity, which have been emphasized generally in the tradition, applies especially to preaching. The Calvinist sermon is not ostentatious or pretentious but plain, roughhewn, and powerful. In considerable measure the content, clearly and distinctly presented, is the rhetoric as well as the message. Reinhold Niebuhr, one of the great preachers of the twentieth century, tells in his diary that he very soon in his ministry had to decide if he were going to be a "pretty" preacher. He decided against "pretty" in favor of the rough-hewn and plain-spoken sermons that the Reformed tradition has so much admired.[44]

## The Organized Church and Pastoral Care

Calvin believed that the organization of the Christian community was critically important for the nurturing of the life of faith and obedience. The human phenomena of church structures and procedures of worship are means of grace and must be appropriate for the work of the Spirit. Hence neither Calvin nor his successors were indifferent to structures. Yet the structures were not important in themselves but as means of grace.

The focus of Calvin's concern with church organization is pastoral care and the "cure of souls." Calvin not only wrote the office of pastor into his church structure, but he was himself a pastor above all. In the official order for the church's existence in Geneva, he provided for visitation of prisoners and of the sick, and for catechetical instruction and examination prior to admission to the Lord's Supper. The confession of sins and the promise of forgiveness of sins, which are in the Sunday liturgy, can also take place in the meeting of Christian with Christian and, in particular, in the pastoral work of the ministers. The deacons were constituted as the church's ministry of compassion to the needy. Yet pastoral care is not only comfort for the bereaved, forgiveness for the guilty, and help for the sick and needy; it is pre-eminently the renewal of life in the image of Christ. Pastoral care has as its purpose not only the giving of comfort but also the redirection of life.[45] In his voluminous correspondence Calvin exercised pastoral care all over Europe, not only giving comfort but also calling Christians to the heroic, demanding, and dangerous service of Almighty God.

Jean-Daniel Benoit in a substantial study *Calvin: Director of Souls* finds that Calvin was first a pastor and then a theologian or, better, that he was a theologian in order to be a pastor. He also concluded that it was as a pastor, not as a theologian, church organizer, or powerful personality that Calvin significantly influenced history. For in the care of souls, Calvin not only was concerned for the salvation of the individual; but he also united this salvation with the advancement of the reign of Jesus Christ.[46]

## The Disciplined Life

Personal discipline was a characteristic of the early Protestant reformers of all persuasions, as it is of most persons who accomplish much. Yet even among highly disciplined people, Calvin stands out not only in his personal achievement but also in his insistence that discipline should characterize the Christian life and community. He attempted to make discipline a part of the structure of the organized life of the church, especially in the work of the elders in the consistory or session.[47]

In the early years of the Reformed movement Zurich differed from Calvin's Geneva on the achievement of discipline. Bullinger feared that the Oecolampadian-Calvinist way would issue in a "papal tyranny." He kept discipline separate from the Lord's Supper and left it to the Christian magistrate. As J. Wayne Baker has argued in *Heinrich Bullinger and the Covenant: The Other Reformed Tradition* (1980), Bullinger developed an alternate way of being the Christian community with his doctrine of magisterial sovereignty.

Discipline, as the Reformed tradition has advocated it, can best be understood as the deliberate and economic use of the energies and vitalities of human existence in the pursuit of loyalty to God and the advancement of God's cause in the world. John T. McNeill has found that economy is a word that is descriptive of the Puritan.[48] It is certainly descriptive of Calvin's personal life and churchmanship. Yet neither Calvin nor the Puritans were ascetic in an attempt to escape an evil world. They were ascetic or disciplined in that they believed in the economical use of a good world. They exulted in the vitality of existence, but they also believed that momentary desires must sometimes be denied for the sake of a later good. Within a disciplined life there was and is a place for fun and even frivolity, but this place is fitted into a larger order.

Max Weber, the German sociologist, and Ernst Troeltsch, the historian of the social teachings of the churches, were impressed by the self-discipline of the Calvinist as it applies to work.

> To a people who have been educated on Calvinistic principles the lazy habit of living on an inherited income seems a downright sin; to follow a calling which has no definite end and which yields no material profit seems a foolish waste of time and energy, and failure to make full use of chances of gaining material profit seems like indifference towards God.[49]

Calvin rejected the monastery, but he made the whole world the place of disciplined living and the pursuit of goals that have their end in God and his cause on earth. The discipline of work applied not simply to the productivity of business or labor but also to political and social reform.

The early Calvinist was too reserved to be an exhibitionist in personal feelings or in personal piety. Yet here too Calvin and his followers stood for the discipline of private and public worship. Reformed life can never be reduced to private piety, but it is never without it.[50]

The discipline of the Reformed tradition, especially as illustrated by Calvin and the Puritans, was not regarded as a burden. It was a manner of life that was freely chosen and that was believed to be the means of the joyful and responsible freeing of life's energies and vitalities.

## *Simplicity*

Simplicity is a recurring theme in all of Calvin's writings, and it was a characteristic of his practice.[51] He opposed all redundancy. He was the enemy of the ostentatious, the pompous, the contrived, the needlessly complicated. His style was plain and direct. He opposed needless spending and consumption, but he also opposed other forms of waste. Simplicity is closely related to Calvin's emphasis on authenticity and sincerity. Every activity or device that covers up reality must be rejected.

Simplicity was a general principle with Calvin. He applied it to liturgy, polity, and style of life. He also applied it to literary style, and this application serves well as an illustration of the way this motif shaped his own life. Early in his professional life, when writing his commentary on Romans (1539), Calvin deliberately set out to write his commentary with *"lucid brevity,"* and he did not hesitate to rebuke the older and distinguished Bucer for being verbose and lacking in clarity.[52] Calvin deals with style in greater detail in his commentary on 1 Corinthians 1:20. As Calvin understood the situation, Paul's method of preaching had been plain and he (Paul) objected to "wicked and unfaithful ministers" at Corinth who sought to recommend themselves with a show of words and masks of human wisdom. The simplicity of the gospel was disfigured; the Corinthians themselves "were tickled with a silly fondness for high-sounding style." Hence Calvin speaks approvingly of Paul's "rude, coarse and unpolished style." Yet Calvin does not reject human eloquence. God is its author, and every person ought to rejoice in it, but only as it is used to convey truth and to uncover reality. It is never an end in itself. Eloquence can get in the way of truth. "In a plain and unpolished manner of address, the majesty of truth might shine more conspicuously." Language is the servant of truth, of reality.

That eloquence, therefore, is neither to be condemned nor despised, which has no tendency to lead Christians to be taken up with an outward glitter of words, or intoxicate them with empty delight, or tickle their ears with its tinkling sound, or cover over the cross of Christ with its empty show as with a veil; but, on the contrary, tends to call us back to the native simplicity of the gospel, tends to exalt the simple preaching of the cross by voluntarily abasing itself, and, in fine, acts the part of a herald to procure a hearing for those fishermen and illiterate persons, who have nothing to recommend them but the energy of the Spirit.[53]

Simplicity is very close to sincerity. It clears away the ornaments, the ostentations, the contrivances, the pretenses that obscure the real.

------

There is no one model of Reformed life-style or personality. Furthermore the characteristics of the Reformed ethos listed in this discussion are not exclusively Reformed or in some cases Christian. They can be found elsewhere in Christian and human communities. Yet they have persistently and frequently characterized the Reformed community. In a variety of patterns they have been embodied in personalities and communities that are Reformed. Furthermore they have been integrally related to Reformed theologies, polities, and worship.

# IV

# THEOLOGY
# AND
# THE REFORMED TRADITION

The Reformed tradition has emphasized the vocation of the Christian to be a theologian and, more specifically, a responsible theologian of Christian faith. Augustine, perhaps the greatest of Christian theologians, insisted that there is a faith commitment in all understanding.[1] Life is so constructed that faith of some sort is inevitable. Human existence demands that every person must decide and act, and every person decides and acts in the light of some faith commitment about the nature of the universe and the meaning of human existence. To be human is to live by faith. There is no other option. Therefore, to be human is also to have a theology. So every person is in some sense, however vague, a theologian. The uniqueness of the Reformed tradition is not that it insists that everyone is a theologian but that it insists that everyone should be a responsible theologian who can speak intelligibly about the faith.

Theology, as an inevitable task for every human being, is rooted in a threefold necessity. Theology is required work for the Christian by Biblical warrant. The warrant is implicit in the admonition of Jesus to consider how the lilies grow (Matthew 6:28). It is explicit in the great commandment, "Thou shalt love the Lord thy God . . . with all thy mind." (Matthew 22:37) The Apostle Paul insisted that the believer must take every thought captive to Christ (2 Corinthians 10:5). The author of 1 Peter declared, "Always be prepared to make a defense to any one who calls you to account for the hope that is in you." (1 Peter 3:15)

For the believer, theology is grounded in the nature of faith itself. " . . . faith is incipient theology."[2] Every faith commitment involves a spoken or unspoken assertion about the final nature of things and about the meaning of human existence. In addition, faith always seeks understanding (intelligibility), in part because the person who believes is a self with a mind as well as a heart, and in part because faith as well as the self seeks to bring all things, all the diversities of life, into some intelligible, coherent whole.

For every human being (or almost every human being), theology is demanded by the mystery that encompasses all created things. Karl Barth has well said that life is lived in brackets, or to put it another way, in parentheses.[3] The words in parentheses only make sense in the light of the words outside the parentheses. Yet if one is within the parentheses, there is no way to know what is outside the parentheses. Within the parentheses much can be known and done, many problems solved, but the meaning of the parentheses remains unknown.

The mystery that encompasses all created things must not be confused with problems that can be solved with greater knowledge.[4] Problems are due to ignorance; mystery is due to the nature of human existence. Problems can be solved by work and by knowledge, but knowledge enhances mystery. Modern culture that has been amazingly successful in solving problems is tempted to confuse the two. The journey to the moon, for example, solved many problems; but it only enhanced the mystery of the moon and the earth. The picture of the earth taken from the moon surely has as much spiritual significance as any photograph of our time. For here is this pendent ball, the earth, our home, floating in the darkness of space, reflecting the light of the sun.

Every human being encounters the boundaries, the brackets, the parentheses that enclose the existence of all created beings.[5] At the boundary of existence some encounter a reality which they can only understand as impersonal and materialistic. Yet most human beings have at the boundary of their existence, on occasion at least, encountered a mystery, however vague and diffused, that can only be understood as a "Thou" and for which the word God has seemed the most appropriate response. These experiences can never be commanded; they come as a "gift" in moments when we *know* we are utterly dependent, when we *know* that we are free and responsible, when we *know* we must tell the truth no matter the hurt, when we confront our final earthly destiny in death. The encounter with mystery may also come in reflection upon the universe and an existence that is not self-explanatory. Theodore Dobzhansky, a prominent authority on the evolution of life on this planet, concluded his investigation with the question that has troubled thoughtful people in every age and that is not answered by the data. "Whose enterprise is this, and with what aim and for what purpose is it undertaken? The four centuries of the growth of science since Copernicus have not dispelled this mystery; the one since Darwin has made it more urgent than ever."[6] The important point is that most people have had experiences either at the boundary of their lives or in critical reflection which only the word God makes intelligible. Theology is reflection upon these crucial experiences of the mystery that encompasses human life in the light of "revelatory moments" that transmute the mystery into meaning.[7] The Christian community lives by the conviction that the mystery that encounters all people at the boundaries of human experience is made known in Jesus Christ, who is the embodiment of the wisdom of God and of the power of God.

## What Is Theology?

Theology in its broadest sense is critical reflection about the meaning of human existence and about the nature of the universe. *Christian* theology is critical reflection about God, about human existence, about the nature of the universe and about faith itself in the light of the revelation of God recorded in Scripture and particularly embodied in Jesus Christ, who is for the Christian community the final revelation, that is, the definitive revelation which is the criteria of all other revelations. Christian faith does not exhaust the theological possibilities as is evident in the existence of a great variety of theologies, for example, Islamic theology. Every theology, however, is based upon a faith commitment to what is conceived to be the revelatory event that is transparent and open to the ultimate nature of things. The revelatory event is the event that makes all other events intelligible, the event in light of which all other events are understood.[8] It occurs as a gift that becomes the clue to the meaning of all of experience. It results in insight into the nature of things that enables the believer to bring some unity into the diversity of life and to surrender life to a loyalty and a devotion that fulfills it.

No proof is possible for any revelatory event. Any revelation must be self-authenticating. Yet the decision of faith is not arbitrary; it is validated in or rejected by personal and social experience. The acceptance of a revelation is never the conclusion of an argument; yet the believers are always grasped by revelation in such a way that they believe their lives are illumined and saved by it. Furthermore, the revelatory event is subject to critical evaluation.

The problem of faith for every human being is first to identify the "revelatory moments" in the light of which life is lived and secondly to examine those "revelatory moments" as to their nature. These "moments" may be superficial, and they may "reveal" far less than the Creator of heaven and earth. The Christian community has subjected the claim that Jesus Christ is the decisive revelation of God to exacting investigation, particularly in the working out of the doctrine of the Person of Christ in the fourth and fifth centuries (Nicene Creed and Definition of Chalcedon) and in the historical studies of the past two centuries. The Christian claim may be wrong, but no one can deny that it has been critically evaluated by the community itself. Christians have the right to ask those who find life's "revelatory moment" in other experiences to subject those experiences to the same critical examination.

Every faith ought to be tested by human experience and by its capacity to do justice to facts of experience. For Christians the critical revelatory event is Jesus Christ. In his light, all other events become intelligible. The Christian claim is that the presence of God in Jesus Christ does more justice to the facts of life, makes more sense out of life, and gives more meaning to life than any other "revelation" whatsoever.[9]

It is very important to note that *every* person lives his life in the light of certain experiences or events that reveal for him the real nature of human existence and the world. These experiences may occur in business or in play, in moments of happiness or sadness, in the presence of the mystery of nature or of life, in personal history or in the history of the nation. Many persons are not consciously and critically aware of these experiences that shape their lives. Hence, the preliminary theological question is one of self-examination. Every self-critical person must ask: what is the revelatory event or events in my life? What is the experience or experiences that are the clue or clues for understanding all experience? The decision of faith is the decision as to which experience will provide the clue to the meaning of all other experiences. Most "revelatory experiences" are not adequate to account for or to support human existence. They reveal only false gods, only idols, that divide life and that in the end leave the believer desolate. Most people are never so integrated that they live in the light of any one "revelation" but are torn by many conflicting "revelations." H. Richard Niebuhr has rightly pointed out, however, that human lives are not only torn by conflicting loyalties to many false gods but that life is crushed by the "twilight of the gods" when their inadequacy is uncovered.[10] Christian faith is rooted in the conviction that the *Creator* of heaven and earth and the *Source* of human life is revealed in Jesus Christ. In Jesus Christ the God who is the end of the gods, who is the destroyer of idols, who is worthy of human devotion and loyalty, reveals himself. The Christian claim is that Jesus of Nazareth embodied the wisdom and the power of God, the Creator of heaven and earth.

Theological reflection as the explication of the faith by which one lives is a *human* work and subject to all the limitations of human existence. For this reason, there is no perfect theology. Human finiteness means that no theologian ever exhausts the meaning of Christian faith. The limitation of time means that every theology is most appropriate for a particular time and place and must be revised as time changes. Sin, as well as the limitation of every human perspective, means that every theology is in some measure an ideology; that is, a means of justifying the theologian's own situation and intentions. Karl Marx (1818–1883) said that theology is inordinately determined by the way the theologian makes his living and by his economic situation.[11] Ludwig Feuerbach (1804–1872) and Sigmund Freud (1856–1939) contended that theology was the projection of the human spirit, its wishes and its needs.[12] In some measure, both judgments are true of every theology. Therefore, no theology is ever *the* theology or the final statement of Christian faith. God's Word is final, but the human apprehensions of that Word are never complete or wholly accurate. No tradition has understood the human limitations of the theological enterprise better than the Reformed. Yet because the Reformed tradition has valued the role of theology so highly, it has been tempted at times to place too high a value on its own theological efforts. It is very difficult to hold together the conviction that theology is critically important and that every theologian must be the best possible theologian with the equally important conviction that all theologies, including one's own, fall short of the truth.

Theology as a *human* enterprise must be carried on in the Christian *community.* The Reformed theologian is never a lone individual doing his own thing but a member of the community participating in the dialogue of the community. Reformed theology is done for the universal, catholic church. It intends to be a statement of *the Christian* faith. Again, the task of combining the acceptance of the limited perspective of a particular tradition with the catholic or universal task of theology is not simple. Yet this is the intention of every truly Reformed theologian. Fortunately, the ecumenical movement has enlarged the perspectives of most theologians. Today responsible theologians not only represent as best they can their own tradition, but they also read, argue with, and assimilate the theological work of theologians of every Christian tradition. Moreover, the dialogue is carried on not only on the contemporary horizon, but back through the centuries. To be a church theologian is to appropriate or to recapitulate the theological work of the church in all times and places. No theologian can ever do this completely, but every theologian must do this as far as possible.

Theology which is a *human enterprise* and a *communal responsibility* is best understood as a *continuing dialogue.* [13] (1) The primary focus of the dialogue is the revelation of God, as it is contained in the Bible. The Holy Spirit, speaking through Scripture, is the final judge of all theological issues. Yet, theology is not simply a dialogue between the theologian and revelation. (2) The theologian is also in dialogue with the history of doctrine; for the history of doctrine, including the church's official confessions of faith, is the way the church has understood the revelation in other times and places. (3) The theologian is concerned with the actual experience of the Christian community, the way in which the believing response to revelation has been embodied in human life and community. Some theologians, Schleiermacher (1768–1834) pre-eminently, have defined theology as the explication of Christian experience. The Reformed tradition as a whole, however, has always insisted that the theologian's engagement with the experience of the Christian community is always secondary to revelation. Yet, no doctrine is fully understood until it is studied in actual experience. (4) A further facet of the dialogue is with culture. Physical and social sciences, political, social, and economic movements all raise questions about human life that are questions for the theologian. New knowledge, as for example, new information about the origin of human life on this planet, and new questions such as those raised by the various social movements of the past two decades, help the theologian to see and hear what has not been previously seen and heard in the divine revelation. (5) Christian theology must also be done in dialogue with the living religions of mankind which testify that all people encounter "mystery" and that God has not been without witnesses to his presence everywhere. In his last lectures, Paul Tillich indicated that if he were writing his systematic theology again, he would write it in dialogue with the living religions of mankind rather than with Enlightenment man.[14] (6) The theologian has to be involved with language and with the way the faith is to be expressed in meaningful words and symbols. (7) Finally, the theologian has to take seriously the claims of logic and the warrants that justify any assertion. Theologians can be typed by the way in which they engage in this many-faceted dialogue.[15] Reformed theologians have been characterized by their heavy involvement with the Bible and with the history of doctrine, but at their best they have not neglected the other facets of the dialogue. Yet they have always insisted that the perspective and framework in which theological discussion takes place is set by revelation, not by the movements, pressures, and perspectives of human history itself. A contextual theology

> is to be distinguished from the imperialism by which the theologian presumes to speak with authority in matters pertaining to other disciplines and arts. It is equally to be distinguished from the theologization of the human which is unable to distinguish between what God does to shape and to interpret what is human, and what man, even at the highest levels of creativity, makes of himself and his world. A contextual theology aims at the humanization of theology in the sense of being open to every human enterprise while continuing to speak its own piece.[16]

There is no one theological method, just as there is no one scientific method. The actual starting point and procedures of theology are determined by many factors, some of which are very accidental, such as the personal predilections of the theologian or the pressures of the moment. In fact, the great theologians have generally given only secondary attention to method. Hence, it is impossible to describe theological work in simple, definable procedures. The method of Reformed theology can best be described as a relentless wrestling with the divine revelation in the full context of the church and of life. Joseph Sittler, a Lutheran theologian, has written, "My own disinclination to state a theological method is grounded in the strong conviction that one does not devise a method and then dig into the data; one lives with the data; lets their force, variety, and authenticity generate a sense for what Jean Daniélou calls a 'way of knowing' appropriate to the nature of the data."[17] Karl Barth's *Church Dogmatics* illustrates, sometimes to the point of boredom, a relentless wrestling with the data of theology, especially the Bible and the history of doctrine, in such a way as to allow Christian faith to be expressed in the contemporary situation in a way that is true to the data from which it arises.

Theology is more the work of an artist than a craftsman. Its character is more that of an organism or a portrait than a machine. Christian theology cannot be divided into parts which stand independently of the whole. Every doctrinal problem or issue involves the whole Christian vision. Systematic theology, the attempt to state the whole of Christian faith in a coherent and consistent way, is an organic whole very much as a portrait is. It is not a machine with discrete parts. This organic character of theology accounts in part for its diversity, for the various facts never come together precisely in the same way for different theologians in different contexts. The way in which the various dimensions of Christian faith come together in the Reformed tradition varies from theologian to theologian, but the different theologies have certain typical emphases, nuances, and patterns that distinguish this tradition from other theological traditions.

## Characteristics of Reformed Theology

*(a) A theology of the holy catholic church.* Reformed theologians have built upon the work of the ancient church. It is worth noting that the formulation of Christian theology in the comprehensive way that one finds in the Reformation confessions or in Calvin's

*Institutes* would not have been possible in the early church. Theology always builds upon the work of the past, and comprehensive statements of the faith are achieved only with the passing of time. The Protestant Reformation accepted with little modification the great formulations of the ancient catholic church, namely the Apostles' Creed, the Nicene Creed, and the Chalcedonian Definition of the person of Jesus Christ. The Nicene Creed defines the decisive and final character of the revelation of God in Jesus Christ. All who affirm it are united in the basic Christian affirmation that God is defined by Jesus Christ. On this point the Protestant Reformation and the Reformed tradition had no doubts.

Protestantism and the Reformed tradition in particular had grave misgivings about many of the doctrinal developments of the medieval church. The doctrines of the church and sacraments were greatly elaborated in the period between the fall of Rome (410) and Protestant Reformation (1517). During this time, the church had to deal with barbarians of northern Europe who could neither read nor write and who had no traditions of either Christian or classical ethics. It is understandable that the church placed increasing emphasis on sacraments, on representation of Christian truth and data in pictures and statutes, and on church discipline. The doctrine of transubstantiation received official formulation at the Fourth Lateran Council in 1215, and yearly confession was made obligatory at the same time. The doctrine of the seven sacraments (baptism, confirmation, penance, the mass, marriage, ordination, and extreme unction) was made official at the Council of Florence (1439). All of these doctrines of the church and sacraments were radically revised by the Reformers. The Apocrypha, gradually accepted in the Old Testament canon by inclusion in the Vulgate, was rejected. Even the doctrine of man as formulated at the Council of Orange (529) was revised to place more emphasis on the invincibility of divine grace and the bondage of human sin. In particular, the Protestant Reformation concentrated upon God's way of salvation and insisted that salvation is wholly by the grace of God and not by any merit of man.

*(b) A theocentric theology.* The central theme of theology, as Reformed theology has understood it, is not man and his plight or his possibilities, not even Jesus Christ, but God, who is the crea-

tor and who was uniquely present in Jesus Christ. To put it more exactly, Christian theology has to do with the Triune God, who is the unfathomable creator of all things, . . . who has made himself known in Jesus Christ, and who, as the Holy Spirit, is the Lord and life-giver and who speaks by the prophets.[18] Unitarianism of the Father, of the Creator, leaves out of account the Redeemer and Sanctifier. The unitarianism of the Son forgets the Creator and the Sanctifier. Finally, the unitarianism of the Spirit becomes absorbed in the work of God in the inner life of the believer to the exclusion of his other works. Each unitarianism distorts the understanding not only of God but also of the Christian life that is a response to God's claim. Christian theology has to do with the one God who is personally and always related to his creation in three ways.

Writing some sixty years ago, a great Calvin scholar, Émile Doumergue, insisted that Calvin was theocentric, not Christocentric, in his theological work.[19] The significance of Jesus Christ is so great for Christian theology that Christian piety has always been tempted to believe that no theology can be too Christocentric. For the Christian, God is defined by Jesus Christ; and Jesus Christ is centrally important for all Christian theology. The Nicene Creed, which affirms that in Jesus Christ the believer confronts God himself, is the basic Christian confession. Jesus Christ is the decisive clue to the nature of the Creator and the Spirit. Our knowledge of the Father and the Spirit would be most diffused and thus not Christian without the Son who was incarnate in Jesus of Nazareth. Yet it is equally true that in his works God is indivisible and his works cannot be separated from his unity. It is a fundamental Christian affirmation that the God who redeems is also the God who creates and who gives life and speaks by the prophets.

The insistence that the object of faith is the Triune God has been a characteristic of Reformed theology. This theology has had little patience with any Jesusology type of piety, as is seen in sentimental, self-oriented hymnology. It has likewise had little sympathy with so-called charismatic movements that become absorbed in the introspective analysis of one's own psyche.[20] The God whom Christians worship is the Lord God who creates the heavens and the earth and the Holy Spirit who gives comfort, as well as the God who encounters his people and redeems them in Jesus Christ. A unitarianism of the Father leads to an austere, creativistic faith. A unitarianism of the Son leads to the sentimentalism of Jesusology. A unitarianism of the Spirit leads to emotional irresponsibility. Reformed theology acknowledges the Triune God.

The triune God is the Lord of heaven and earth. On this point Reformed theology has never been in doubt, and this conviction has given a distinctive character to the faith of the Reformed community. H. Richard Niebuhr has, as well as any contemporary theologian, analyzed faith in a way that is compatible with Reformed theology.[21] On the one hand, faith is trust in God. It is more than mental assent. It is the confidence that is born of the personal assurance that God is sovereign. Calvin loved the Psalms because of the assurance that they give that God is the ruler of nature and history and the protector of his people. Significantly, the Psalms that first attracted the attention of Calvinist worship were those that affirmed trust in God amid the turbulence of life. Faith is also, H. Richard Niebuhr insisted, loyalty to God and his cause in the world. Here, too, Niebuhr has given contemporary expression to a fundamental theme of Reformed faith. The Christian life for Calvin was in no small measure loyalty to God and his cause.

The theocentric character of Reformed faith sets it over against every ethic of self-realization, against inordinate concern with the salvation of one's own soul, against excessive preoccupation with questions of personal identity. The great fact is God, and the true vocation of every human being is trust in him and loyalty to his cause. Again, H. Richard Niebuhr has expressed with great insight this Calvinist conviction that the final fact with which any person has to do is God.

> We may call it the nature of things, we may call it fate, we may call it reality. But by whatever name we call it, this law of things, this reality, this way things are, is something with which we all must reckon. We may not be able to give a name to it, calling it only the 'void' out of which everything comes and to which everything returns, though that is also a name. But it is there—the last shadowy and vague reality, the secret of existence by virtue of which things come into being, are what they are, and pass away. Against it there is no defense.[22]

> God, I believe, is always in history; he is the structure in things, the source of all meaning, the 'I am that I am,' that which is that it is. He is the rock against which we beat in vain, that which bruises and overwhelms us when we seek to impose our wishes, contrary

to his, upon him. That structure of the universe, that creative will, can no more be said to interfere brutally in history than the violated laws of my organism can be said to interfere brutally with my life if they make me pay the cost of my violation.[23]

There is no Reformed theology that does not articulate the majesty and the glory of God. Likewise, there is no Reformed piety that does not experience the "Otherness" of God. The God of Reformed faith cannot be domesticated or commanded by any human being. He is the living God.

*(c) A theology of the Bible.* Reformed theology has always been intensely Biblical. The first theses that Reformed theologians presented for debate with medieval catholicism declared without equivocation that in theology the Bible is the decisive authority. The first two theses of Berne (1528) declare:

> (1) The holy Christian Church, whose only head is Christ, is born of the Word of God, and abides in the same, and listens not to the voice of a stranger.
> (2) The Church of Christ makes no laws or commandments apart from the Word of God; hence all human traditions are not binding upon us except so far as they are grounded upon or prescribed in the Word of God.

Zwingli, whose work began the Reformation in Zurich, deliberately set out, as has been noted, to preach through books of the Bible so as to present the Christian Gospel in its fullness. He brought all of his skills as a humanist scholar to the explication of the Biblical text in its literary or natural meaning.

There can be no question that John Calvin intended to be a Biblical theologian.[24] In his will, he identified himself as "I, John Calvin, Minister of the Word of God in the church of Geneva."[25] One of the most striking characteristics of Calvin's work as theologian is his synthesis of the work of the exegete, the systematic theologian, and the preacher. This synthesis was rooted in Calvin's conviction that all theology stands under the Word of God and also in his insistence that theology is a practical science. In a perceptive article "The Modernity of Calvin's Theological Method," Gilbert Rist has written that Calvinist theology is located between the Biblical text and preaching.

> It is necessary to recognize that with Calvin theological effort is not the final consideration; it gives way to what precedes it and what

follows it; it is only the discourse which permits preaching to take root in Holy Scripture; it is only a key, an opening, an entrance to the profitable reading of both the Old and New Testaments. Theology is a service for all men and not a purpose in itself, intelligible only to clerics. Doctrine is contained in the Holy Scripture, not in dogmatics, and this is why theology is only able to echo the biblical text, to reflect it constantly without being able to add anything to it.[26]

The interaction of theology, sermon, and commentary was carefully thought out by Calvin and programmatically developed. In the preface to the 1539 edition of the *Institutes,* Calvin stated that his object was to prepare students for the sacred volume. The *Institutes* had the modest purpose of being a manual for the reading of Scripture in contrast to the grandiose design of summas. As such, the *Institutes* are intentionally related to the reading and study of the Scriptures and the commentaries.

This purpose persisted even with greater emphasis through all the editions of the *Institutes.* The 1559 preface declares again, ". . . it has been my purpose in this labor to prepare and instruct candidates in sacred theology for the reading of the divine Word, . . . ." In the preface to the French edition of 1560, which was meant for a more popular audience, Calvin expressed the hope that the *Institutes* will be a "key to open a way for all children of God into a good and right understanding of Holy Scripture. . . . Although Holy Scripture contains a perfect doctrine, to which one can add nothing, . . ."[27] Most readers, Calvin knew, would need some guidance. Calvin's *Institutes* were not designed for the theologically elite but for the Christian as a reader of Scripture.

It is significant that the development of the *Institutes* paralleled the writing of the commentaries. In the years between the Romans commentary in 1539 and his death in 1564, Calvin commented on every book in the New Testament except Second and Third John and Revelation. He also published commentaries on the Book of Genesis and a harmony of the rest of the Pentateuch, Joshua, Psalms, Isaiah, Ezekiel 1–20, Daniel, Jeremiah, Lamentations, and all the Minor Prophets. In addition, Calvin preached frequently. This enabled him to comment on many books on which he did not produce commentaries including Job, Judges, First Kings, and Second Samuel. The only books not commented on in the *Institutes* are Esther, Nahum, Second John and Third John. It is wrong therefore to think that the *Institutes* developed simply as a result of theological controversies or demands for theological coherence and completeness. The section on predestination, for example, was enlarged as a result of Calvin's study of the Gospel of John, not simply because of his controversies on the subject.

Theology has the task of clarifying the Biblical message. Theology is more than the repetition of Biblical words. In justifying the terminology of trinitarian theology, Calvin wrote,

> If they call a foreign word one that cannot be shown to stand written syllable by syllable in Scripture, they are indeed imposing upon us an unjust law which condemns all interpretation not patched together out of the fabric of Scripture. . . . we ought to seek from Scripture a sure rule for both thinking and speaking, to which both the thoughts of our minds and the words of our mouths should be conformed. But what prevents us from explaining in clearer words those matters in Scripture which perplex and hinder our understanding, yet which conscientiously and faithfully serve the truth of Scripture itself, and are made use of sparingly and modestly and on due occasion?[28]

Calvin's theology can properly be described primarily as commentary upon Scripture as a whole and secondarily as commentary upon the way the church had read Scripture in its theology and creeds. Theology clarifies and focuses the message of Scripture in the idiom of a particular situation.

Explaining Scripture in "clearer words" meant, in practice, explaining it in conversation with humanist culture and in controversy with scholastic theology. Calvin was a participant in the humanist culture of his day, and every paragraph of theology that he wrote reflects this fact. His theology was worked out in dialogue with the thought forms of his age, even though he wrote no programmatic essays proposing to do this. The theological basis for a theology alive to its culture is found in the universal activity of the *Logos.* Those who have "even tasted the liberal arts penetrate with their aid far more deeply into the secrets of the divine wisdom."[29] Wencelius in *L'esthétique de Calvin* has demonstrated how Calvin used poetry in his theological task.[30]Calvin as a theologian was very much in conversation with the humanist culture, and he posed the question of faith sharply for his humanist friends, who refused his Protestant and Christian commitments.

Theology, however, has the task not simply of clarifying Scripture but also of ordering the message of Scripture. This problem, apparently, was a major concern for Calvin. In the preface to the 1559 edition of the *Institutes,* he declared that he had never been satisfied until then with the arrangement of his theology. He takes satisfaction in the conviction that ". . . I have so embraced the sum of religion in all its parts, and have arranged it in such an order, that if anyone rightly grasps it, it will not be difficult for him to determine what he ought especially to seek in Scripture, and to what end he ought to relate its contents."[31] In this sense, Calvin was a systematic theologian, providing in the *Institutes* the "system," the coherent statement of Christian faith, that was mirrored in his commentaries.

Another characteristic of Calvin's use of Scripture is the emphasis upon the whole canon of Scripture. Calvin had his favorite books: Romans, Psalms, Matthew, John, First Corinthians, and Genesis, for example; but as much as any major theologian ever has, he attempted to establish his theology upon the whole of Scripture. Critics have contended that one of his faults as a theologian was the failure to distinguish adequately between the lights and shadows of Scripture, and the tendency to treat all Scripture as on the same level.[32]

From the beginning in the sixteenth century to Karl Barth in the twentieth century, Reformed theologians have been in intention and in fact theologians of the Bible. Reformed theology has always been more Biblical than philosophical, just as it has been more practical than speculative. This has been its strength and its weakness. While Reformed scholars have not always been the most venturesome Biblical scholars, they have been unexcelled in steadfastness and solid work. They have been in the forefront in the work of the Bible translation societies, in the study of the original texts of Scripture, and in commentaries upon them.

*(d) Predestination.* Reformed Christians are universally associated with predestination. This association is well grounded in the theologies, confessions, and the controversies of the tradition. Hence, predestination can be taken as a special mark of Reformed theology. All Christians have some doctrine of predestination, but Reformed Christians have been unique in their emphasis on it and in the rigor with which they have developed it.

Predestination brings the Reformed understanding of God to focus upon the believer and the church. God, as has been indicated, was understood by Reformed theologians in a very dynamic way, as activity, force, will, intentionality. God is the Lord, the all-governing creator. The origin of the faith of the believer and of the church must be found first in the action of God, not in any human effort. Reformed theologians have always known that psychologically and historically the life of faith and the life of the church were the work of the people of God. Yet, they also insisted that the root of this life was not first in the decision of individuals or of the community but in the election of God.

Predestination means that human life is rooted in the will and the intention of God. Reformed theologians used to speak of the decrees of God. In more modern language, they were speaking of the purpose of God and declaring that behind everything that exists is the will and purpose of God. No human life is ever the simple result of the forces of biology and history. Every human life has its first source in God's intention. God thought of each person before he was and called him into being, giving him his name, his individuality, his identity as a child of God, and his dignity that no man should dare abuse. In view of the historical, biological, and pyschological factors involved in the birth of babies, this is a tremendous affirmation of faith. Yet, the Reformed were so overwhelmed by the power and activity of God that they dared to make this affirmation.

Reformed theologians went further and declared that God not only called all people into being, but that he had also elected them, or at least some, to a high and holy destiny. The human predicament, as Reformed theology has understood it, is that every person, as the result of sin, is self-centered when he ought to be God-centered. There is no way for a self-centered person to become unself-centered by trying hard any more than he can forget himself by trying hard. Many of the deepest experiences in life are beyond the power of the human will. We cannot by trying hard feel grateful or even love someone else. Gratitude, love, self-forgetfulness are always elicited by something that happens to us. So it is with faith. Human beings do not believe in God by their own efforts but as a result of the outreaching grace of God, perhaps in the maturation during childhood, perhaps in a crisis experience, that elicits trust and confidence.

Reformed theologians have known that faith, as well as gratitude, love, and self-forgetfulness is a psychologically and historically completely human act, but they have also insisted that faith is first of all the act of God that elicits the human response. Predestination was Calvin's most emphatic way of saying that salvation is the work of God's grace, just as justification by grace through faith was Luther's most emphatic way of saying the same thing.

Calvin was confronted by the fact that some persons apparently did not respond to the claim of God on their lives.[33] With his powerful sense of God's activity and governance of the world, Calvin could not leave this fact in mystery. He had to root unbelief in the will of God, and he believed that he had Biblical justification for this. Hence, he said that God in his sovereignty and for the glory of his justice passed over some people and in condemnation of their sin ordained them to eternal death. This was hard doctrine, though logically satisfying; and Reformed theologians, including Calvin himself, have had difficulty living with it.

Several special emphases in Calvin's theology help to relieve but do not solve the difficulties of Calvin's doctrine of predestination. First of all, Calvin insisted that the God who elects is the God whom we know in Jesus Christ.[34] Secondly, Calvin insisted that God does not deal with human beings as though they were sticks and stones but as persons.[35] Therefore, predestination must be understood in personal rather than mechanical metaphors. Love, the most unique human act, is the best human clue to what happens in predestination. No person ever falls deeply in love through his own efforts. The primary fact in love is the impact of another life that elicits love. "We are elected into love." Yet love is also wholly one's own act. Furthermore, when a person loves another person, he is never so free as when he does the will of the person he loves. Thirdly, Calvin insisted that Christian people are elected not to privilege but to the service of God.[36] Finally, Calvin preached the doctrine of predestination as a source of comfort. Salvation does not depend upon the faltering human efforts but upon the mercy and power of God.[37]

Calvin located the doctrine of predestination in the ordering of his theology after his discussion of the Christian life. This suggests that predestination can best be understood not at the beginning but at the conclusion of the life of faith. It is the testimony of the believer that what has happened in the life of faith has not been the result of one's own efforts about which one can boast but of the grace of God.

Predestination is never a source of arrogance or of presumption. It may be, as Calvin believed it was, a source of comfort in the dark night of the soul. The same can be said of the related doctrine of the perseverance of the saints. This doctrine cannot, when rightly understood, be a source of arrogance or presumption, but it too can be for the believer in the dark night of soul or for the parent whose baptized child rebels a source of comfort and hope. Predestination and the perseverance of the saints are most likely to be helpful to believers when they are appropriated as prayers, as hope based on faith in God; and this is the way Calvin at least intended for them to be appropriated.

Calvin's formulation of the doctrine was never fully satisfactory. In later centuries Arminius (1560–1609) in Holland, Amyraut (1596–1664) in France, Jonathan Edwards (1703–1758) in America, and Karl Barth (1886–1968) in Switzerland would all seek a more satisfactory statement of the Reformed doctrine; and none would wholly succeed. The paradox, which is grounded in Christian experience as well as Scripture, remains. From the perspective of human history and psychology, salvation and the life of faith is wholly a human act and achievement. Yet it is also a fact of experience that faith is a response to a "power" that has grasped a person and elicited the response. The Reformed never tired of insisting that God's act is prior to man's act, that God first loved us and that his grace is "prevenient"; that is, it goes before. And more than this, they dare to trust that God's grace is invincible.

Calvin once said that predestination is nothing less than the knowledge of the adoption of God, a love that persistently and invincibly pursues the distraught and the alienated.[38] This was and is the saving meaning and power of the doctrine. Francis Thompson, a Roman Catholic poet, has given the essence of it powerful expression in his poem "The Hound of Heaven."[39]

> I fled Him, down the nights and down the days;
>    I fled Him, down the arches of the years;
> I fled Him, down the labyrinthine ways
>    Of my own mind; and in the mist of tears

I hid from Him, and under running laughter.
    Up vistaed hopes I sped;
    And shot, precipitated
Adown Titanic glooms of chasmèd fears,
    From those strong Feet that followed, followed after.
    But with unhurrying chase,
    And unperturbèd pace,
    Deliberate speed, majestic instancy,
    They beat—and a Voice beat
    More instant than the Feet—
"All things betray thee, who betrayest Me."

    . . . . . .

    Ah! must—
    Designer Infinite!—
Ah! must Thou char the wood ere Thou canst limn with it?
My freshness spent its wavering shower i' the dust;
And now my heart is as a broken fount,
Wherein tear-drippings stagnate, split down ever
    From the dank thoughts that shiver
Upon the sighful branches of my mind.
    Such is; what is to be?
The pulp so bitter, how shall taste the rind?
I dimly guess what Time in mists confounds;
Yet ever and anon a trumpet sounds
From the hid battlements of Eternity;
Those shaken mists a space unsettle, then
Round the half glimpsèd turrets slowly wash again;
    But not ere him who summoneth
    I first have seen, enwound
With glooming robes purpureal, cypress-crowned;
His name I know, and what his trumpet saith.
Whether man's heart or life it be which yields
    Thee harvest, must Thy harvest fields
    Be dunged with rotten death?
    Now of that long pursuit
    Comes on at hand the bruit;
That Voice is round me like a bursting sea;
    "And is thy earth so marred
    Shattered in shard on shard?
Lo, all things fly thee, for thou fliest Me!
    Strange, piteous, futile thing!
Wherefore should any set thee love apart?
Seeing none but I make much of naught" (He said),
"And human love needs human meriting:
    How hast thou merited—
Of all man's clotted clay the dingiest clot?
    Alack, thou knowest not

How little worthy of any love thou art!
Whom wilt thou find to love ignoble thee
    Save Me, save only Me?
All which I took from thee I did but take,
    Not for thy harms,
But just that thou might'st seek it in My arms.
    All which thy child's mistake
Fancies as lost, I have stored for thee at home:
    Rise, clasp My hand, and come."

        Halts by me that footfall:
        Is my gloom, after all,
    Shade of His hand, outstretched caressingly?
        "Ah, fondest, blindest, weakest,
        I am He Whom thou seekest!
Thou dravest love from thee, who dravest Me."

*(e) The distinction between Creator and creature ("finitum non est capax infiniti").* Calvin's theology and Reformed theology in general is significantly shaped by a radical distinction between the creator and the creature, between the self-existent being of God and the dependent being of the creature. This distinction is another way of stating the doctrine of the sovereignty of God, and it also helped to shape Calvin's entire theology. It accounts for a strong emphasis upon history and ethics in his doctrine of salvation, upon the humanity of Jesus Christ in his doctrine of the person of Jesus, upon liturgy as a human work, upon the rejection of any confusion of the bread and the wine in the sacrament with divine reality. It results in the capacity to accept things as things and to rejoice in the "thingness" of existence, without divinizing or unduly exalting any created object. It frees the individual and the church from either claiming too much or too little for human achievements.

This emphasis on the distinction between creator and creature was at the center of the Reformed-Lutheran debates of the seventeenth century concerning the nature of the presence of Christ in the sacrament and the problem of the relation of the divine and the human in the person of Jesus Christ.[40] In this debate the Reformed distinction between the creator and the creature was refined as the theological principle, *"Finitum non est capax infiniti."* The finite cannot contain the infinite. This formulation of the principle does not seem to be found in Calvin's writings, but it has its basis in the distinction that he did make between creator and creature. His own vivid apprehension of the presence of God as the Almighty Father, creator of heaven and earth no doubt guided his reading of Scripture; but this is something less than a principle to which every theological statement is referred for development. Nevertheless, the distinction between creator and creature is one of the most pervasive motifs of his theology, polity, and worship.

Calvin's emphasis on the distinction between creator and creature is balanced by his emphasis on the immanence of God. God is purposefully at work in his whole creation. The divine reality and the human reality do unite in one acting subject in Jesus Christ. The Holy Spirit does dwell in the church and in the person of the Christian. The infinite and indeterminate God does work in his finite and determinate creation. God "accommodates" himself, Calvin continually emphasized, to the human condition.

*(f) Theology as a practical science.* At the beginning of his great *Summa Theologica,* (ca. 1265–ca. 1274) one of the theological masterpieces of Christian history, Thomas Aquinas, the thirteenth-century theologian, asks whether sacred doctrine is a practical science. He concludes that it is both speculative and practical, but his emphasis lies on the side of the speculative.[41] The vision of God rather than the kingdom of God is the controlling motif. The emphasis in Reformed theology is precisely the reverse. Calvin tried as best he could to limit speculation, and he made the capacity to edify a basic test of sound theology.

Theology is not an end in itself. The *Institutes of the Christian Religion* had practical purposes. First of all, it was a guide for readers of the Bible, so that they would be able to see individual texts in the light of the whole of Scripture and so that the words of Scripture would be explained in language readers would better understand. Secondly, Calvin's theological work was closely related to preaching and pastoral care. Calvin was a theologian in order to preach and to do the work of a pastor. Thirdly, theology had as its purpose the formation of human life and society in conformity to the will of God. Calvin had no use for theology that answered idle questions. He put his position with biting clarity in the question he posed to Sadolet:

> Do you remember what kind of time it was when the Reformers appeared, and what kind of doctrine candidates for the ministry learned in the schools? You yourself know that it was mere sophis-

try, and so twisted, involved, tortuous, and puzzling, that scholastic theology might well be described as a species of secret magic. The denser the darkness in which any one shrouded a subject, and the more he puzzled himself and others with nagging riddles, the greater his fame for acumen and learning.[42]

Calvin was aware that Augustine had been faced with the question about what God was doing before he created the world. Augustine thought such a question deserved a serious answer, not the flippant popular response, "making hell for those who ask such questions." Calvin had sympathy with this latter response.[43] Again when faced with the questions about the incarnation, Calvin replied:

> My answer is brief: Since the Spirit declares that these two were joined together by God's eternal decree, it is not lawful to inquire further how Christ became our Redeemer and partaker of our nature. For he who is tickled with desire to know something more, not content with God's unchangeable ordinance, also shows that he is not even content with this very Christ who was given to us as the price of our redemption.[44]

This practical outlook and theological method may in part have been due to the fact that Calvin was a busy man with much to do. Life was too real, too demanding for the luxury of speculation. It is difficult, however, to account for so pervasive an outlook in terms of the pressures of the moment. The practical bent is rooted in Calvin's personality and in his understanding of the nature of theology. He was himself a humanist scholar before he was a reformer.[45] His interests were historical and literary. He was a graduate in law. The experience of the authority of God speaking through the Bible had been an important element in his conversion to Protestantism. Finally, God's will as the law of human life was basic to his whole understanding of the Christian life. Hence the metaphysical concerns and cosmic dimensions of Christian faith received very little attention from Calvin. In this Calvin set the pattern for later Reformed theology.

Calvin placed great emphasis upon the test of fruits. By its fruits a theology reveals its fundamental character. Theology that is written in textbooks must be written in lives. Calvin insisted that the truest test of a person's faith is love for the neighbor. The emphasis on theology as a practical science robbed the theological tradition of its full measure of intellectual creativity and richness, but it did give theology a focus in the everyday life of people and nations that has distinguished it from other theological traditions.

*(g) Theology as wisdom.* Word and Spirit were the basic and essential factors in Calvin's interpretation of Scripture and in his theology.

> For by a kind of mutual bond the Lord has joined together the certainty of his Word and of his Spirit so that the perfect religion of the Word may abide in our minds when the Spirit, who causes us to contemplate God's face, shines; and that we in turn may embrace the Spirit with no fear of being deceived when we recognize him in his own image, namely in the Word.[46]

The study of the natural meaning of the words of Scripture, which Calvin advocated, leads by itself to an objective knowledge of Scripture and religion, as does the scientific study of any object. Dependence on the Spirit alone leads to irrational aberrations ranging from snake handling to sacred sex. The combination of word, the objective study of Scripture and of the faith, with Spirit, the personal assimilation of the data by the self under the illumination of the Spirit, leads, as Lucien Joseph Richard has pointed out, to wisdom.[47] Theology to a far greater degree than any other area of scientific knowledge grows out of the interaction of the critical reflection of the mind with the profound experience of the presence of God in personal life and with a life of obedience. A person who has lived deeply and experienced the presence of God is a better judge of the reality of God than a person who has studied about God, even in the Bible, but who has not experienced God's presence. John Calvin, who lacked the critical tools of modern Biblical scholars, is still one of the masters of Biblical interpretation.

The separation of theology as objective knowledge from the life of devotion and obedience may result either from the intention of the theologian who wishes to divorce technical skill from commitment and obedience or from the desire of the believer who wishes to adore God without bothering to understand.[48] Theology without commitment and devotion without intellectual understanding are alike ruled out by Calvin's insistence on the indissoluble unity of word and Spirit in the study of the Bible and of theology. In the twentieth century Karl Barth has declared that theology without prayer is inconceivable.[49] Theology is, there-fore, neither technical knowledge nor emotion but wisdom; for it is the judgment of the whole self, uniting the critical reflection of the mind with the experience of the presence of God and with the life of obedience. As there is a wisdom of human maturity, reason, experience, and perception, so there is a theological wisdom of Christian maturity, experience, reason, and revelation. The words and propositions of systematic theology cannot be separated from their embodiment in individual lives and in community life. For this reason parable and biography are proper forms of theology, and for this reason systematic theology with its concerns for greater precision and clarity still uses the concrete, parabolic language of human and Christian experience.

## The Development of Reformed Theology

*(a) The nature of theological change.* The writing of Reformed theology has been going on now for more than 450 years. Zwingli published *On True and False Religion,* a major theological work, in 1525; and Calvin published the first edition of the *Institutes of the Christian Religion* in 1536. The last volume of Karl Barth's *Church Dogmatics* appeared in 1968. Theology is like manna. It must be written for the day. While great theologies of the past can be appropriated by later generations, they cannot be simply repeated without going bad. Every generation must write its own theology for its own time and place.

The task of writing theology in every new generation and situation raises the question of doctrinal change and development.[50] The difference between systematic theologies of the sixteenth century, to say nothing of the twentieth, and the writings of the New Testament is so great as to evoke from some the question of whether there can be any continuity between them. Furthermore, the difference between a theology written in the sixteenth century and one written in the twentieth is obvious even to the beginner in theological study. Change and development in theology raise the question as to whether the gospel is the same yesterday, today, and forever. The answer must always be yes and no. The gospel that God proclaimed in the words, deeds, death, and resurrection of Jesus Christ is unique, once and for all. It does not change. The Christian community's apprehension of the gospel does change from time to time and from place to place. Furthermore, Christians who have the benefit of the testimony and witness of Christians in many times and places should hear and understand the gospel better than many who stood closer in time to the years when Jesus lived as a man. "Later" certainly does not inevitably mean a deeper understanding of the gospel. It does, however, offer new possibilities of hearing and understanding.

The ways in which theology grows and develops are many.[51] On the simplest level the restatement of a doctrine in a new language and culture brings with it new nuances and even new meaning. The Nicene Creed refers to God as light, a word that had great meaning in the fourth-century Mediterranean culture but little now.[52] Secondly, doctrine grows and develops by making explicit what was implicit in early statements. Many of the great texts of the New Testament are found to have far wider application and significance when studied carefully by succeeding generations. Thirdly, doctrine develops in response to challenges to Christian practice and belief. For example, the Christian community spoke of Jesus as God and man. For a time this could be done in a most general and unreflective way. Eventually, in response to questions that Christians raised or that were asked from outside the Christian community, theologians had to say more precisely in what sense they believed Jesus Christ to be God and man and how they could make both affirmations about one acting subject. The doctrine of the Person of Jesus Christ as defined at Nicea and Chalcedon is not in the New Testament in one sense, but in another sense the doctrine is necessary to make explicit and clear what Christians believe to be in the New Testament. Fourthly, Christian doctrine develops through its own reflection and refinement. The development of Christian doctrine requires time. The comprehensive statements of Christian faith that were produced by the Protestant reformers of the sixteenth century simply could not have been produced in the early church. The Christian community had not had time to think through the meaning of the Christian faith, to develop adequate concepts, or to put individual doctrines together in some consistent statement.

Changing cultural and theological contexts necessitate theological development. After Calvin's death, for example, theologians continued to reflect on the doctrine of predestination; they asked whether God thought of man as creatable, or as created and fallen, when he elected him. It is impossible to find a clear answer to this question in Calvin's writings, for he had not thought specifically about this question. Again, Charles Darwin published his *Origin of the Species* in 1859, three centuries after Calvin. Calvin did not relate the Christian doctrine of creation to facts that are now known about human origins on this planet. Historians today dispute about Calvin's doctrine of inspiration of the Bible, and they dispute about this because they ask the question in the light of critical studies of the Bible as literature and history that again came three centuries after Calvin.

A careful definition of the nature and limits of doctrinal development is not simple, and differences at this point are one of the sharpest divisions between Protestants and Roman Catholics.[53] Roman Catholics, though insisting that in some sense their dogmas are in the New Testament, allow greater latitude to development than Protestants. The Dogmas of the Immaculate Conception (the doctrine that Mary was born without sin) and of the Assumption (the doctrine that the body of Mary was taken uncorrupted to heaven) appear to Protestants to develop out of the experience of a portion of the Christian community, not out of the New Testament. Protestants, and the Reformed in particular, believe that all Christian doctrine must be clearly attested in Scripture. Nevertheless, one of the finest statements on the development of doctrine comes from the pen of an influential Roman Catholic theologian, Karl Rahner.[54] He finds an analogy to doctrinal development in the experience of human love. A man may fall in love with a woman in such a way that his life is radically transformed. There is no question that this experience of love is real, that it is his own experience. Yet it may be that in an intellectual and reflective way the lover understands very little of what has happened to him. He may be able to speak of it only in a halting and stumbling way. The reflection of others on this experience and his own reflection at a later time may disclose hidden depths in the experience of which he was unaware intellectually, as well as meanings for future development that he did not anticipate. The experience belongs to the person who is involved in it in a way it cannot belong to anyone who reflects on it from the outside or even to the person himself as he reflects on it later. Nevertheless, the later reflection is not unrelated to the experience itself. As a result of the reflection, similar experiences of others may be illuminated and the experience of the original lover may be enlarged.

The disciples of Jesus experienced the presence of God in Jesus Christ in a way that has been decisive for Christians ever since. Yet it is possible that Christians, as they have lived the life of faith in changing contexts and as they have reflected in study, have discovered meaning and significance that the first disciples could never have perceived or articulated. The immediacy of the experience of being a contemporary of Jesus has its own unique significance. Christians cannot get along without the Apostles. Every authentic Christian doctrine must be attested by the witness of Scripture. Yet it is also true that the devotion and reflection of Christians through the centuries have opened up the meaning of what God did in Jesus Christ and have given it a breadth and depth that the first disciples did not know. Church history is in large measure the record of how Christians have read the Bible and have attempted to be disciples of Jesus Christ. "Later" in Christian history does not necessarily mean better theology, but it does mean that Christians now have the resources that come from the developing understanding of what God did in Jesus Christ.

Christian theology has to avoid extremes in its relation to the past. On the one hand, it cannot repeat the theology of the past. This is the way of spiritual death. On the other hand, it must avoid "lust for novelty and narcissistic delight in being different."[55] Hence Reformed theology in its development must be received with gratitude and with critical judgment. Continuity is maintained not by sterile and rote repetition but by each generation's appropriating its theological heritage in a living way as it articulates the faith in its own language and in its own life situation. Reformed theology can be best understood as it has developed through five distinct, though never sharply defined periods.[56]

**(b) Classical reformed theology, 1517–1564** (*Ninety-five Theses, October 31, 1517—Death of Calvin, May 27, 1564*). The turbulence in the soul of an Augustinian monk named Martin Luther, who was concerned about how he, a sinful man, could stand in the presence of a righteous God, was the immediate occasion of the

Protestant Reformation. Political, economic, and social factors helped foster but also sometimes restrained the Reformation movement, but the Reformation was essentially a deeply religious revival. The heart and center of it was no peripheral theological concern but the nature of salvation itself. As Roland Bainton has insisted, the Reformation was a religious revival that set back the secularization of Europe.[57]

The central thrusts of the Protestant Reformation are stated with verve and enthusiasm by Martin Luther in his great writings of 1520: "The Babylonian Captivity of the Church," "Treatise on Good Works," "The Freedom of a Christian," and "To the Christian Nobility of the German Nation Concerning the Reform of the Christian Estate." In these writings Luther affirmed that the final authority in the church is not pope, council, or state but the word of God. He declared that a person is not saved by his own merit, works, or achievement but by God's grace through faith. He insisted that every believer is a priest who is responsible for himself and for his neighbor before God. No priest or institution can answer for any human being. Every human being is accountable. Every person must believe for himself because every person dies by himself. Luther not only abolished the division between the lay Christian and the religious; he also abolished the distinction between sacred and secular works. A person's daily work is not something done in addition to being a Christian or in spite of being a Christian. A Christian's daily work is one of the ways in which the Christian lives out his Christian faith. Finally, Luther insisted that faith is necessary to the reception of the sacraments. By insisting upon faith, a personal, responsible act, he ruled out magic, every attempt to by-pass conscious responsible decision, in matters of religious faith.

John Calvin was a second-generation reformer. When he was born, Luther was already a theological teacher and had arrived at his position on the authority of Scripture. Consequently, more of Calvin's attention was given to matters of church organization and church life, to problems of Christian ethics in personal life and society. He could build upon the theological work of Luther and others who had gone before him. Hence it was possible for Calvin to write a comprehensive statement of Christian faith, *The Institutes of the Christian Religion,* the most influential summary of Protestant theology. Yet Calvin, too, wrote his theology with great intensity and depth of feeling. His gifts for language and for logical, orderly thought gave his writings a "finished" quality that belies the intensity and haste with which they were written. Yet students of Calvin's theology have detected a lack of precision in definition and a failure to work through some theological problems that would require later attention.[58] Luther, Calvin, and most of the early reformers were first of all preachers. They were not academic theologians, and their work reflects the needs of the congregation, not the concerns of the scholar as such.

*(c) Protestant scholasticism, 1564–1755.* The first phase of the Protestant movement was completed by the time of Calvin's death. Luther had died in 1546. Calvin's final edition of the *Institutes of the Christian Religion* had been completed in 1559. The great Reformation confessions had been written by the end of the 1560s. Patterns of church organization, if not finally fixed, were clearly recognizable by this date. Three new pressures began to shape the life of the Reformed communities.

First of all, the internal development of church life required that more attention be given to a refinement of theology and polity. Many loosely defined procedures and theological concepts now had to be precisely defined since they were no longer sustained by the original enthusiasm. A second pressure that moved in the same direction arose from the controversies that developed within the Reformed communities, between the Reformed and Lutheran communities, and between the Reformed and the Roman Catholics. Intricate controversies concerning predestination developed in France and in Holland. The Canons of the Synod of Dort, 1619, answered these controversies in a moderate way. One focus of the battle was between the infralapsarians and the supralapsarians. The infralapsarians declared that in election God regarded human beings as created and fallen. The supralapsarians insisted that in election God regarded the human race as creatable. This latter position seems to make creation and the fall a means to election or reprobation and was regarded as the harsher position, though Karl Barth has insisted that it was not without its virtue in that it emphasized that grace preceded creation.[59] Today most people regard such controversies as abstruse and presumptuous, which they were; but they also represented serious theological work that was more important than the anti-intellectual pressures of the twentieth century will allow anyone to recognize. The controversies of the seventeenth century were inevitable in the development of the church's life, and they were aggravated by the debates that arose between the Lutherans and the Reformed on the Lord's Supper as well as on predestination and related issues.

The Roman Catholics carefully defined their faith at the Council of Trent (1545–1563). Medieval Catholicism was fluid theologically, allowing for many points of view. The Protestant and the Roman Catholic reformations ran it through two funnels and thus limited the theological options for Protestants and Catholics alike. It was inevitable that the Protestant and Roman Catholic definitions of the faith should be shaped in some measure over against each other as well as against the teachings and practices of the medieval church.

A third factor in the development of theology in this period was the loss of the original enthusiasm of the early period and the disappointed hopes of movements that were thwarted by the failures in the life of the religious communities themselves. Hence the Reformed as well as other church groups had a tendency to turn in upon themselves. Pietism, a pattern of Christianity that emphasized personal religious life, replaced the hope for the Christian society. Theology ceased to be in dialogue with the intellectual movements of the time and concentrated upon its own inner development. When it became apparent that the social, political, economic, and intellectual life of the world was not to be taken captive, the church's piety and theology tended to withdraw from the general culture and built walls of protection.

Scholasticism, the term usually applied to the theology of this period, is hard to define. It has its roots in medieval scholasticism, but any Protestant scholasticism is modified by the Protestant doctrines of the authority of Scripture and justification by grace through faith. It is sufficient here to note that scholasticism is a type of theology that places a great emphasis upon precision of definition and upon logical, coherent, consistent statements. It represents a high, technical level of theology. These virtues gave scholastic Reformed theology great power. The theologies of this period are today still impressive and indispensable for their intellectual thoroughness. The danger of scholastic theology is that in seeking careful and precise definitions, theology becomes very abstract and remote from life. It forgets that life is more than reason.

The scholastic theologians incorporated into the Reformed consensus covenant theology as it had been developed by the English Puritans and by continental theologians such as Cocceius (1603–1669) and Witsius (1636–1708). Covenant theology which organized theology around the various covenants shifted attention from the decrees of God to the working out of the decrees in history. It obviated the increasing arbitrariness of the divine activity as pictured by theology, and it emphasized human responsibility. The covenant of works that God made with Adam conceptualized the obligation of every human being to the creator, and thus gave the theologian a basis on which to speak to those outside the Christian community. Covenant theology served to make theology more human and reasonable. It has also been argued that it undercut the sovereignty of God and conceived of the Christian life in a legalistic and rationalistic way.[60]

The scholastic theologians succeeded in ruling out the liberalizing theology of Arminius (1560–1609) on predestination and human freedom and the work of the Saumur theologians: Amyraut's (1596–1664) modification of the doctrine of predestination; Placeus' (1596–1665 or 1655) opposition to the doctrine of the immediate imputation of Adam's sin; Louis Cappel the Younger's (1585–1658) work on the text of Scripture and the denial of the Mosaic authorship of the Hebrew vowel points.

The most persistent effort to modify the dominant seventeenth century Reformed theology without challenging its basic presuppositions was carried out by New England theologians beginning with Jonathan Edwards (1703–1758). Theological work now had to take into account three new developments. Isaac Newton (1642–1727) in his *Principia Mathematica* (1686) had described an orderly world which operated according to its own laws. God was increasingly unnecessary in a universe that seemed to be self-operating and intelligible in accordance with its own rules. Second, John Locke (1632–1704) had incorporated this new knowledge in a philosophy that emphasized the empirical basis of all knowledge and the reasonableness of Christianity. Third, the religious revivals in which Edwards himself participated raised the old question of human freedom and divine sovereignty.

Edwards in contrast to Calvin analyzed the human will with great care and under the guidance of new insights into human nature including those of Locke. He argued that the human will is under the necessity of being itself. To speak of the power of contrary choice as belonging to the will did not make sense. Moral inability consists in the want of inclination or the strength of a contrary inclination. The will is free in that it does as it pleases. This was Edwards' answer to the Arminianism which seemed to picture human beings poised between the choices of salvation or damnation, and it was also his demonstration of the need of grace. Yet the center motif of Edwards' reasonable Reformed faith was the being of God whom he conceived more in terms of being, of goodness, and of beauty than did Calvin. Edwards also intended a Biblical, historical statement of the faith which he never finished. He was attempting to adjust the traditional Reformed faith to the new cultural and religious situation with intellectual curiosity and with theological freedom and creativity.

Edwards' modification of the Reformed theology was continued by a remarkable succession of theologians including Jonathan Edwards, Jr., Samuel Hopkins, Joseph Bellamy, Timothy Dwight, Bennet Tyler, coming to a conclusion in the work of Nathaniel William Taylor (1786–1858). With Edwards they wrestled with the problem of human freedom and grace and with the intelligibility of the Christian conception of God. They sought to make accommodations in the doctrines of original sin and the atonement. They opened the way to bursts of Christian activity in missions and social reform, and they prepared their people for the more difficult questions that the nineteenth century posed. Yet, they remained within boundaries of the traditional Reformed Orthodoxy and the Westminster Confession. In the 1880s they would be replaced by liberal theologians who were less bound by the tradition.

*(d) The crisis of the enlightenment and the nineteenth century, 1775–1918.* The Scientific Revolution, the Enlightenment, the Industrial Revolution, and the various cultural and intellectual movements of the century that ended with World War I undoubtedly constitute one of the most radical changes in intellectual and cultural history.

First, there was what Van Harvey has called a "new morality of knowledge."[61] Until the seventeenth and eighteenth centuries "the morality of knowledge" had emphasized dependence on authorities. In 1637 Descartes wrote his essay on method and advocated doubt of all authorities as a means of arriving at the truth.[62] A person, who does not want to be deceived, subjects the authoritative books, persons, institutions, even the wisdom of the race, to radical doubt. What survives the crucible of doubt can be trusted. This new attitude caused alarm in some church circles, arousing the particular concern of Voetuis, a prominent Dutch theologian.[63] Yet it was a productive way of arriving at truth, and it shaped the future.

Secondly, there was a new attitude toward change; it had been regarded as unusual. The static, the unchanging was normal. Joachim of Fiori (1145–1202) had challenged this view in the twelfth century. Increasingly, change was accepted as the normal condition. By the middle of the twentieth century the velocity of social change had increased to a speed that threatened all but the strongest with disorientation.

Thirdly, the scientific revolution changed drastically man's picture of the world in which he lived. The pre-Copernican world was easy to imagine in theological terms. There was a certain appropriate relation between space and theology. God was "up there" and hell somewhere "below." But after Copernicus (1473–1543), God no longer had an address, as a nineteenth-century theologian declared. Furthermore, there was the terror of infinite spaces, as Pascal noted.[64] In the nineteenth century the immense range of time and man's late appearance in the history of the universe created further problems. The crisis in the relation between science and religion reached an emotional peak in the Darwinian controversies that began in England in the 1860s just after the publication of *Origin of Species* in 1859 and that produced a crisis for the church in the southern part of the United States in 1925 with the Scopes trial. Much of the controversy, as at the Scopes trial, must be judged as nonsense; but underneath it lay a basic issue. Is the ultimate fact in the universe purpose, intention, and love or impersonal, capricious force?

A fourth development that disturbed the life of the church was the serious application of a critical, historical methodology to the Bible. Historians honed to a sharp edge their tools of analysis that enabled them to detect the composite character of literary documents and to understand the character of the writing itself. Moreover, with better methods of studying history there also developed a historical consciousness, a new awareness of the way in which individuals, societies, and institutions, as well as writings, are shaped and formed by the circumstances out of which they come. When these tools were applied to the Bible, especially in the last third of the nineteenth century, the results shocked many churchmen. Faith had been tied too closely to views *about* the Bible. Furthermore, it was clear to most Christians that historical study could undermine Christian faith. For example, if compelling evidence could be produced that Jesus never lived or that the gospel account was not a reliable record of what he said and did, then Christianity would not be possible as a faith for most Christians. The result was fear and anxiety. Furthermore, historians such as Frazer in *The Golden Bough* explained religion away as a stage in human development beyond magic but before science.

Fifth, Karl Marx (1818–1883), who sponsored with Engels the *Communist Manifesto* in 1848 and published *Das Kapital* in 1867, created problems for the Christian community also. Marx uncovered the ideological character of faith; that is, the way in which religion, even prayer, can be used to promote one's own interest. He claimed that the church was not in the vanguard for justice but was a protector of injustice. In addition, he insisted that the way a person earns his living and his economic status shapes his theological and ethical thinking, and thus he explained away religion in economic terms.

Sixth, Sigmund Freud (1856–1939) likewise raised questions for the theological community. Freud himself declared that as modern knowledge had taken away the status of man's location in the universe (Copernicus) and the uniqueness of his origin (Darwin), he would take away the dignity of his freedom.[65] Furthermore, Freud explained religion in terms of the fulfillment of human need and fantasy.[66] Ludwig Feuerbach early in the nineteenth century had contended in *The Essence of Christianity* that theology was the projection of the human spirit.

Seventh, the Western world became aware of the religions of mankind in a new and vivid way in the nineteenth century. The Christian community had always had contact with Judaism and with the Islamic faith and had accommodated itself to them. Now the issue of the significance of the existence of the living religions of the world for Christian doctrine was raised in a critical way.

Eighth, the Industrial Revolution coincided with the intellectual developments and radically altered the way people lived. Agriculture and rural villages were no longer the norm. An industrial, urban society with rapidly increasing capacities for movement and for communication provided new opportunities but also took away many of the props that had supported human life in the past.

Theological time, it must be noted, is not the same as chronological time. The significance of many of the new intellectual and cultural developments were in some quarters only slowly realized. Many who have known about Freud and Marx in their minds have not known about them in the depths of their personal existence. In every congregation there are those who, while living chronologically in 1976, theologically live in 1800 or 1900 or 1940. Some may be living theologically close to 1977; but some, perhaps fewer now than in the late sixties, are attempting to live in 2000 A.D.

The impact of the cultural and social developments of the nineteenth century on Christianity was very great. Three theological movements—Fundamentalism, Liberalism, and the Social Gospel—were all spawned by this crisis; but these movements ought not to be identified with the liberal or conservative spirit or even the Social Gospel with social concern. There have always been liberals and conservatives in the church, and some churchmen have always been concerned about social issues. The impact of the Enlightenment and the nineteenth century was so great, however, that the particular responses of these different attitudes or dispositions were galvanized into fixed positions. They were no longer ways of relating to problems but specific positions formulated at a particular time that could be simply repeated in a new situation. It is, therefore, important to distinguish Fundamentalism, Liberalism, and the Social Gospel from attitudes or dispositions that always exist in the church and to understand them in terms of their historical origin.[67]

Fundamentalism both ignored and defied the new developments. Pietistic fundamentalists continued to pray and to read the Bible as though nothing had happened. They were not angry or even disturbed about the situation. The fideistic fundamentalists were angry. They defied the new knowledge and declared that Darwin, Freud, and the others were all wrong. They formulated Christian faith in opposition to the new knowledge, and in addition they went forth to search out the heretics who had been corrupted by the new knowledge.

The Liberals accepted or welcomed the new developments. Furthermore, they intended to be Christians and modern people at the same time. They attempted to incorporate as much of the new knowledge as they could into Christian understanding and faith. In so far as the Liberals rightly understood the permanent quality of the new knowledge and in so far as they wrestled as Christian theologians with this new data to discover its meaning for Christian faith, they left a lasting imprint on Christian theology. No responsible theologian can write off the Liberals, for they rightly understood that Christian faith had to come to terms with what had happened. Theology may go through and beyond Liberalism but not behind it. Yet the Liberals in their attempt to be modern and Christian at the same time sometimes gave up the distinctive affirmations of Christian faith while attempting to hold on to the emotionally laden symbols.

The Social Gospel was the effort of Christians to work out the way in which Christians live in the new, urban, industrial society. Christians knew how to live in rural, small-town, and agricultural societies.[68] Now they were faced with an entirely new situation. What does it mean to be honest if you happen to be president of General Motors or the United Automobile Workers? Many of the first efforts of the social gospelers were overly simple. They underestimated the complexity of the problems and the nature of human sin. They attempted in one of the most popular tracts of the movement, *In His Steps,* to meet the new situation by asking: what would Jesus do? It is easy to criticize the failures of the Social Gospel, but the social gospelers began a task that is not yet finished and displayed a courage and integrity that deserves the highest praise.

*(e) The new reformation theology, 1918–1955.* In the optimistic days at the beginning of the twentieth century, Christians had sung of the day of dawning brotherhood. World War I and the ensuing depression heralded a new era.[69] In 1917 Karl Holl

began the modern study of the Protestant reformers with an essay on Luther's understanding of religion, an essay that insisted that ethics issues from religion, not the other way around, as progressive religious thought had assumed since Kant. The great herald of the new era in theology was Karl Barth's commentary on Paul's Letter to the Romans (1918), and especially the second edition, published in 1922. The nineteenth-century theologians had been impressed by the new knowledge; but Barth was impressed by the word of God, which stands in judgment over all human achievement and knowledge. God is in heaven. Man is on earth; therefore let his words be few. The liberal theologians had emphasized continuity—the continuity between God and the world, between Christian and non-Christian, between God's revelation in Jesus Christ and God's revelation everywhere. Barth emphasized the discontinuity, the difference. Furthermore, God is the Creator, who is sovereignly free. He speaks when and where he chooses. He is not at man's beck and call. In short, Barth reaffirmed the classic Christian affirmations about God, about man's condition and his salvation.

Barth reaffirmed the classic Christian affirmations; yet he did so as a person of the twentieth century. He accepted the fact that the nineteenth century had happened. He did not deny the reality of the scientific revolution, of historical-critical study, or of the Industrial Revolution. He was neither a fundamentalist nor a liberal, and both alike were unhappy with him.

The new era in theology began in America with Reinhold Niebuhr's book *Moral Man and Immoral Society,* published in 1932. The religious liberal had believed that injustice could be overcome by religion. The secular liberals such as John Dewey put their faith in education. Niebuhr accepted the Marxist analysis that had pointed out that both religion and reason can be and are used by the self to maintain injustice. Moreover, Niebuhr found the optimism of liberal thought to be unwarranted in the light of man's impulsive nature and the power of his self-centeredness. The best that man can hope for is a society in which force will be a continuing factor and in which centers of power will be sufficiently reduced and balanced against each other so that a tolerable justice will be possible.

Barth and Niebuhr ushered in one of the greatest eras in the history of theology. Theological works of lasting significance followed closely after each other. The ecumenical movement contributed to a new catholicity of the theological task as it brought theologians together from different traditions. The continuing devastation of the great depression and the rise of terribly evil political and social movements such as National Socialism and the advent of World War II provided a context of seriousness and urgency.

*(f) A time of theological puzzlement and experimentation, 1955-forward.* By the 1950s it was apparent that the Barthian theological movement had lost much of its vigor.[70] Rudolf Bultmann and Paul Tillich, whose theologies reflected far more of the older liberalism, shared the theological stage with Barth and Reinhold Niebuhr in the later 1940s and 1950s. Moreover, it was becoming apparent to many that the theology of the past thirty years had answered too many questions of the nineteenth century too easily and that these questions would have to be reopened. One question had to do with the nature and extent of the historical knowledge of Jesus Christ. Even the language of theology was called in question, and some declared that the word "God" was neither true nor false but meaningless. The Barthian theologians had spoken much about God and man's sin. The theologians of the secular wanted to speak more about the world and human responsibility. In addition, no theologians appeared with the commanding authority of a Barth or a Niebuhr.

The theology of the two decades since 1955 has not been without its excitement. It has included a great variety of movements and concerns: the new quest for the historical Jesus, the nature of God-talk and the death-of-God theologies, Vatican II and its aftermath, the theology of the secular and the revival of Bonhoeffer, the civil-rights movement, the women's liberation movement, the theology of hope, the theology of liberation, the peace movement, among others. Many theologians moved from one theology or movement to another so rapidly that the charge of faddism in theology was raised. Others worked more prosaically with the older masters, hoping to find in them the clue to Christian understanding in the new time. The theological upheaval of the period underlined the importance of standing in a living tradition from which a theologian can engage in conversation and debate with all the new movements and theologies without losing direction or being blown about by every wind of doctrine. Such a theologian could hope that in all the novelty and searching the foundations were being laid for another great era in theology.

## Representative Theologians

*(a) John Calvin (1509–1564)*: *The Institutes of the Christian Religion.* Calvin's *Institutes of the Christian Religion* (First edition, 1536; final Latin edition, 1559) is the most influential statement of Reformed theology in particular and of Protestant theology in general. It is also a literary landmark. Calvin wrote as a master of the Latin language, and he was the first major theologian to use French as a medium for theology. He deliberately chose the language of common speech over against the special vocabulary of the scholastic theologians. His purpose was to persuade, to convince.[71] The *Institutes* have the unity of a great portrait, not of a machine with finished parts fitted together. The unifying theme is the knowledge of God and the knowledge of man in their inner relationships. As Calvin put it, no one can speak of man without speaking of God, and no one can speak of God without speaking of man.

The *Institutes* are divided, according to Calvin's division of the Apostles' Creed, into four parts: I. The Knowledge of God the Creator, II. The Knowledge of God the Redeemer, III. The Way in Which We Receive the Grace of Christ, IV. The External Means or Aids by Which God Invites Us into the Society of Christ and Holds Us Therein. Within the fourfold division, Calvin on two occasions suggests a twofold division of the *Institutes* according to the twofold knowledge of God: Knowledge of God the Creator, I,1–II,5, and Knowledge of God the Redeemer, II, 6–IV, 20.

The *Institutes* represent the effort to state the message of the Bible in a coherent and orderly way in the language of ordinary discourse. Calvin writes as a churchman concerned with organization, preaching, worship, and pastoral care. Above all he writes as an exegete of Scripture. Possibly no theologian in history has so well combined the powers of Biblical exegesis, of clear and logical thought, of literary expression, and of pastoral concern in one powerfully integrated personality. This unity of Bible, logic, literary expression, and pastoral concern is the strength and greatness of the *Institutes*. Its weakness is a lack of philosophical curiosity and imagination.

*(b) William Ames (1576–1633): The Marrow of Theology.* Ames grew up as a part of the Puritan movement in England. He studied under William Perkins and, like most Puritan theologians, was greatly influenced by the logic of the Huguenot martyr Peter Ramus (1515–1572). Forced to flee England, he lived his mature life in Holland. Here he wrote *The Marrow of Theology,* a succinct, tightly organized, coherent statement of Christian faith from the Augustinian, Reformed, and Puritan perspective. Like Johannes Wollebius' (1586–1629) *Compend of Christian Theology* (1626), William Ames' *The Marrow of Theology* (1623) is easy to read and easy to retain in memory. A contemporary translator describes the *Marrow* as "fundamentally a teaching document about Christian life in the Puritan style."[72] It was widely read and very influential in England and New England.

*(c) Francis Turretin (1623–1687): Institutio Theologiae Elencticae.* Francis Turretin did his theological work one century after Calvin.[73] It was his intention to consolidate and preserve the Reformed theology. He sought to do so by using the theological methods of scholasticism, which laid emphasis on definition, logic, and method. This development was necessary because Calvin had written his theology out of the exuberance of a revival of faith without time for sufficient attention to theological niceties. Though Calvin had a logical mind, his theology is an organic whole, held together by the existential relationship between God and man rather than by any logical pattern. While Calvin worked hard for the proper order for his theology, he did not attempt to press all Christian doctrines into a system whose parameters were fixed. Hence much of his theology, while orderly placed in his overall statement, remains open-ended. Consequently, a careful reading of the *Institutes* reveals "contradictions," or themes that are never adequately correlated. While Calvin tried to resolve some of the paradoxes of his theology, as in the case of his doctrine of "double predestination," many of the seemingly contradictory statements remain. This procedure is annoying to rational people, but apparently contradictory assertions or correlative themes held in tension may be nearer to the truth than any forced resolution of the tension. A good illustration of the unresolved dilemmas in his theology is Calvin's insistence on the

bondage of the human will and the freedom of the human will. Even when all problems of terminology have been cleared up and when all qualifications have been noted, the tension between the inevitability of sin and human freedom and responsibility remain.

Furthermore, during the century after Calvin, theological debates with the Roman Catholics, the Lutherans, the Anabaptists, and among the Reformed themselves placed a premium upon definition and logic. As a churchman, Turretin also felt an obligation to battle the rising tide of secularism. Turretin's work was a significant technical achievement, and the theologian today can learn from Turretin's analysis of the issues. His theology was the basis of the Princeton theology, and his *Institutio* was used as a text in many seminaries. Even though Turretin's theology was abstract, Charles Hodge demonstrated that it could be united with a warm piety and evangelical concern.

*(d) Charles Hodge (1797–1878): Systematic Theology.* [74] Charles Hodge was not an imaginative or creative theologian, but he was one of the most influential theologians in American history. More than three thousand students passed through his classes at Princeton; and his *Systematic Theology,* which summarized in a readable form the Princeton theology, has been one of the most widely used textbooks in American theological education. Hodge began his work as a Biblical scholar. He also studied church history. This early orientation helped to shape the later theologian, for Hodge was never interested in philosophical problems. He defined theology as the

> exhibition of the facts of Scripture in their proper order and relation, with the principles or general truths involved in the facts themselves, and which pervade and harmonize the whole.[75]

Theology is concerned with the "facts and principles of the Bible," not with questions that arise out of human existence as such. Hodge studied in Germany, where he came to know such scholars as Neander and developed a long friendship with Friedrich August Tholuck. German study did not influence Hodge in the liberal, critical direction that it did so many American students in the nineteenth century. His sponsor, Archibald Alexander of Princeton, had advised him that "it will be worth while to have gone to Germany to know that there is but little worth going for."[76]

Historically, Hodge was a disciple of Turretin, who had greatly influenced Alexander. Turretin, Hodge wrote, is

> on the whole, the best systematic theological writer with whom we are acquainted; and notwithstanding the tincture of scholasticism which pervades his work, it is remarkably adapted to the present state of theology in this country.[77]

Yet Turretin's statement of Reformed theology undergoes certain changes as it passes through Hodge's mind and personality. Personally, Hodge was a warm-hearted man and "congenitally pious." The American context in which he lived and worked was attempting to meet the needs of the frontiers through the methods of revival and the camp meeting. Hodge's theology, John Oliver Nelson has observed, applied the Calvinist doctrine of the sovereignty of God to conversion and united the evangelical principle of "heart religion" with Reformed theology.[78] Hodge had no doubt that his theology and that of the reformers was the same. He did not seek to be original. Yet theology did change with him. Nelson has observed that Calvin wrote in an uncertain time when the lightning of history was flashing. Hodge wrote for a stable and comfortable society which faced no critical dilemma. There is merit in this judgment even though Hodge lived through a civil war which was far more traumatic for the South than for Princeton and through the nineteenth century, whose full impact was just beginning to be felt when Hodge died. He did concern himself with Darwin, but the real impact of the evolution controversy would come later. Hodge was conservative, but he was not a fundamentalist, though his theology could be turned into fundamentalism by sterile repetition in a new situation. The warm-hearted and pragmatic qualities of Hodge's theology were lost in fundamentalist controversies that engaged Hodge's son, A. A. Hodge, and Benjamin B. Warfield, the remarkably able scholar who succeeded to the theological leadership at Princeton.

*(e) William Adams Brown (1865–1943): Christian Theology in Outline.* [79] William Adams Brown graduated from Union Theological Seminary in New York in 1890. He then studied in Berlin under Adolf Harnack, the great church historian and pre-eminent representative of liberal theology. Brown returned to Union Theological Seminary in New York as a teacher in 1892 and remained connected with that institution until his retirement in 1936. His

professional life began amid the fundamentalist-liberal controversies of the 1890s that led to heresy charges against several professors from Union Theological Seminary (New York) and to the severance of its relation with the Presbyterian Church in the U.S.A. His active work ended just as the theological climate in the United States was changing under the impact of Reinhold Niebuhr and the writings of Barth and Brunner.

William Adams Brown is an outstanding representative of evangelical liberalism. This theology owed four characteristics to its nineteenth-century heritage: (1) devotion to truth, (2) tentativeness, (3) emphasis on principle of continuity, and (4) liberal spirit. To its evangelical background (Dwight L. Moody had figured in Brown's own development) it owed (1) the authority of Christian experience, (2) the centrality of Jesus Christ, (3) loyalty to the historic faith, (4) missionary compassion. Two characteristics of evangelical liberalism were the slogan "Back to Christ" and the emphasis on a theology of Christian experience.[80] Evangelical liberalism accepted as facts evolution, historical-critical study, the Industrial Revolution, and other new developments of the nineteenth century. At the same time it insisted on the uniqueness of Jesus Christ and the necessity of divine salvation by the grace of God. Brown believed that the most important problem faced by theologians was "to present the permanent elements in the Christian message in a form to appeal to those who have thus broken with the past" and to address those who feel at home in the church, who value the past "but who do not always see clearly how to relate this treasure to the world of thought in which they are living."[81] For this reason Brown, following William Newton Clarke, discarded the old "scholastic" language of theology and sought to use the pure English of common experience. Brown's theology was unsatisfactory to fundamentalists and conservatives, but there is no question of its distinctively Christian character and of its great influence during the first four decades of the twentieth century.

*(f) Karl Barth (1886–1968): Church Dogmatics.*[82] Karl Barth, like William Adams Brown, began his theological career as a liberal and also as a student of Harnack. He was first a pastor, and concern for the preacher's message was an enduring characteristic of his work. He began his break with liberalism during the time

of World War I as he sought to preach the word of God to his congregation. The weak reaction of liberals like Harnack to the war contributed to his disillusionment. As has been noted, his commentary on Romans (second edition, 1922) shook the theological world. Barth no longer had confidence in the liberal effort to make the gospel intelligible. The theological task was the purification of the Christian message.[83] "Dogmatics as such does not inquire what the Apostles and Prophets have said, but what we ourselves must say 'on the basis of the Apostles and Prophets.' "[84] Theology is the church testing its message as to its authenticity. Dogmatics or theology examines the agreement of the word of God and man's word in the form of church proclamation. It does this by measuring church proclamation by the word of God in Holy Scripture so far as Scripture is a witness to the original word of God in revelation. Barth was more concerned with heresy than with paganism or unbelief. The church's great problem is not with the hearer, not with modern man, but with the authenticity of its own message.

Near the conclusion of his *Church Dogmatics* Barth defines theology as the accountability of the church for its message and its activity.

> In theology the community gives a critical account, both to itself and to the world which listens with it, of the appropriateness or otherwise of its praise of God, its preaching, its instruction, its evangelistic and missionary work, but also of the activity which cannot be separated from these things, and therefore of its witness in the full and comprehensive sense and in relation to its origin, theme and content. In the ministry of theology the community tests its whole action by the standard of its commission, and finally in the light of the Word of the Lord who gave it.

Barth succinctly stated his theological method, which is a good summary of his total theological stance.

> At each point I listen as unreservedly as possible to the witness of Scripture and as impartially as possible to that of the Church, and then consider and formulate what may be the result.[85]

**(g) Reinhold Niebuhr (1892–1971) and H. Richard Niebuhr (1894–1962)** were neither in intention nor in fact simply Reformed theologians.[86] They were born into a tradition that blended Lutheran and Reformed emphases. They were also formed by the intellectual and pragmatic traditions of American culture, and they intentionally theologized in a catholic (ecumenical) context. They were the most influential American theologians of the twentieth century, and they did transmit elements of the Reformed tradition with unusual power. H. Richard Niebuhr expounded the sovereignty of God with originality and with a vigor that deserves more attention than it has received. He also related culture and faith, revelation and reason in a contemporary way that is closer to John Calvin than is the theology of Karl Barth at this point. Reinhold Niebuhr, surely better than any contemporary theologian, did justice to the Reformed doctrine of sin; and he put together salvation as justification and sanctification, God's grace as mercy and God's grace as power, in a typically Reformed but in a contemporarily relevant and powerful way. Reinhold Niebuhr demonstrated the power of Christian categories to illuminate political, social, and economic problems. More than any theologian in recent centuries, he received the attention of intellectuals and men of affairs outside the church. Neither H. Richard Niebuhr nor Reinhold Niebuhr wrote a systematic theology. H. Richard Niebuhr's *Meaning of Revelation* and Reinhold Niebuhr's *Nature and Destiny of Man* are classics of twentieth-century theology.

## Reformed Confessions

The Reformed community in the sixteenth and seventeenth centuries was busy writing confessions of its faith.[87] A confession was a particular community's understanding of the Christian faith at a particular time and place, and there was a great hesitancy to give any confession greater status than that. The writing of confessions slowed in the eighteenth century only to revive in the twentieth century. The reasons for the paucity of creeds in the eighteenth and nineteenth centuries are numerous: awakenings and revivals with an emphasis on emotion rather than intellect; cultural movements that undermined the faith and to which the church found difficulty in responding; and certainly of equal significance, the "finished" character of the seventeenth-century confessions, which gave them an appearance of permanence and universality.

The first distinguishing feature of the Reformed confessions is their number and variety. Unlike the Lutheran confessions, written for the most part in a period of eight years by Melanchthon and Martin Luther in one geographical area, the Reformed confessions were written by many different people in a great variety of places and time. Theologians have despaired of writing *the* theology of Reformed confessions; only *theologies* of Reformed confessions can be written. No one can provide an official list of Reformed confessions, for no one has the authority to set the boundaries. The Reformed community produced at least fifty confessions of some note in the first 150 years.

The theologically distinctive marks of the Reformed confessions are the same as those of Reformed theology. The confessions all place great emphasis upon God and his Lordship, upon the authority of the Bible, upon ethics and even discipline. Some of the confessions, notably the Second Helvetic Confession, the Scots Confession of 1560, and the Heidelberg Catechism, express the faith with emphasis on its appropriation by the community. The Westminster and the Belgic Confessions, on the other hand, are more objective in their statement of the faith.

The importance of confessions for Reformed church life is great. The confession of faith is a significant act of Christian life and worship. Furthermore, the Reformed emphasis on the importance of doctrine and upon the importance of the life of the mind in the service of God has contributed further to the role of confessions in the life of the church. (See Appendix of chapter for listing of Reformed confessions.)

The earliest Reformed confessions were theses for debate or defenses of the faith. As such they were composed of concise and pointed statements of the Reformers' basic commitments. An example is "The Conclusions of Berne" (1528), which declared, "The Holy Christian Church, whose only head is Christ, is born of the Word of God, and abides in the same, and listens not to the voice of a stranger." In theses such as this the Reformers proclaimed their faith.

As the Reformation matured, the confessions became comprehensive statements of the faith. The Gallican Confession of 1559 is a notable example. It had its origin in a statement of faith drawn up by endangered Reformed pastors in Paris as their proclamation and defense. They sent a copy to Geneva. When the French Protestants held their first National Assembly in Paris in 1559, a delegation from Geneva carried with them a confession which revised and expanded the original eighteen articles. Calvin participated in the preparation of this Confession, which reflects his theology and which was adopted with revisions by the Assembly as the confession of the French Church. It was reaffirmed by the Synod which met at La Rochelle in 1571, again with minor revisions. The Gallican Confession is an orderly, precise, and balanced statement of the Reformed faith, particularly as it had been formulated in Geneva, characteristics it shares with the Belgic Confession of 1561.

The Second Helvetic Confession (1561, 1566) is a strikingly different kind of confession. Originally written by Heinrich Bullinger (1504–1575) of Zurich as a personal testimony, it received synod approval in 1566 and became the most widely endorsed of the continental confessions. In contrast to the Gallican Confession, it is discursive rather than concise; it is concerned with the experience of the faith as well as the objective statement of the faith; it is generous in spirit. It also contains an extensive treatment of the ethos and structure of the Christian community's life.

The Scots Confession of 1560 was written in four days at the request of the Scottish Parliament as a part of the reformation of the church. The authors were a commission of six men, including John Knox. The Confession embodies the intensity of the moment and the personal quality of the confession of believers who were staking their lives on the issues before the church. It has been described as "the warm utterance of a people's heart." Yet it states the Protestant faith in plain language, "revealing conviction, determination, and enthusiasm." It is more pictorial and historical than abstract in style.

The confessions of the seventeenth century have a distinctive character. Behind them was more than a hundred years of Protestant and Reformed theological work. They were written not in the context of a religious and theological revival, but in an established church with internal debates and external controversies not only with Roman Catholics but also with other Protestant churches. The Canons of Dort were drawn up by the Synod of Dort (1619), which met to resolve a controversy concerning difficult problems of God's Lordship and human freedom. (See pages 38–39).

The Westminster Confession and catechisms, written by the Westminster Assembly (1643–1647), became the basic Reformed confession of English-speaking Presbyterians, and with revisions, of Congregationalists as well as of many Baptists. This Confession has all the virtues of a highly developed, precise, technically refined theology, as well as the particular imprint of English Puritanism. Its virtues are also its weaknesses. In places it knows too much about God and God's will, and it lacks both the generosity of the Second Helvetic and the personal and experiential warmth of the Scots and Second Helvetic confessions.

The prolific character of Reformed confession writing came to an end with the "finished" statements of the seventeenth century. The challenging developments of the last two hundred years have increased the tempo of confession writing, but few confessions have gained the status of the earlier confessions which reflect the deep background of piety and learning out of which they were written. Among the more notable of the recent confessions are those which came out of the Reformed community in Germany in the 1930s: "Dusseldorf Theses" (1933), "Declaration Concerning the Right Understanding of the Reformation Confession of Faith" (1934), and the "Barmen Declaration" (1934); "Statement of Faith of the United Church of Christ" (1959); and the "Confession of 1967" of the United Presbyterian Church, which not only dealt with specific theological issues but related the faith to contemporary social problems.

The Reformed tradition has also been characterized by great emphasis upon catechetical instruction. Some of the catechisms were prepared with as much care as confessional documents, which indeed they were, but cast in a form for the instruction of the people, in particular children. Calvin himself gave catechetical instruction a high priority and regretted that he did not have time to revise his own catechism. The most influential of Reformed catechisms were the Heidelberg Catechism (1563) and the Westminster Shorter Catechism (1647). The Heidelberg Catechism, written by Olevianus and Ursinus, reflects the influence of Lutheran theology and has the warm, experiential quality of the Scots and Second Helvetic Confessions. It begins with the notable question, "What is thy only comfort in life and death?" The Westminster Shorter Catechism has the virtues and weaknesses of the Westminster Confession.

Many Reformed pastors gave a high priority to catechetical instruction and to the development of the arts of and the materials for effective teaching. The production of catechisms was prolific, especially during the Puritan period. Catechetical instruction not only provided specific and easily mastered answers to theological questions, but also raised the questions themselves. Along with the role of confessions in the life of the church, it was a very significant source of the strength of the Reformed community until the Second World War, when it declined under the attack of new theories of education, a secular and pluralistic society, and the theological malaise of the churches.

## *Appendix D:*

# REPRESENTATIVE REFORMED SYSTEMATIC THEOLOGIES

CLASSIC REFORMED THEOLOGY
> Ulrich Zwingli: *The True and False Religion,* 1525
> Heinrich Bullinger: *Fifty Godlie and Learned Sermons, Divided into Five Decades Containing the Chiefe and Principall Points of Christian Religion,* 1549
> John Calvin: *Institutes of the Christian Religion,* 1536, 1559

SEVENTEENTH CENTURY
CONTINENTAL
> Johannes Wollebius: *Compendium of Christian Theology,* 1626
> Francis Turretin: *Institutio Theologiae Elencticae,* 1688

PURITAN
> Dudley Fenner: *Sacra Theologica,* 1585
> William Perkins: *A Golden Chaine,* 1590
> William Ames: *The Marrow of Theology,* 1623

EIGHTEENTH CENTURY
> Benedict Pictet: *Christian Theology* (1696, English translation— 1834)
> Samuel Willard: *A Compleat Body of Divinity,* 1726

NINETEENTH- AND TWENTIETH-CENTURY PATTERNS OF THEOLOGY
CONSERVATIVE
AMERICAN
> Charles Hodge: *Systematic Theology,* 1871
> A. A. Hodge: *Outlines of Theology,* 1860
> Robert Lewis Dabney: *Systematic and Polemic Theology,* 1878
> Henry B. Smith: *System of Christian Theology,* 1884
> William Shedd: *Dogmatic Theology,* 1888
> Augustus Hopkins Strong: *Systematic Theology,* 1906
> Louis Berkhof: *Reformed Dogmatics* (Dutch tradition), 1932

DUTCH[88]
> Herman Bavinck: *Gereformeerde Dogmatiek* (1895–1901) *Our Reasonable Faith* (1909)
> Gerrit Cornelis Berkouwer: *Studies in Dogmatics*

GERMAN
> Heinrich L. Heppe: *Reformed Dogmatics,* 1861

FRENCH
> Auguste Lecerf: *An Introduction to Reformed Dogmatics,* 1931 (English translation, 1949)

LIBERAL

Friedrich Schleiermacher: *The Christian Faith,* 1821, 2nd ed., 1830 (Schleiermacher considered himself Reformed, but the judgment has been questioned. In any case, every theologian has to give attention to him. Brian Gerrish in *Tradition and the Modern World* (1978) has argued cogently for his inclusion.)

Alexander Schweizer: *Die Glaubenslehre der Evangelisch—Reformierten Kirche,* 1844–1847

William A. Brown: *Christian Theology in Outline,* 1906.

NEW REFORMATION THEOLOGY, 1918 FF.

Karl Barth: *Church Dogmatics,* 1932–1967 (English translation, 1936–1969)

Emil Brunner: *Dogmatics,* 1946–1960

Otto Weber: *Grundlagen der Dogmatik,* 1955

## REPRESENTATIVE CATECHISMS

Catechisms present systematic theology usually in a question and answer form and for elementary instruction in the Christian faith.

Geneva Catechism (John Calvin) 1542

Emden Catechism 1555

The Heidelberg Catechism (Zacharias Ursinus and Caspar Olevianus) 1563

Craig's Catechism 1581

The Zurich Catechism of 1609

Brief Method of Catechising (William Gouge) 8th Ed. 1631

Short Catechism Containing the Principles of Religion (John Ball) 18th Impression 1637

The New Catechism 1644

Endeavour of Making the Principles of Christian Religion, namely, the Creed, the Ten Commandments, the Lord's Prayer, and the Sacraments, Plaine and Easie (Herbert Palmer) 6th Ed. 1645

The Shorter Catechism (Westminster Assembly) 1648

The Larger Catechism (Westminster Assembly) 1648

The Principle of Christian Religion with a Brief Method of the Doctrine Thereof (James Ussher) 1654

Draft Catechism of the Church of Scotland 1954

# Appendix E:

## REPRESENTATIVE REFORMED THEOLOGIES

(This listing includes theologies that focus on a theme or an issue, in contrast to systematic theologies that attempt a comprehensive and coherent statement of Christian faith. Karl Barth has labeled them "irregular dogmatics" in contrast to "regular" or "school" dogmatics that emphasize completeness of treatments. *Church Dogmatics* 1/1 pp. 316–318)

Most of the theologies listed below are in the mainstream of the Reformed tradition, and all have some contact with it. The theologies have been located in the most appropriate period, though in some cases this involved chronological dislocation.

### 1517–1564

Martin Bucer (1491–1551): *De Regno Christi* (1550)
Peter Martyr (1500–1562): *The Common Places* (E. T. 1583)

### 1564–1775

Theodore Beza (1519–1605): *Confession de la foy chrestienne* (1558)
Girolamo Zanchi (1516–1590): *The Doctrine of Absolute Predestination* (1562)
Jacob Arminius (1560–1609): *The Declaration of Sentiments* (1608)
Moïse Amyraut (1596–1664): *Brief Traitté de la Prédestination* (1634)
Gisbert Voetius (1589–1676): *Selectae Disputiones Theologicae* (1648–1669)
John Owen (1616–1683): *Works*
Johannes Cocceius (1603–1669): *Summa doctrinae de foedere et testamento Dei* (1648)

### 1738–1880

#### NEW ENGLAND THEOLOGY

Jonathan Edwards (1703–1758): *The Works of President Edwards*
Samuel Hopkins (1721–1803) *System of Doctrines* (1793)
Nathaniel Taylor (1786–1855) *Lectures on the Moral Government of God* (1859)

#### CONSERVATIVE

James Henley Thornwell (1812–1862): *Collected Works*
William Cunningham (1805–1861): *Historical Theology* (1862)
James Orr (1844–1913): *The Christian View of God and the World* (1890, 1891)
Abraham Kuyper (1837–1920): *Calvinism* (1899)
Benjamin Warfield (1851–1921): *Calvin and Calvinism*

LIBERAL

John W. Nevin (1803–1886): *The Mystical Presence* (1846)*

Horace Bushnell (1802–1876): *God in Christ* (1849)

John McLeod Campbell (1800–1872): *The Nature of the Atonement* (1856)

Andrew Martin Fairbairn (1838–1912): *The Philosophy of the Christian Religion* (1902)

James Denney (1856–1917): *The Christian Doctrine of Reconciliation* (1917)

Hugh Ross Mackintosh (1870–1936): *The Person of Jesus Christ* (1912)

John Oman (1860–1939): *Grace and Personality* (1917)

John Baillie (1886–1960): *The Interpretation of Religion* (1929)

Henry P. Van Dusen (1897–1975): *The Plain Man Seeks for God* (1933)

Robert L. Calhoun (1896–    ): *God and the Common Life* (1935)

*Liberal in sense of opening up new perspectives

1918–1955

P. T. Forsyth (1848–1921): *The Person and Place of Jesus Christ* (1909)

George Hendry (1904–    ): *God the Creator* (1935, 1937)

Hendrik Kraemer (1888–1965): *The Christian Message in a Non-Christian World* (1938)

Reinhold Niebuhr (1892–1971): *The Nature and Destiny of Man* (1941, 1943)

Robert L. Calhoun, et al.: "The Relation of the Church to the War" (1943)†

Donald Baillie (1887–1954): *God Was in Christ* (1948)

Josef L. Hromadka (1889–1969): *Theology Between Yesterday and Tomorrow* (1957)

H. Richard Niebuhr (1894–1962): *Radical Monotheism and Western Culture* (1960)

A. A. van Ruler (1908–1970) *The Christian Church and the Old Testament* 1955 (E. T. 1972)

†[An ecumenical document that bears imprint of the chairman of the committee, Robert L. Calhoun; it can be found in John Leith, *Creeds of the Churches* (Richmond: John Knox Press, 1974), pp. 522–554].

1955–1976

Paul Lehmann (1906–    ): *Ethics in a Christian Context* (1963)

Helmut Gollwitzer (1908– ): *The Existence of God* (1963, E. T. 1965)

Jürgen Moltmann (1926– ): *Theology of Hope* (1964, E. T. 1967)

Thomas F. Torrance (1913–    ): *Theology in Reconstruction* (1965)

James Gustafson (1925–    ): *Ethics in a Theological Perspective* (1981)

IN NEW CULTURAL CONTEXTS

Ruben A. Alves (1933– ): *A Theology of Human Hope* (1972)

Allan Aubrey Boesak (1946– ): *Black Theology, Black Power* (1978)

Choan-Seng Song (1929– ): *Third Eye-Theology: Theology in Formation in Asian Settings* (1979)

*Appendix F:*

## REPRESENTATIVE BIBLICAL STUDIES BY REFORMED SCHOLARS

William Robertson Smith (1856–1894): Article on Bible in Ninth Edition of *Encyclopaedia Britannica, The Prophets of Israel* 1882
Lectures on the Religion of the Semites 1889

A. B. Davidson (1831–1902): *The Theology of the Old Testament* 1904

Charles A. Briggs (1841–1913): *A Critical and Exegetical Commentary on the Book of Psalms* 1906
An Editor of the *International Critical Commentary*

Adolf Schlatter (1852–1938): *The Theology of the New Testament and Dogmatics* 1909 (E.T. 1973)

James Moffatt (1870–1944): *Introduction to the Literature of the New Testament* 1911
*A New Translation of the Bible* 1935 (O.T. 1924–1925; N. T. 1913)

Karl Barth (1886–1968): *The Epistle to the Romans* 2nd edition 1922 (E.T. 1933)

J. Gresham Machen (1881–1937): *New Testament Greek for Beginners* 1923
*The Virgin Birth of Christ* 1930

T. W. Manson (1893–1958): *The Teaching of Jesus* 1931

Walther Eichrodt (1890–    ): *Theology of the Old Testament* 1933–1939 (E. T. 1961–1967)

C. H. Dodd (1884–1973): *The Bible Today* 1947

Theodorus Christiaan Vriezen (1899–    ): *An Outline of Old Testament Theology* 1949 (E. T. 1958)

Oscar Cullmann (1902–    ): *Christ and Time* 1947 (E. T. 1950)

George Ernest Wright (1909–1974): *God Who Acts: Biblical Theology as Recital* 1952

John Bright (1908–    ): *A History of Israel* 1959 (rev. ed. 1972)
*The Authority of the Old Testament* 1967

Walther Zimmerli (1907–    ): *Old Testament Theology in Outline* 1972 (E. T. 1977)

Eduard Schweizer (1913–    ): *Jesus* 1968 (E. T. 1971)

Hans-Joachim Kraus (1918–    ): *Die biblische Theologie. Ihre Geschichte und Problematik* 1970

*Appendix G:*

## REPRESENTATIVE REFORMED CONFESSIONS OF THE SIXTEENTH AND SEVENTEENTH CENTURIES

I. EARLY THESES

Zwingli's Sixty-Seven Articles, 1523
Theses of Berne, 1528
Theses of Rive, 1535
Theses of Lausanne, 1536

II. CONFESSIONS OF ZURICH AND BASEL

The Confession to Charles V (Zwingli), 1530
The Confession to Francis I (Zwingli), 1531
First Confession of Basel, 1534
First Helvetic Confession, 1536
Second Helvetic Confession, 1566

III. CONFESSIONS OF GENEVA, FRANCE, AND THE NETHERLANDS

Confession of Geneva, 1537
Consensus of Geneva, 1552
Gallican Confession of Faith, 1559
Belgic Confession, 1561

IV. THE ZURICH CONSENSUS (TIGURINUS), 1549

*(Joint statement on Lord's Supper of representatives of viewpoints of Geneva and Zurich)*

V. THE RHINELAND

The Tetrapolitan Confession, 1530
Heidelberg Catechism, 1563

VI. OTHER EUROPEAN CONFESSIONS

Confession of Czenger (Hungary), 1557 or 1558
Consensus of Sendomir, 1570
Confession of Sigismund, 1614

VII. ENGLISH LANGUAGE CONFESSIONS

Scots Confession of 1560
Thirty-Nine Articles, 1563 (Reformed in articles on predestination and the Lord's Supper)
Irish Articles of 1615

VIII. SEVENTEENTH-CENTURY CONFESSIONS

Canons of Dort, 1619
Westminster Confession, 1647
Declaration of Thorn, 1645
Helvetic Consensus Formula, 1675
London Confession, 1677, 1689

**JOHN CALVIN**
1509-1564

Minister of the Word of God, Geneva
Theologian, Preacher, Pastor, Churchman

**JOHN KNOX**
1505-1572

Minister, Reformer, and Historian
of the Church in Scotland

## JEANNE D'ALBRET
### 1528-1572

Jeanne d'Albret was the only daughter of Marguerite of Navarre. The daughter is said to have been the only sovereign of the sixteenth century who put no one to death for religion. The same could be said of her son Henry IV and of Philip of Hesse, but her tolerance impressed her generation.

...She expected her subjects to subscribe to the confession of La Rochelle but did not prosecute those who declined.

Bainton, Roland H., *Women of the Reformation in France and England.* Minneapolis: Augsburg Publishing House, 1973, Chapter 2, pp. 43, 68.

## JOHN WITHERSPOON
### 1723-1794

President of the College of New Jersey
(Princeton University)
Signer of Declaration of Independence; Churchman

Picture from Firestone Library, Princeton University

## CHARLES HODGE
### 1797-1878

Churchman and Theologian
Professor, Princeton Theological Seminary

The original portrait from which this picture was made is in the possession of the Presbyterian
Historical Society in Philadelphia, Pennsylvania.

**JAMES HENLEY THORNWELL**
1812-1862

Churchman and Theologian
Professor and President of South Carolina College
(University of South Carolina)
Professor, Presbyterian Theological Seminary
Columbia, South Carolina

## HERMAN BAVINCK
### 1854-1921

Theologian
Professor of Dogmatics at Kampen, 1882-1903
Free University, Amsterdam, 1903-1921

## WOODROW WILSON
### 1856-1924

President of the United States
1913-1921

...Woodrow Wilson was a Presbyterian Christian of the Calvinistic persuasion. He stands pre-eminent among all the inheritors of that tradition who have made significant contributions to American political history. Indeed, he was the prime embodiment, the apogee, of the Calvinistic tradition among all statesmen of the modern epoch.

Arthur S. Link, "Woodrow Wilson and His Presbyterian Inheritance" in *Essays in Scotch-Irish History*, edited by E. R. R. Green, New York: Humanities Press, 1969, p. 2.

## HOLLIE PAXSON WINSBOROUGH
### 1865-1940

Pioneer in the work and organization
of the women of the church

## WILLIAM HENRY SHEPPARD
### 1865-1927

He was missionary of the Presbyterian Church, United States in Belgian Congo (which is now Zaire) from 1890–1910, effective critic of the exploitation of the Congo, elected member of the Royal Geographic Society of London.

## ROBERT E. SPEER
### 1867-1947

"Champion of the Cause of Missions"
(Citation for honorary degree, Princeton University)

Board of Foreign Missions, Presbyterian Church in the
United States of America, 1891–1937.

**JOHN BAILLIE**
1886-1960

Theologian
Principal of New College and
Dean of the Faculty of Divinity,
University of Edinburgh, 1950-1956
President of World Council of Churches, 1954-1960

Picture furnished by I. F. Baillie, son of John Baillie

**EMIL BRUNNER**          **KARL BARTH**
1889-1966        and        1886-1968

    Pre-eminent Reformed theologians of the twentieth century greet each other in a meeting in 1960.

## JOHN ALEXANDER MACKAY
### 1889-

Churchman and Missionary (South America)
President of Princeton Theological Seminary, 1936-1959
President, Board of Foreign Missions
of Presbyterian Church, U.S.A., 1945-1951
President of World Presbyterian Alliance, 1954-1959
Chairman, International Missionary Council, 1948-1958

Picture from Princeton Theological Seminary

## WILLEM VISSER 'T HOOFT
1900-

Dr. Visser 't Hooft has had a single career—that of ecumenical statesman and international Christian organization staff leader for more than fifty years. He contributed substantially to the founding of the World Council of Churches and was its first general secretary from 1939 to 1966.

**SUZANNE DE DIETRICH**
1891-

Teacher of the Bible

# V

---

# POLITY
# AND
# THE REFORMED TRADITION

Reformed Christians, especially those who speak English, are best known by their polities, as, for example, the Presbyterians and the Congregationalists. This fact indicates the great importance of the organized life of the church for this tradition and justifies a chapter on polity in any study of the Reformed tradition.

## *The Significance of Polity*

A good starting point is this question: why have Reformed Christians regarded church polity, or the organized life of the church, of crucial importance? The first answer must be the very deep conviction that God calls the Christian to a life of obedience in and through the polity of the church. The ultimate basis for the organized life of the church is not human wisdom but the will of God. The ministry and the polity of the church is God's gift to the church. On its simplest level this conviction found expression in the belief that God had revealed one pattern of church organization in the Bible. This belief was sometimes espoused by Presbyterians in their advocacy of the divine right of Presbyterianism.[1] The conviction that polity is God's will for the church, however, is not necessarily tied to this particular belief. In a more general way it embodies the conviction that God is concerned about the church's organized life and wills for it to exist in particular ways even though these ways may be diverse and impossible to define precisely. Church organization is never merely functional or a matter of human convenience.

Calvin found in "order" an important concept for understanding Christian faith and life. The proper ordering of life in creation and human existence is established by God's ordination, but this order has been distorted by sin. Calvin conceived of the church, according to one recent study, as "the history of the restoration of order."[2] The Christian, according to another study, is "elected or called to order." "He who is elected in Christ finds his personhood by taking his place in the harmonious structure of the holy community."[3]

Presbyterians have also taken polity seriously because of its significance for theology. Faith cannot be separated from the form in which it expresses itself. In part, faith determines the form of its expression; but the form of expression also determines faith. This is especially true of the government, discipline, and worship of the church. Christian people learn theology, even when they cannot articulate it, not only from words in preaching and teaching but also from their manner of life in the church. Personality is shaped by practice and worship.

The form of the church, for example, either encourages or discourages a person to exercise the responsibility of faith or to depend upon the church as an institution for decisions that should be personal responsibility. The priesthood of all believers, therefore, is encouraged or discouraged by the form and shape of the church's life. Representative church government, in contrast to congregational church government or monarchical church government, was based by Calvin and other Reformed theologians, such as Thornwell at a later time, upon theological considerations, especially anthropology. In the contemporary ecumenical movement, the significance of Christology for polity and of polity for Christology has been clearly emphasized. Doctrine and polity are indissolubly united, influencing each other and being shaped by each other.

A third reason polity is important is its significance in maintaining the integrity of the church. Calvin was surely convinced, as is amply documented in the fourth book of the *Institutes* and in the struggles of his ministry, that the structure of the church's life contributes either to the integrity or to the apostasy of the church. Calvinists themselves have indicated the importance of the ordering of the church's life for the church's very existence in their temptation to make discipline the third mark of the church.[4] Discipline is necessary, or at least has been so regarded by some Calvinists, for the right preaching of the word and the right administration of the sacraments. In contemporary history the significance of polity for the church's life has been illustrated in the German church's struggle and in the experience of Protestant churches in the South in the United States in connection with racial conflicts after World War II.

## The Subordination of Polity to the Gospel

The Reformed tradition is distinguished not simply by its insistence that polity is important but also by its radical subordination of polity to the gospel. Reformed theology has never made the existence of the church dependent upon polity. The one thing necessary and indispensable to the church's existence is the word of God or the gospel, a conviction that the Reformed share with the Lutherans.

Calvin himself is very clear on this point. "Wherever we see the Word of God purely preached and heard, and the sacraments administered according to Christ's institution, there, it is not to be doubted, a church of God exists."[5] As for individuals Calvin writes, "we recognize as members of the church those who, by confession of faith, by example of life, and by partaking of the sacraments, profess the same God and Christ with us."[6]

The Calvinist insistence on the prevenience of God's grace and upon the church as the company of the elect undercuts even the significance of the sacraments and, much more, the necessity of any structures of polity. One of the most inclusive definitions of the church appears in an important Reformed creed, the Second Helvetic.

> . . . we do not so strictly shut up the Church within those marks before mentioned, as thereby to exclude all those out of the Church who either do not participate of the sacraments (not willingly, nor upon contempt; but who being constrained by necessity, do against their will abstain from them, or else do want them), or in whom faith does sometime fail, though not quite decay, nor altogether die: or in whom some slips and errors of infirmity may be found. For we know that God had some friends in the world that were not of the commonwealth of Israel.[7]

Calvin's conviction that the gospel alone is necessary for the church's existence made possible a catholicity in relation to other churches of the Reformation and even toward Roman Catholicism that would not have been possible otherwise. Full agreement as to polity was not necessary for Christian unity. On the other hand, the claim that some church structure or that anything other than the gospel was necessary for the church's existence did violence to Calvin's understanding of the gospel and of the Christian faith. The church is constituted by the action of God, and only the word of God is essential for its existence.

Reformed churches sometimes made discipline a third mark of the church along with the preaching of the word and administration of the sacraments, as in the Scots Confession of 1560 and the Belgic Confession of 1561. Calvin himself exalted discipline, but he never made it a mark of the church's existence. When the tradition did make discipline a mark of the church's existence, discipline was understood to be necessary to the proper preaching of the word and administration of the sacraments. Professor James S. McEwen in his study of John Knox has written,

> The discipline which the Reformed Church insisted upon exercising was in no sense whatever an expression of legalism. It had nothing to do with legalism, or with any idea that God would be pleased with strict adherence to rules and regulations. Nor was it an expression of an over-scrupulous moralism. Its basis was this sense of the "numinous", or the "altogether holy", in the Lord's Supper— and the deep conviction that this holiness must not be profaned by allowing the careless or the deliberately wicked to approach the Holy Table, at the sacred moment when the Lord and the participants were (as Knox puts it) "knitted together".[8]

## The One, Holy, Catholic, Apostolic Church

Reformed polities all reassert the ancient affirmation of the one, holy, catholic, and apostolic church. For them the historical reality of the church, as it must be for contemporary man, was an article of faith. The Christian does not believe *in* the church, a community of forgiven but sinful people, as one believes *in* the Holy Spirit, the Lord and giver of life. The force of the creedal affirmation is rather the assertion that in the mixed body that forms any congregation, there *is* the people of God, the church as the "earthly-historical form of existence of Jesus Christ Himself."[9] Calvin never doubted that even in the darkest hour for faith, the church exists; and he expressed his conviction in these remarkable sentences.

> Although the melancholy desolation which confronts us on every side may cry that no remnant of the church is left, let us know that Christ's death is fruitful, and that God miraculously keeps his church as in hiding places. So it was said to Elijah, "I have kept for

myself seven thousand men who have not bowed the knee before Baal." [I Kings 19:18 p.][10]

Karl Barth in the twentieth century boldly declared that the church is the "earthly-historical form of existence of Jesus Christ," but he likewise knew that the actuality of the church is visible only to faith. The church as a human phenomenon does not have to be believed. It is simply there as organization structures, buildings, and paraphernalia. But:

> What Christianity really is, the being of the community as "the living community of the living Lord Jesus Christ," calls for the perception of faith, and is accessible only to this perception and not to any other. It has this character in virtue of the reconciling and self-revealing grace of God, in virtue of the mission and work of the Holy Spirit, and therefore in the power of Jesus Christ Himself. Only in this power is it recognisable in this character. The glory of Jesus Christ was hidden when He humbled Himself, when He took our flesh, when in our flesh He was obedient to God, when He destroyed our wrong, when He established our right. So, too, the glory of the humanity justified in Him is concealed. And this means that the glory of the community gathered together by Him within humanity is only a glory which is hidden from the eyes of the world until His final revelation, so that it can be only an object of faith. What it is, its mystery, its spiritual character, is not without manifestations and analogies in its generally visible form. But it is not unequivocally represented in any such generally visible manifestations and analogies. The men united in it and their action are in every respect generally visible. They are so as the elect and called of God, and their works as good works. But the being of the community in its temporal character is hidden under considerable and very powerful appearances to the contrary.[11]

The church as an affirmation of faith does not lead to a depreciation of the church that is accessible to ordinary knowledge. The "invisible" church is visible. The visible being of the church witnesses to its invisibility. The problem of invisibility is based in the inability of any human being to set the boundaries of the church or grasp the reality that is known only to God. The church that we do know must attest and demonstrate as best it can its "invisible" reality, but in its sinful history it can never be exactly identified with the true church of Jesus Christ.

Reformed theologians in the sixteenth century refused to give up the word "catholic," and they boldly held to the unity of the church in the face of fragmentation. Furthermore, Reformed churches did not repudiate Christendom, a Christian society; but rather, during the sixteenth-century Reformation they renewed efforts to make Christendom a reality. A secular society with no official faith commitments or a denominationally differentiated Christian community, especially in one locality, could not have been imagined by Calvin. The early Reformed communities sought to be the one, holy, catholic, apostolic church in their places, and they sought to be coextensive with the community. Protestantism and the Reformed community gave to these four ancient marks of the church a particular nuance in as much as the church was defined primarily by God's action in his word and the sacraments, but the ancient marks of the church were always affirmed.

The church is *one* and *catholic*. If it is truly catholic, it is also one. One of the finest definitions of the catholicity of the church was written many years ago by Cyril of Jerusalem.

> The Church, then, is called Catholic because it is spread through the whole world, from one end of the earth to the other, and because it never stops teaching in all its fulness every doctrine that men ought to be brought to know: and that regarding things visible and invisible, in heaven and on earth. It is called Catholic also because it brings into religious obedience every sort of men, rulers and ruled, learned and simple, and because it is a universal treatment and cure for every kind of sin whether perpetrated by soul or body, and possesses within it every form of virtue that is named, whether it expresses itself in deeds or words or in spiritual graces of every description.[12]

The catholicity and unity of the church is always in peril. From the beginning the church suffered divisions and has existed in many forms. The fragmentation of the church has greatly increased during the last 300 years as the denominational pattern has developed in Protestantism. A denomination by definition is a Christian community which claims to be the catholic church but does not claim to exhaust the reality of the church or to be the only form of the church. By this admission the denominational pattern has been less destructive of the unity of the church than those forms of the church which not only claim to be the catholic church but which also make exclusive claims for themselves. The unity and catholicity of the church is likewise imperiled by class, cultural, racial, and national differences. The very emphasis in

Protestant and Reformed churches on the sermon, on congregational participation in worship, and on fellowship enhances the problems created by these differences.

Reformed theologians have always insisted that the church is *one* and *catholic*, however much its unity and catholicity may be compromised by doctrine, polity, and the social differences that separate Christians. As Calvin put it, "There could not be two or three churches unless Christ be torn asunder."[13] Karl Barth in the twentieth century writes,

> The Church, being different from any other human community, thereby is catholic, that is, universal. She is limited by no barrier, either of state, or of race, or of culture. Exclusively and properly belonging to no one, the Church belongs to everyone.[14]

The church is also *holy.* Some in the ancient church thought this meant that the church is holy because the people are holy.[15] Therefore they excluded from the church those guilty of certain sins, particularly murder, adultery, and apostasy. Others said that holiness was centered in the priesthood.[16] If the church depends upon the holiness of people or ministers, then its existence is precarious. Both people and priests are called to a life of holiness; but as Augustine contended, the holiness which is a basic mark of the church is the presence in the church of God's Spirit and word and of prayer and the sacraments by which believers are renewed.[17] "The holiness of the Church will purely and simply consist in the fact that the Church has both the benefit of listening to the word of God and that of hoping." Holiness refers to God's work, not to man's. The people in the church are not "particularly suited to come near to God." They are there because God has called them.[18]

The church is also *apostolic;* that is, in continuity with the apostles. For some the succession of the apostles is maintained by the succession of bishops.[19] Calvin rejected the historical reliability of an unbroken succession and the possibility that such a succession could guarantee apostolicity.[20] Reformed theologians have cherished the fact that there is a succession of believing men and women stretching back through the centuries. This succession of faith from generation to generation is impressive indeed. Yet authentic succession is rooted primarily in living obedience to the living Lord of the church.

There is one "essential" ministry, the only ministry that is unchallengeably essential. That is the ministry which the Lord Jesus Christ opened in Galilee . . . the ministry which He continues to this day in and through the Church, which is His body. The promise of this abiding presence, and its fulfilment in the early Church, is as well attested as anything in the New Testament. It is in virtue of this presence that it is possible to call the Church the Body of Christ.[21]

## Reformed Polities

Reformed theology has lived comfortably with a variety of polities. As Calvin put it, "we know that church organization admits, nay requires, according to the varying condition of the times, various changes."[22] He recognized this fact in his history of ecclesiastical development in the ancient church, and he accepted a variety of polities as viable forms of the church in the sixteenth century. While Reformed theology has been overwhelmingly associated with presbyterian polity, it has thrived at times with congregational polity and has lived with *functional* and *jurisdictional* episcopal systems.

Historical circumstances in the sixteenth century gave the Reformed communities considerable freedom in working out new patterns of church life. Most Lutheran communities inherited the medieval church structure intact, and the same was true of the Reformation in England. In Switzerland the reformation in doctrine coincided with a repudiation of the old church structures, especially in Geneva. The Geneva polity which from the beginning struggled for a church independent of the state has had more influence in an increasingly secular society than the Zurich polity which emphasized "magisterial sovereignty" in a Christian community which was inclusive of church and state. In France, Holland, and England the Reformed communities frequently were in opposition to the established order and thus were free to work out their forms of church life.

## Calvin's Polity

John Calvin gave more attention to polity than did any other major reformer. One of his creative contributions to theology was the four-fold division of the Apostles' Creed as a basis for his theology, which allowed him to devote the fourth and longest book of the *Institutes* to the church, the sacraments, and the state. Calvin also came into a situation that had preaching but no church organization. The old had been rejected, but the new had not yet developed. He had both the interest and the opportunity to develop a pattern of church life that was expressive of the teachings of Scripture and supportive of Christian faith and life. His immediate range of pastoral oversight was Geneva or, in contemporary parlance, the metropolitan area of Geneva. He did not have responsibility for a polity for a province, much less a nation. Hence the polity of the *Institutes* is open-ended in regard to the needs for large geographical areas.

The *Ecclesiastical Ordinances,* which Calvin drew up for a "well-ordered" church in Geneva, became one of his most influential writings. It provided for four orders which he believed to have been instituted by God. Pastors were to have responsibility for preaching the word, for administering the sacraments, for instructing, and, along with the elders, for disciplining. Doctors were to be the teachers with responsibility for the "instruction of the faithful in true doctrine."[23] The doctors closest to ministers were the lecturers in theology, but the order included a comprehensive school program. The elders were to have with the pastors oversight "of the life of everyone."[24] The deacons were the church's ministry of compassion, especially to the poor and sick.

One notable feature of this polity is Calvin's emphasis upon pastors who are noted for their integrity and competence. Integrity and competence were maintained by careful examination of life, of ability in theology, and of capacity for the communication of the Christian message. Calvin had an exalted view of the ministry. He sometimes incautiously called ministers the mouth of God.[25] The significance of the minister was not, however, *status* but *function.* Calvin regarded the minister as the theologian of the church who discharges the responsibility of preaching, of leadership in worship, of teaching, and of pastoral care. He believed this function was critically important for the well-being of the church. The significance of the function accounts for Calvin's stringent demands upon the minister.

A second notable achievement is the consistory (session), made up of the ministers and the elders.[26] One consistory served the metropolitan area. Calvin insisted upon the consistory's responsibility for discipline of the congregation in the areas of morals, of participation in worship, and of Christian knowledge. Calvin fought for and, after a struggle of many years (1541–

1555), achieved for the consistory a measure of independence and freedom from the state in the performance of these tasks. As the church developed in later years, particularly in the last century, the consistory (session) had to assume responsibility for the increasing complexity of church life. The rise of denominations and the development of a secular culture undercut the power of the consistory in discipline of morals and public life.

Calvin was determined that the church should be what it claimed to be; namely, the people of God. Discipline was never an end in itself. The church sought to maintain discipline for three ends: (1) that the glory and honor of God should be affirmed again, (2) that evil should not corrupt the good, and (3) that those who had fallen into sin should be helped to wholeness.[27] Calvin drew back from the stringent discipline of the Anabaptists, who sought a separate and pure church; and he never made the church's existence dependent upon discipline. Within these limits, Calvin's ministry in Geneva is distinguished by his efforts to establish a disciplined Christian community.

A third feature of Calvin's polity is his emphasis on catechetical instruction. Calvin was convinced that Christians must know what they believed and why they believed it. Ignorance was sufficient to bar one from the sacrament of the Lord's Supper and full participation in the life of the church. Therefore, a regular program of catechetical instruction was necessary for a well-ordered church.[28]

A fourth emphasis of this polity is the office of the deacon as the church's ministry of compassion.[29] Calvin's Geneva outlawed begging and did away with many festival days because they took people from their work. Yet few communities have made more careful efforts to take care of those who could not care for themselves. Calvin himself was concerned with such matters as adequate employment and the heating of homes.[30] He built into the structure of the church an official order for service to human need; namely the office of deacon. This order was never fully developed, but its importance for Calvin and for the church is not the less for its lack of development along lines Calvin intended. In the evolution of the Presbyterian churches in the United States, the deacons sometimes became more concerned with the business affairs of the church than with the ministry of compassion.

The fifth and most notable feature of Calvin's polity is his primary emphasis on the acts of God by his Spirit through word and sacraments that create the church. All formal marks of the church and all structures are subordinate to the grace of God. Jesus Christ is the head of the church.

L. J. Trinterud has summed up Calvin's view of church government as follows:

> The primary elements of Calvin's theory of church government may be summed up in three. The church is a community or body in which Christ only is head, and all other members are equal under him. The ministry is given to the whole church, and is there distributed among many officers according as God has gifted and called them. All who hold office do so by election of the people whose representatives they are. The church is to be governed and directed by assemblies of officeholders, pastors, and elders, chosen to provide just representation for the church as a whole.[31]

## Presbyterianism

Presbyterianism is not a fixed pattern of church life but a developing pattern that has both continuity and diversity.[32] Many features of the system, such as lifetime or term service as tenures for elders, vary from time to time and place to place. American Presbyterianism developed from the congregation and presbytery to the synod, to the general assembly, while Scottish Presbyterianism developed from the General Assembly down. The consequences of these diverse developments are very apparent to any observer at the respective assemblies today.

The word "presbyterian" began to be used in the first half of the seventeenth century in Scotland when polity was a critical issue,[33] and it has ever since been the designation of the largest portion of the English-speaking Reformed community. No one pattern of church life can be designated as the definitive and final form of Presbyterianism. No one definition is adequate. Four definitions of Presbyterianism by nineteenth- and twentieth-century exponents may be accepted as indicating its salient features in a diverse spectrum.

Charles Hodge and James Henley Thornwell were the most influential American Presbyterian theologians of the nineteenth century. Each of them gave a great amount of attention to polity. While they debated vigorously certain issues of ecclesiastical polity and practice, they were agreed about Presbyterianism in general. Hodge defined Presbyterianism in terms of the following general principles:

1st. That all the attributes and prerogatives of the Church arise from the indwelling of the Spirit, and consequently, where He dwells, there are those attributes and prerogatives.

2d. That as the Spirit dwells not in the clergy only, but in the people of God, all power is, *in sensu primo,* in the people.

3d. That in the exercise of thse prerogatives, the Church is to be governed by principles laid down in the word of God, which determine, within certain limits, her officers and mode of organization; but that beyond those prescribed principles and in fidelity to them, the Church has a wide discretion in the choice of methods, organs and agencies.

4th. That the fundamental principles of our Presbyterian system are first, parity of the clergy; second, the right of the people to a substantive part in the government of the Church; and third, the unity of the Church in such sense, that a small part is subject to a larger, and a larger to the whole.[34]

James Henley Thornwell defined Presbyterianism as follows:

> The term *Presbyterian* is primarily distinctive of our notions of church-polity, and in this relation, it has a wider and a narrower application. In its widest application, it includes all those who deny that the government of the Church is entrusted to an order of men higher than Presbyters or Elders—who, in other words, maintain the official parity of the ministry. In this sense it is simply the opposite of Prelatic or Episcopalian, and extends to all denominations who deny the Divine appointment of Diocesan Bishops. Hence it includes Independents, and even Methodists. All who affirm the official equality of the rulers of the church are essentially Presbyterian. In its narrow application, it embraces only those who place the government of the Church in the hands of representative assemblies, composed exclusively of Presbyters or Elders.[35]

In defining this latter use of the word "Presbyterian," Thornwell goes on to state the principles of Presbyterian church government in general.

1. "The first principle is that of the unity of the Church. As the body of Christ the Church is one." All who are incorporated into him must therefore constitute one organized whole, which is the Holy Catholic Church. A church, therefore, which cannot realize the visible unity and thus aim to coincide with the invisible church, is self-condemned; and any constitution which does not

recognize this fact is convicted of being unscriptural. This principle of the unity of the church lies at the foundation of presbyterian polity.

2. "The second principle of the Presbyterian system is, that unity is realized by representative assemblies. The government of the Church is not entrusted to individuals, nor to the mass of believers, but to councils."

3. "The third principle is, that the elements which make up these representative assemblies are Elders, who are rulers chosen freely by the people."

4. "The fourth principle is, that the power is primarily in the body and is exercised through organized courts. . . . The Session, the Presbytery, the Synod, the Assembly, are properly called *the Church* as they manifest its living power."[36]

The differences between Thornwell's and Hodge's understanding of Presbyterianism reflect pervasive ambiguities in the development of the polity. Thornwell opted for a polity based upon Scripture; Hodge called for Scripture warrant for general principles but allowed details without positive Scriptural warrant. Thornwell also insisted that the "church in her organized capacity is a society for all spiritual purposes," that the church is itself a missionary society and does not use independent boards to do its own work. Hodge and Thornwell differed decisively on the office of elder. For Hodge, the elder was the lay representative of the people. For Thornwell, ministers and ruling elders were alike elders. The elder is essentially a ruling elder to which the functions of preaching and teaching may be superadded. Thornwell's emphasis is reflected in the polity of the Presbyterian Church in the United States, which requires ruling elders to participate in the ordination of ministers. This conflict over the nature of the eldership is rooted in an ambiguity in presbyterian polity that goes back at least to Calvin and remains unsettled.[37]

Two twentieth-century historians of Presbyterianism have defined Presbyterianism in the following ways. James Moffatt writes:

> Presbyterianism is the name for belief in the Apostolic and catholic Church as governed by presbyters. [The] constitutive principles, as they are now in operation, may be described as follows: (a) the parity of presbyters; (b) the right of the people, through their representatives or lay elders, to take part in the government of the

Church; and (c) the unity of the Church, not simply in faith and order, but in a graduated series of Church courts which express and exercise the common authority of the Church as a divine society.[38]

G. D. Henderson, a careful Scottish student of Presbyterianism, defines it as follows:

Presbyterianism is strictly a form of church government adopted by certain Christian and Protestant Churches, in which the main characteristic is control by a graded series of ruling bodies whose members are ordained ministers and lay elders, all ministers having equal status and all the elders having the same rights and responsibilities as the ministers in the matter of discussion and voting.[39]

In these definitions of Presbyterianism four basic principles are most prominent.

1. The authority of Scripture. One persistent characteristic of Presbyterian polity has been its appeal to Scriptural authority. Some have claimed that Presbyterianism is *the* form of church government prescribed by Scripture, but all have appealed to the decisive authority of Scripture.

Calvin clearly indicates that church order is prescribed by God. He speaks, for example, of "the order by which the Lord willed his church to be governed,"[40] of "that order and that form of polity which he has laid down,"[41] and of that "spiritual government such as our Lord showed and instituted by his Word."[42] The Gallican Confession of 1559, which is closely associated with Calvin, declares that the true church "should be governed according to the order established by our Lord Jesus Christ."[43]

Calvin recognized that many details of polity cannot be established from Scripture, and thus he did not advocate a legalistic obedience to Scripture or servile imitation of the primitive church. The following paragraphs are quoted in detail as they present very clearly Calvin's viewpoint.

We see that some form of organization is necessary in all human society to foster the common peace and maintain concord. We further see that in human transactions some procedure is always in effect, which is to be respected in the interests of public decency, and even of humanity itself. This ought especially to be observed in churches, which are best sustained when all things are under a well-ordered constitution, and which without concord become no churches at all. Therefore, if we wish to provide for the safety of the church, we must attend with all diligence to Paul's command that "all things be done decently and in order" [I Cor. 14:40].[44]

We therefore have a most excellent and dependable mark to distinguish between those impious constitutions (which, as we have said, obscure true religion and subvert consciences) and legitimate church observances. We have this if we remember that the end in view must always be one of two things, or both together—that in the sacred assembly of believers all things be done decently and with becoming dignity; and that the human community itself be kept in order with certain bonds of humanity and moderation. For when it is once understood that a law has been made for the sake of public decency, there is taken away the superstition into which those fall who measure the worship of God by human inventions. Again, when it is recognized that the law has to do with common usage, then that false opinion of obligation and necessity, which struck consciences with great terror when traditions were thought necessary to salvation, is overthrown. For here nothing is required except that love be fostered among us by common effort.[45]

Let us take, for example, kneeling when solemn prayers are being said. The question is whether it is a human tradition, which any man may lawfully repudiate or neglect. I say that it is human, as it is also divine. It is of God in so far as it is a part of that decorum whose care and observance the apostle has commended to us [I Cor. 14:40]. But it is of men in so far as it specifically designates what had in general been suggested rather than explicitly stated.

By this one example we may judge what opinion we should have of this whole class. I mean that the Lord has in his sacred oracles faithfully embraced and clearly expressed both the whole sum of true righteousness, and all aspects of the worship of his majesty, and whatever was necessary to salvation; therefore, in these the Master alone is to be heard. But because he did not will in outward discipline and ceremonies to prescribe in detail what we ought to do (because he foresaw that this depended upon the state of the times, and he did not deem one form suitable for all ages), here we must take refuge in those general rules which he has given, that whatever the necessity of the church will require for order and decorum should be tested against these. Lastly, because he has taught nothing specifically, and because these things are not necessary to salvation, and for the upbuilding of the church ought to be variously accommodated to the customs of each nation and age, it will be fitting (as the advantage of the church will require) to change and abrogate traditional practices and to establish new ones. Indeed, I admit that we ought not to charge into innovation rashly, suddenly, for insufficient cause. But love will best judge what may hurt or edify; and if we let love be our guide, all will be safe.[46]

Doumergue has written that Calvin's polity had its sources in the Bible, in reason, and in history, a judgment that is supported by the above citations.[47] There are, nevertheless, certain essential principles of polity which are of divine right and which have normative value in the life of the church.

Later Calvinists and Presbyterians were more assertive of the Biblical authority of Presbyterianism. Walter Travers, in *A Full and Plaine Declaration of Ecclesiastical Discipline Out of the Word of God and of the Declining of the Church of England from the Same,* insists that polity must be strictly Biblical:

> I call therefore Ecclesiastical Discipline, the pollicie of the Church of Christ ordained and appointed of God for the good administration and government of the same: that I make here God the Author of Discipline . . . had need be more fully proved, because it is denied by many, who dare affirm that there is no precept given touching this matter but contend that it is wholly left unto judgment of the Magistrate and of the Church. The rule and patterns of discipline is not to be drawne from the ordinances and fantasies of men, but from the Word of God, which thing as it hath long time preserved purity and sincerity in those Churches wherein all things are reformed according to God's word; so all the corruptions which are in our Church this day, spring from no other head than this, that we have followed popish dreams and fantasies, as most stincking sinks and channels leaving the pure fountains of the word of God.
>
> That our particular lawes ground upon this foundation and let so much bee admitted for Ecclesiastical discipline, as may be confirmed by the voice and authority of God himselfe.[48]

*The Book of Discipline,* which was edited by Travers and was influential at the Westminster Assembly, began with the assertion:

> The Discipline of Christs Church that is necessary for all times is delivered by Christ, and set downe in the holy Scriptures. Therefore the true and lawfull Discipline is to be fetched from thence, and from thence alone. And that which resteth upon any other foundation ought to be esteemed unlawful and counterfeit.[49]

It is significant, however, that while asserting the sole Scripture authority for Presbyterianism, Travers continued to serve as a clergyman in the Episcopal Church of England. It is inconceivable that he would have acquiesced, as he did, if the gospel had been at stake.

The sum of the matter seems to be that Calvinists and Presbyterians have been very insistent that polity stands under the sovereignty of the word of God; but they have, with a few exceptions, refused to say finally that acceptance of Presbyterianism was necessary for the existence of the church or that it had the exclusive authority of Scripture. The mainstream of Presbyterianism runs between a Biblical legalism and indifference to the Bible. It insists that Presbyterianism is agreeable to the word of God, and it refuses to allow Presbyterianism or any structure of church government to be considered necessary for the church's existence.

2. The unity of the church through representative assemblies. A second principle of Presbyterianism is the unity of the church through church courts composed of elders elected by the people. The word "church" is given to the local congregation and to the whole body of believers. There can be no church without local congregations and no local churches except as they participate in the universal church.

Here Presbyterians rejected both congregationalism and episcopacy. Over against the congregationalists, especially at the Westminster Assembly, Presbyterians insisted that a congregational court, elected by the congregation and representative of the congregation, could act on its own authority independently of the congregation. They also maintained that local congregations are not independent units but are under the authority of a graded series of church courts or councils. Over against Episcopalianism, Presbyterians maintained that the unity of the church is secured through church courts, not through the episcopacy.

Church courts were a gradual development in Presbyterianism, especially in France and Scotland, where they were established on a national basis. The principles are clearly stated, however, by Calvin. Calvin, who emphatically opposed rule by individuals, advocated courts that provided for joint rule. He also emphatically opposed rule by ministers alone and advocated courts that provided a way for preaching and ruling presbyters to rule together.

The fundamental Presbyterian principle of representative church government was rooted in Calvin's anthropology, which insisted on one hand that no person was good enough to be entrusted with rule and on the other that the mass of people were not qualified to make the critical decisions that must be made in the life of the church. Calvin feared alike the pretensions and tyranny of individual rule and the fickleness and disorder of the masses. In state and church he approved on theological grounds democracy tempered by aristocracy; i.e., by the qualified. The will of God is more likely to be done if decisions are made neither by individuals nor by all the people but by those who have been chosen for their special qualifications. In his commentary on Acts 15:2 Calvin writes that:

> holy synods assembled since the beginning, that grave men and such as were well exercised in the word of God might decide controversies, not after their own pleasure, but according to the authority of God.[50]

In his commentary on Acts 15:6 Calvin writes:

> It may be, indeed, that the disputation was had in presence of the people. But lest any man should think that the common people were suffered hand over head to handle the matter, Luke doth plainly make mention of the apostles and elders, as it was more meet that they should hear the matter and to decide it. But let us know, that here is prescribed by God a form and an order in assembling synods, when there ariseth any controversy which cannot otherwise be decided.[51]

James Henley Thornwell expressed this same conviction:

> In the Church the representative government is not, as in the State, even ultimately the creature of the people: it is the direct appointment of Christ, and the powers and duties of ecclesiastical representatives are prescribed and defined in the Word of God, the real Constitution of the Church. They are represented as rulers, and not as tools; they are to study and administer the laws of the Saviour, and not bend to the caprices of the people; and they are to listen to no authoritative instructions but those which have proceeded from the throne of God. Christ never gave to the people, as a mass, any right to exercise jurisdiction or to administer discipline. They cannot appear in Session or Presbytery. It is not only inconvenient that they should be there in their collective capacity, but they have no right to be there. The privilege of attending as members, as component elements of the court, would be destructive of all the ends which representation is designed to secure: it would subvert the whole system of government. The business of the people is to elect the men who give sufficient evidence that they are fitted by the Spirit to fill the offices which Christ has appointed.[52]

3. Parity of the ministry. A third principle of Presbyterianism is the parity of the ministry. This principle is put very clearly in the Second Helvetic Confession.

Now the power, or function, that is given to the ministers of the Church is the same and alike in all. Certainly, in the beginning, the bishops or elders did, with a common consent and labor, govern the Church; no man lifted up himself above another, none usurped greater power or authority over his fellow-bishops. For they remembered the words of the Lord, "Let the leader among you become as one who serves." (Luke xxii.26); they kept themselves by humility, and did mutually aid one another in the government and preservation of the Church. . . . Notwithstanding, for order's sake, some one of the ministers called the assembly together, propounded unto the assembly the matters to be consulted of, gathered together the voices or sentences of the rest, and, to be brief, as much as lay in him, provided that there might arise no confusion.[53]

The same point is made in the Gallican and Belgic Confessions.

We believe that all true pastors, wherever they may be, have the same authority and equal power under one head, one only sovereign and universal bishop, Jesus Christ; and that consequently no Church shall claim any authority or dominion over any other.[54]

As for the Ministers of God's Word, they have equally the same power and authority wheresoever they are, as they are all Ministers of Christ, the only universal Bishop, and the only Head of the Church.[55]

Calvin used the terms "bishops," "presbyters," "pastors," and "ministers" interchangeably. "For all who carry out the ministry of the Word it [Scripture] accords the title 'bishops.' "[56] There is no question that Calvin disliked the term "hierarchy" and the framing "of a principality or lordship as far as the government of the church is concerned."[57] While Calvin took a positive attitude toward the development of government in the early church, he opposed "dominion," ostentatious pomp, and tyranny in any church office.

4. Right of the people to call a pastor and elect officers. A fourth principle of Presbyterianism is the right of the people to call their own pastors. John Calvin writes:

Someone now asks whether the minister ought to be chosen by the whole church, or only by his colleagues and the elders charged with the censure of morals, or whether he ought to be appointed by the authority of a single person. . . .
We therefore hold that this call of a minister is lawful according to the Word of God, when those who seemed fit are created by the

consent and approval of the people; moreover, that other pastors ought to preside over the election in order that the multitude may not go wrong either through fickleness, through evil intentions, or through disorder.[58]

Calvin's emphasis on the rights of the people was attenuated partly by the existing situation and partly by his own aristocratic tendencies.[59] Sometimes this right was little more than approval of a decision that had already been made. The full right of the people to elect their own officers was later claimed by Presbyterians in Scotland and America to the fullest extent possible under presbytery.[60]

5. The Reformed tradition has always hesitated to declare itself fully in regard to the office of deacon, and for this reason the office of deacon cannot be made a principle of Presbyterianism. However its importance deserves attention. Eugene Heideman in his study of Reformed polity has noted that Calvin gave the office cultural as well as ecclesiastical significance. He summarizes the role of the office at its best in the Reformed tradition.

> . . . the Reformed tradition has maintained that the deacon represents the righteousness of God, which has been made known in the world in the form of helping the poor and the sick, in watching over the widows and the orphans, and in the message of social righteousness. Thus the deacon in his alms-gathering and charitable work does not stay on a lower level than the other office bearers, but, when properly understood, plays an essential role among the office bearers in the midst of the church. These three offices thus do not represent a hierarchy of offices with the minister enjoying the highest rank and the deacon receiving the lowest status; on the contrary they stand in a horizontal relationship to each other, even though their functions must be distinguished in such a way as to avoid undue confusion.[61]

## Episcopacy

Reformed theology has lived at times in harmony with episcopal communities. Many English bishops and even archbishops were Calvinists or Reformed in theology during the sixteenth century. Reformed churchmen also experimented with forms of episcopacy in sixteenth- and seventeenth-century Scotland. The very loose Scottish polity of the 1560s was not committed to Presbyterianism. A firm commitment came after the work of Andrew Melville and after the efforts of the English to impose episcopacy upon the Scottish church. Today the Hungarian Reformed Church has bishops, who have administrative responsibility but no theological significance.

Episcopacy like Presbyterianism has developed, and the word means different things in different times and places. After 1662, the date of the religious settlement following the Puritan revolution in England, episcopacy began to acquire a new meaning. Before 1662 there is good evidence that ordination by presbytery and by bishop was mutually recognized.[62] After 1662 the bishop became increasingly regarded as necessary for ordination and for the existence of the church. The doctrine of apostolic succession was firmly tied to the bishopric. Reformed theology, as defined by Calvin and the classic documents of the tradition, while compatible with a functional episcopacy, is incompatible with a theological episcopacy, as defined by Kenneth Kirk in *The Apostolic Ministry.* [63]

In recent years a number of Calvin scholars have sought to establish that Calvin's polity is open to episcopal development. Since this is a debated point, the best procedure is to review the most important passages in Calvin's writings that bear on this issue.

In the *Institutes* Calvin discusses the office of bishop under the theme "The Condition of the Ancient Church, and the Kind of Government in Use Before the Papacy."

> All those to whom the office of teaching was enjoined they called "presbyters." In each city these chose one of their number to whom they specially gave the title "bishop" in order that dissensions might not arise (as commonly happens) from equality of rank. Still, the bishop was not so much higher in honor and dignity as to have lordship over his colleagues. But the same functions that the consul has in the senate—to report on business, to request opinions, to preside over others in counseling, admonishing, and exhorting, to govern the whole action by his authority, and to carry out what was decreed by common decision—the bishop carried out in the assembly of presbyters.
>
> And the ancients themselves admit that this was introduced by human agreement to meet the need of the times. . . . Afterward, to remove seeds of dissensions, all oversight was committed to one person. Just as the presbyters, therefore, know that they are, according to the custom of the church, subject to him who presides, so the bishops recognize that they are superior to the presbyters more according to the custom of the church than by the Lord's actual arrangement, and that they ought to govern the church in co-operation with them. . . .
>
> A certain area was assigned to each city from which its presbyters were drawn, and it was thought of as belonging to the body of that

church. Each college was under one bishop for the preservation of its organization and peace. While he surpassed the others in dignity, he was subject to the assembly of his brethren. But if the field under his episcopate was too large for him to be able to fulfill everywhere all the duties of bishop, presbyters were assigned to certain places in the field, and carried on his duties in lesser matters. These they called "country bishops" because they represented the bishop throughout the province.[64]

That each province had one archbishop among the bishops, and that at the Council of Nicaea patriarchs were ordained to be higher in rank and dignity than archbishops, were facts connected with the maintenance of discipline. However, in this discussion it cannot be overlooked that this was an extremely rare practice. These ranks, therefore, were established so that any incident in any church whatever that could not be settled by a few might be referred to a provincial synod. If the magnitude or difficulty of the case demanded larger discussion, the patriarchs, together with a synod, were summoned, from whom there was no appeal except to a general council. Some called the government thus constituted a "hierarchy," an improper term (it seems to me), certainly one unused in Scripture. For the Holy Spirit willed men to beware of dreaming of a principality or lordship as far as the government of the church is concerned. But if, laying aside the word, we look at the thing itself, we shall find that the ancient bishops did not intend to fashion any other form of church rule than that which God has laid down in his Word.[65]

John T. McNeill finds that in this passage "Calvin distinctly approves a jurisdictional and disciplinary episcopate if guarded against arbitrary domination, and he dislikes the term 'hierarchy.' "[66] This is the most that can be argued from this passage. At most, Calvin approves but does not advocate episcopacy. The argument that Calvin did not advocate episcopacy because of the special situation in Geneva is unconvincing because Calvin *did* advocate other practices in the life of the church which were prohibited in Geneva.[67]

Calvin's comments on Philippians 1:1 provide a very good summary of his position.

*Bishops.* He names the pastors separately, for the sake of honour. Moreover, we may infer from this, that the name "bishop" is common to all the ministers of the Word, inasmuch as he assigns several to one Church. Therefore, bishop and pastor are synonymous. And this is one of the passages which Jerome quotes for proving it in his epistle to Evagrius, and in his exposition of the Epistle to Titus.

Afterwards the custom prevailed that only the one whom the presbyters in each Church appointed over their college was called
bishop. This originated in a human custom and rests on no Scriptural authority. I acknowledge indeed, that, as the minds and manners of men are, order cannot be maintained among the ministers
of the Word without one presiding over the others. I speak of
individual bodies, not of whole provinces, far less of the whole
world. Now, although we must not contend for words, it would be
better for us in speaking to follow the Holy Spirit, the Author of
tongues, than to change for the worse forms of speech disposed by
Him. For from the corrupted signification of the word this evil has
resulted, that, as if all presbyters were not colleagues, called to the
same office, one of them, under the cloak of a new name, usurped
dominion over the others.[68]

In actual practice Calvin accepted the episcopal system where
it existed so long as it was purged of the trappings of imperial
status and tyranny and so long as bishops were active in preaching, teaching, and pastoral care. He treated Cranmer with respect.[69] In his long and thoughtful letter to Somerset on the
reform of the English church, he seems to accept the fact of
bishops and speaks of their duty to care for the church.[70] In a
similar letter to the king of Poland, he rejects the papacy and
apostolic succession through bishops; but again he accepts the
fact of episcopal government, including archbishops.[71] Calvin's
acceptance of the fact of episcopacy in these letters is in accord
with his discussion of the historical development of the episcopal
system in the ancient church, which he understood as a development dictated not by Scripture but by the needs of time.

The coexistence of Reformed theology and Reformed life-
styles with episcopal government is a fact of history, and a *functional* episcopacy was accepted as a viable form of the life of the
church by so definitive a theologian as Calvin. It is also true (1)
that Calvin never advocated episcopal government, especially in
his definitive work, the *Institutes,* (2) that the presbyterial government that he established in Geneva develops easily into presbyterial government on a national scale, and (3) that so close an
associate as Beza advocated in a vigorous way presbyterian
church government in France during Calvin's lifetime. Beza like
Calvin was willing to accept episcopal government as a valid form
of the church, but again like Calvin he did not advocate it.[72]

## *Congregationalism*

Congregationalism made its first appearance, at least in the Reformed tradition, in the 1560s when the pattern of church government was being worked out in France. Its great advocate was Jean Morély, who enlisted in its support some of the French nobility, as well as the distinguished logician Peter Ramus. Morély was an ardent Calvinist; and he sought to present his proposal for church order to Calvin, who was too busy to respond to it. Morély wanted discipline to be carried out by the congregation rather than by the consistory (session), and he wanted the congregation to elect its own ministers, not simply approve them after the company of pastors had nominated them. Morély was suspicious of councils other than the local congregation, and he openly advocated greater democracy in the life of the congregation. Calvin's close friends and ardent supporters, Theodore Beza and Chandieu, led the opposition to Morély. The French church was organized along presbyterian lines; and Morély's movement was wiped out by the St. Bartholomew's Massacre in 1572, as his supporters were located in areas that were the hardest hit.[73]

Congregationalism made its appearance a little later in the Reformed community in Great Britain. Robert Browne's *A Treatise of Reformation without Tarying for Anie* was published in 1582. Other major advocates of congregationalism included John Robinson, who was the pastor of the Pilgrims, John Cotton of New England, and John Owen. English congregationalism emphasized the "local church, in which each member has his spiritual responsibility." It also insisted

> the purpose of church polity is that Christ, and Christ alone, may rule in His church. We believe that the instrument whereby Christ rules in the local church is the church meeting, at which all the covenant members of the church seek together by prayer and discussion to discover the will of Christ and are guided into a common mind by the Holy Spirit.[74]

Congregationalism also rejected any coercive authority on the part of church synods, though in some situations congregationalism has been able to absorb much of the associational or synodical pattern. Another principle of congregationalism has been voluntarism; that is, only those who voluntarily choose to do so belong to the church that is gathered by the Spirit. Holiness of life has been a related emphasis.[75]

The priesthood of all believers, the insistence on the right and responsibility of believers to answer for themselves and for their neighbors was one of the cardinal principles of the Protestant Reformation. This principle inevitably bore fruit in church organization. Congregationalism is the result of this Protestant conviction. The congregationalists also believed that their church order was based on New Testament practices. Congregationalism as a pattern of church life has been hampered by two weaknesses. First, it is an order of church life that is designed for saints and has had difficulty with nominal Christians. Secondly, it has had difficulty realizing the catholicity or universal character of the church with its emphasis on the local congregation.

Reformed theology and life have thrived with congregational patterns of church life, especially in Britain and America, where congregationalism has been productive of great theologians and creative churchmen. Many factors contribute to this productivity; but some are rooted in the polity, such as its provision for responsible freedom. The Reformation doctrine of the priesthood of all believers and the congregational polity no doubt still have much to contribute to the church of the future. The writings of two of the leading Reformed theologians of the twentieth century, Karl Barth and Emil Brunner, point in this direction. Yet congregationalism too can become a sterile and doctrinaire pattern of church life; and for this reason theologians who are open to future patterns of church life and who insist on the existential character of the church as a hearing, believing, obeying fellowship hesitate to endorse any fixed church order.

Emil Brunner and Karl Barth have given support to many congregational emphases without finally identifying themselves with congregationalist polity. Brunner was concerned to develop "the Biblical *self-understanding* of *ekklesia,* "[76] and he does this with a great emphasis on the church as community which is created and governed by the word and the Spirit of God and which lives a common life in the Spirit. In his earlier writings this seemed to entail the rejection of organization, but in the *Dogmatics* he insists that his emphasis on community should not be interpreted as the rejection of organized churches. Organization is a secondary question, however; and all church organization must be criticized.

> The evil I turn against is the confusion of any church at all with the *ekklesia* of the New Testament, that is, the life in community with each other based on communion with God generated by God's Spirit.[77]

Karl Barth has laid emphasis upon the church as a community that is awakened, gathered, and ruled by Jesus Christ. While Barth is critical of Brunner's early emphasis upon the spiritual nature of the church and insists that Jesus Christ gives his church a law, he too is critical of all existing church orders.

> No Church order is perfect, for none has fallen directly from heaven and none is identical with the basic view of the Christian community. Even the orders of the primitive New Testament community (whatever form they took) were not perfect, nor are those of the Western Papacy, the Eastern Patriarchate, the Synodal Presbyterianism which derives from Calvin's system, Anglican, Methodist, Neo-Lutheran or other forms of Episcopacy, or Congregationalism with its sovereignty of the individual community. . . . There is no reason to look down proudly and distastefully from one to the others. At one time they may all have been living law sought and in a certain exaggeration found in obedience, and therefore legitimate forms of the body of Jesus Christ. Indeed, they may be this still.[78]

The church for Barth is surely an "event" constituted by the hearing of the Word. Yet the church has a form and an enduring character that is of subordinate but real significance. It is not only awakened and gathered by the Holy Spirit but sent into the world as servant. Its task is the "proclamation, explication, and application" of the gospel as the Word of God to a particular time and place. The form of this ministry, Barth declares in a notable section of *Church Dogmatics* (Par. 72, 4), is twofold: SPEECH: (1) to praise God, (2) to proclaim the gospel "in the assembly of the community, in the midst of divine service," (3) to teach, (4) to evangelize, (5) to send missions to non-Christian lands. ACTION: (6) prayer, (7) pastoral care, (8) Christian life, (9) service of human needs, (10) prophetic action, and (11) Christian fellowship.

From Calvin to Barth there has been a strong emphasis in all Reformed thinking about the church upon the initiative and the Lordship of God. The church is the body of Jesus Christ, and it lives by hearing his voice. For this reason Calvin, in spite of all of his emphasis on polity, could never make any polity a necessary mark of the church's existence. For this reason Barth insisted that Christians with humility and freedom must be critical of all polities without minimizing the relative significance of choosing polities that help and do not hinder the reality of the community of faith.

*Appendix H:*

## REFORMED POLITIES

I. Continental Polities

1. John Calvin, *Institutes of the Christian Religion,* Book IV.

"Articles Concerning the Organization of the Church and Worship at Geneva," (1537) *Library of Christian Classics* (Philadelphia: Westminster Press, 1954), Vol. 22, pp. 45–55.

"Draft Ecclesiastical Ordinances" (Geneva, 1541), *Library of Christian Classics,* Vol. 22, pp. 56–72. Critical texts of the Articles of 1537 and of the Ordinances of 1541 and 1561 can be found in *Joannis Calvini Opera Selecta,* ed. Petrus Barth, Guilelmus Baum, and Dora Scheuner (Munich: Chr. Kaiser, 1926 and 1952), Vols. 1 and 2.

2. The polity of the Reformed Church in France (1559) and other continental polities may be found in *Bekenntnisschriften und Kirchenordnungen der nach Gottes Wort reformierten Kirche,* ed. Wilhelm Niesel (Zurich: Evangelischer Verlag, A. G. Zollikon).

For comprehensive collection see Aemilius Ludwig Richter, *Die Evangelischen Kirchenordnungen des sechszehnten Jahrunderts* (Nieuwkoop: B. De Graff, 1967), Vols. 1 and 2.

II. Presbyterian Polities (English Language)

1. *First Book of Discipline.* May be found in David Laing, *The Works of John Knox,* Vol. 2, (Edinburgh: Woodrow Society, 1848 and in modern English in William Croft Dickinson, ed., *John Knox's History of the Reformation* (New York: Philosophical Library, 1950), Vol. 2. For critical edition, see James K. Cameron, ed., *First Book of Discipline: With Introduction and Commentary* (Edinburgh: St. Andrew's Press, 1972).

2. The Second Book of Discipline. May be found in appendix of Stuart Robinson, *The Church of God* (Philadelphia and Louisville: 1858).

3. *The Book of Discipline of the Elizabethan Presbyterians.* May be found in the appendix of Charles A. Briggs, *American Presbyterianism* (New York: Charles Scribner's Sons, 1885).

4. *Form of Presbyterial Church Government.* May be found in appendix of Stuart Robinson, *The Church of God* (Philadelphia: Joseph M. Wilson, 1858).

*The Confession of Faith, the Larger Catechism, the Directory for Publick Worship, the Form of Presbyterial Church Government* (Edinburgh and London: William Blackwood & Sons, Ltd., 1959).

5. For polity debates in American Presbyterianism see:

*The Southern Presbyterian Review* (contains many articles on polity written during the nineteenth-century debates).

Charles Hodge, *Discussions in Church Polity,* ed. William Durant (New York: Charles Scribner's, 1878).

Thomas Ephraim Peck, *Notes on Ecclesiology* (Richmond, Va.: Presbyterian Committee of Publication, 1892).

John B. Adger and J. L. Girardeau, eds., *The Collected Writings of James Henley Thornwell* (Richmond, Va.: Presbyterian Committee of Publication, 1871).

Thomas Smyth, *Ecclesiastical Republicanism* (New York: R. Carter, 1843).

6. *The Form of Government* and *The Rules of Discipline* used in American Presbyterianism are found in many editions dating from 1789 and continuing down to the present time.

III. CONGREGATIONAL POLITIES

Robert M. Kingdon, *Geneva and the Consolidation of the French Protestant Movement, 1564–1572* (Madison: The University of Wisconsin Press, 1967).

Williston Walker, *The Creeds and Platforms of Congregationalism* (Boston: The Pilgrim Press, 1960).

# VI

## LITURGY
## AND
## THE REFORMED TRADITION

Man defies definition. Some have said that man is what he eats, and there is a measure of truth in this assertion.[1] Augustine said that man is as he loves.[2] This is closer to the truth. A case can also be made that man is as he worships. Personality is shaped by the liturgy, by the very nature of worship itself. For in worship the whole of human existence is focused as in few other acts. Psychologists have noted the very great influence of frequently repeated acts, and no act is more frequently repeated in the public life of the church than that central act of worship on the Lord's Day.

John Calvin, who was an astute observer of human behavior as well as a perceptive theologian, gave careful attention to worship because of its pragmatic and theological significance. Some of the sharpest debates in the Westminster Assembly occurred over the *Directory for the Public Worship of God.* Changing the order of worship in most congregations is a critical concern. Worship both expresses the theological and the ethical convictions of the people and shapes those convictions. Faith is expressed in worship before it is expressed in creed, and it is learned in worship before it is learned in schools. Worship is the heart of the Christian community's common life.

The Reformation along the upper banks of the Rhine and in French as well as German-speaking Switzerland gave special attention to the reform of worship. This reform was an attempt to recover not only the Biblical basis but also the "custom of the ancient church." It also had behind it the work of Christian humanists who had been concerned with the revision of worship for a generation, as Hughes O. Old has demonstrated in a recent study, *The Patristic Roots of Reformed Worship* (1976).

## John Calvin and Karl Barth on Worship

There is no definitive Reformed theology of worship. John Calvin gave serious attention to the theme; and while his thought did not exhaust even the thought of the Reformed community of his own day, it is nonetheless a classic and influential statement of the Reformed position and stance. As pastor of churches in Strasbourg and Geneva, Calvin had to work out a public liturgy; and as an acknowledged pastor and leader he had to instruct the widely scattered Reformed community. The following summary of the main emphasis of this teaching on worship is taken chiefly from his preface to the liturgy and from the *Institutes of the Christian Religion.*

First of all, Calvin insisted upon the Biblical and theological integrity of worship. As has been noted, Calvin was radical in his Biblical criticism of the church's life. He insisted that all practice must be supported by Biblical teaching. "Whatever is not commanded, we are not free to choose."[3] He specifically excluded from this Biblical criticism many incidental matters such as the time or even the day of worship.[4] Many other matters such as the color of the wine in the celebration of the Lord's Supper[5] or the kneeling posture in prayer, which he approved, Calvin regarded as matters of choice so long as purposes of edification were served.[6] He did not needlessly attempt to ascribe theological significance to every act or accessory of worship. Calvin was a man of common sense; yet he applied the Biblical principle relentlessly to all issues that did have theological significance. For example, his application of the second commandment, "Thou shalt not make any graven image," eliminated the visual arts from the worship and meditative life of the church.

His insistence on theological integrity is related to his insistence upon Biblical integrity, for the latter is the chief criterion of the former. Feeling and emotion, aesthetics and beauty were all subordinate to theological soundness. The primary fact in worship is the approach of God, not simply as awe-filled Mystery but as the God and Father of the Lord Jesus Christ who has revealed himself. All true worship is shaped not by human desires but by God's disclosure of himself.

A second principle of worship is theological intelligibility. Worship must not only be correct; it must also be understood.

Calvin did not deny the emotional element in worship. Worship, like faith, is a total personal act.

> A good affection toward God is not a thing dead and brutish but a lively movement, proceeding from the Holy Spirit when the heart is rightly touched and the understanding enlightened.[7]

Yet it is a characteristic of Calvinist worship that Calvin strongly emphasized the understanding. "The tongue without the mind must be highly displeasing to God," he wrote with reference to prayer.[8]

The first step toward intelligibility was the Protestant insistence that worship must be in the language of the people. Yet this was only the beginning. In music care must be taken lest the melody obscure the meaning.[9] In preaching, language must be used to communicate thought, not to impress the hearer with the speaker's learning.[10] Sacramental actions must always be in the context of teaching and preaching, so that the act or the symbol will be clearly understood.[11]

The intelligibility of worship demanded a highly disciplined congregation. For this reason Calvin insisted upon a teaching church. Catechetical instruction preceded the first communion. The Bible was taught in public lectures. Church members were educated in the liberal arts so that they could understand not only the word of God but also the works of God in his world.[12]

A third theme in Calvin's theology of the liturgy is edification. As has been indicated, this was fundamental to his theology. He claimed that the form of liturgy that he presented to the church was "entirely directed toward edification."[13] "Nothing which does not lend to edification ought to be received into the Church."[14] The pragmatic test of worship is increase in love, trust, and loyalty to God and in love for neighbor.

A fourth theme is simplicity. The liturgy must "omit from baptism all theatrical pomp, which dazzles the eyes of the simple and deadens their minds."[15] In the celebration of the Lord's Supper, Calvin objected to the "spectacular" and to the "lifeless and theatrical trifles, which serve no other purpose than to deceive the sense of a people stupified."[16] Concerning ceremonies Calvin wrote, "it is necessary to keep fewness in number, ease in observance, dignity in representation, which also includes clarity."[17] "Ostentation and chasing after paltry human glory"[18] must not determine church architecture. Calvin's worship is not so much austere as it is economical. All unnecessary motions, actions, or words are eliminated. Moreover, the words, actions, and paraphernalia of worship must be appropriate to the reality they communicate or express.

The importance of intelligibility, simplicity, and edification for Calvin came to focus on the role of music in worship. Zwingli, the ablest musician among the reformers, had eliminated music from the worship of the church.[19] Calvin carefully restricted the use of music not because he was indifferent to it but because he was aware of its power to move and to shape human existence. For this reason the songs of worship must be neither light nor frivolous but weighty and majestic. There is a great difference between the music one makes to entertain people at table and in their homes and the psalms which are sung in the church in the presence of God.[20] While Calvin's service book (1545) included a hymn, he was content to limit church music to the Psalms, for they were the inspired word of God.[21] The words of worship must be both honest and designed to edify. The music must contribute to the power and intelligibility of the words. Calvin wanted simple melodies. He opposed organs and elaborate polyphonic music because the music obscures the message.

> "... Spiritual songs can only be sung from the heart. Now the heart seeks after understanding, and in that, according to Saint Augustine, lies the difference between the songs of men and that of birds. For a finch, a nightingale, a parrot may sing well, but they do so without understanding. Now the proper gift of man is to sing, knowing what he says, since the intelligence must follow the heart and the emotions, which can only be when we have the song impressed in our minds in order to never cease singing."[22]

Worship is always a conscious and responsible act and its purpose is the edification of the Christian community.

Karl Barth gives serious attention to worship in his *Church Dogmatics.* No other contemporary theologian of similar status gives it equal attention. "Assembling for divine worship is self-evidently the centre and presupposition of the whole Christian life, the atmosphere in which it is lived."[23] In worship the church "exchanges its working clothes for its festal attire."[24] Barth is concerned with the heart and inner reality of worship, the believing, hoping, obeying encounter with the living word of God.

While Barth is very much aware that preaching is a human work, he emphasizes its unique character. In and through it God acts according to his sovereign will. Therefore, "preaching does not reflect, reason, dispute, or academically instruct. It proclaims, summons, invites, and commands."[25] The human response to this word of God in preaching calls for some public affirmation which Barth contends is first of all the confession of faith. This confession is not only that of the individual but also that of the community.

> Indeed, it cannot really be this unless it is first the confession of the community, in which the human response to the Word of God is the common word of all, and the *mutua consolatio fratrum* does not take place in a corner between individuals but is the objective and obligatory work of all to all. This common response in the common hearing of the Word of God, the confession commonly spoken and received in the renewal of the common knowledge, is the first element in the public worship of Christians. It may include the common recitation of a creed. It will certainly involve singing. But it will take place decisively in free witness, bound only to its object, as the Word of God is proclaimed and published and taught and preached and heard by the community according to the commission of its Lord. As this is done, that which is lawful and right takes place in and for the community. It is constituted as a fellowship of confession: not in the power or weaknesses of the human words spoken and received but because these words are an answer to the Word of God; because in these human words spoken in power or weakness it is a matter of witness to Jesus Christ; because He Himself is present where they are spoken and heard by those whom He has gathered. Thus in the confession of the community that which is lawful and right takes place, and the community is constituted, even though—and when is this not the case?—it sets itself in the wrong with its human speaking and hearing; even in impotent witness and poor proclaiming and publishing and teaching and preaching.[26]

For worship is "at every point a human action. It is men who confess, who baptize, who administer the Lord's Supper, who pray 'Our Father.' "[27]

Once Barth has nailed down the basic character of worship as the human response to the free and sovereign word of God, he is free to deal with the orders and the procedures of worship. As a human action, worship is always reformable. There is no one divinely ordained procedure of worship. Barth writes with typical freedom and zest:

In detail it has to be considered whether the prayers before and after preaching ought not to be brought into much closer connexion with it even externally, not being separated by congregational singing or organ music, but forming a threefold complex opened and closed by singing. Again, it ought to be considered whether these prayers should not always be worked out afresh, so that, instead of recurring in stereotyped fashion from a printed book or sheet, they are newly fashioned and therefore prepared with the sermon for each Sunday in honour of the living Lord of the living community. Again, it must be considered whether the antithesis of the confession of sin and the promise of grace—naturally in the reverse order—would not be better placed in the context of preaching rather than in the opening prayer or the rather questionable little drama which serves as the commencement of divine worship in many places, the opening prayer being reserved for thanksgiving for the call of God which gathers the community and intercession for the presence and activity of the Holy Ghost. Again, it has to be considered whether the Lord's Prayer, best repeated by the whole congregation, would not better come at the end, or even at the beginning, of the opening prayer than at the conclusion of the final prayer. Finally, it must be asked whether this final prayer should not for the most part and decisively, instead of occasionally or not at all, follow the example of the Liturgy of Chrysostom and consist in intercession for the whole state of Christ's Church, for all the semi-Christian or non-Christian world, for all the men who err or sin or suffer in so many ways, and especially for those who hold positions of responsibility, so that at the climax of the service, and in transition to administration of the Lord's Supper, there is the necessary opening of the doors and windows to the outside world, and this in the best possible form, namely, of calling upon God.[28]

Barth is also typical of his own theology and of the Reformed tradition when he writes concerning music.

The praise of God which constitutes the community and its assemblies seeks to bind and commit and therefore to be expressed, to well up and be sung in concert. The Christian community sings. It is not a choral society. Its singing is not a concert. But from inner, material necessity it sings. Singing is the highest form of human expression. It is to such supreme expression that the *vox humana* is devoted in the ministry of the Christian community. It is for this that it is liberated in this ministry.

It is hard to see any compelling reason why it should have to be accompanied in this by an organ or harmonium. It might be argued that in this way the community's praise of God is embedded by anticipation in that of the whole cosmos, to which the cosmos is undoubtedly called and which we shall unquestionably hear in the consummation. The trouble is that in practice the main purpose of instruments seems to be to conceal the feebleness with which the community discharges the ministry of the *vox humana* committed to it. There is also the difficulty that we cannot be sure whether the spirits invoked with the far too familiar sounds of instruments are clean or unclean spirits. In any case, there should be no place for organ solos in the Church's liturgy, even in the form of the introductory and closing voluntaries which are so popular.[29]

Barth's insistence that worship is a human work comes to a focus in the final pages of the *Church Dogmatics* when he calls in question the traditional Roman Catholic, Lutheran, and Reformed doctrine of the sacraments as means of grace and contends that baptism is a human work which corresponds to the divine act and word.

Against it we set the principle that the water baptism which is given by the community and desired and received by the candidates is the human action which corresponds to the divine action in the founding of the Christian life, which goes to meet this, which responds to baptism with the Holy Spirit and cries out for it. It is the human action whose meaning is obedience to Jesus Christ and hope in Him.[30]

Barth finds that Calvin more strongly than Roman Catholic or Lutheran teaching subordinates baptism as an appendix to the written and preached Word of God. Moreover Barth does not flinch over the possibility that his own position will be called Neo-Zwinglian.[31] The full impact of the final paragraphs of the *Church Dogmatics,* published in 1967 just before Barth's death on December 10, 1968, has not yet been felt on the worship and communal life of the Reformed churches.

Karl Barth has renewed the Reformed understanding of liturgy by his emphasis on the centrality of worship in the existence of the church and by his emphasis on the importance of theology over against aesthetic, social, and psychological considerations in worship.

## Reformed Liturgies

There is no one Reformed liturgy. Just as there was no significant effort to impose any one creed so there was no effort to impose any one liturgy. This variety is rooted in historical circumstances and also in the understanding of the liturgy. Calvin gave high priority to the practice of the early church in the shaping of the liturgy, but he did not follow slavishly any one pattern in either the New Testament or the ancient church. Many different practices, words, and formulas have a place in Christian worship and in varying orders. Worship in American Presbyterian churches is rooted in four variants of the Reformed tradition: (1) liturgies of which Calvin's order is an illustration, (2) liturgies of which Farel's service is representative, (3) the Westminster Directory, and (4) the American experience.

The articles for the ordering of the Genevan church in 1537 indicated the need for the development of the worship of the church. Worship was already receiving attention from Calvin as in the *Institutes* of 1536. But it was in Strasbourg where, as pastor of the French Church (1538–1541), Calvin developed his first liturgy. He drew heavily on the work of Diobald Schwarz, who had revised the mass in Strasbourg. Schwarz's revision in German had been celebrated in Strasbourg in 1524 and continued to be revised conservatively but creatively at least seven times by 1539 under the leadership of very able theologians led by Martin Bucer. Calvin appropriated this work in 1539, publishing in 1540 (lost) and in 1542 the *Form of Prayers at the French Church*. In 1542 he published a new edition of this work in Geneva which Hughes Old (*The Patristic Roots of Reformed Worship*, 1976, p. xiii) considers "a good culmination of the Reformed liturgical revisions which preceded it and at the same time the archetype of Reformed worship which followed it." In 1545 Calvin published another revision in Strasbourg which is distinguished from the Genevan liturgy by the inclusion of the assurance of pardon, the commandments, the separation of the prayer of intercession and the communion prayer, and a strong statement fencing the table. These distinctions, Old suggests, are due more to the resistance in Geneva to the Puritanism of Calvin than to the iconoclasm of the Reformation there.

## Calvin's Liturgy of 1545 [33]

This 1545 revision contains some actions that were not allowed in Geneva such as the absolution, and for this reason it may be considered the most complete statement of Calvin's intention for the liturgy.

THE FORM OF CHURCH PRAYERS
AND HYMNS WITH
THE MANNER OF ADMINISTERING
THE SACRAMENTS AND CONSECRATING
MARRIAGE ACCORDING TO THE CUSTOM
OF THE ANCIENT CHURCH

Scripture Sentence: Our help is in the name of the Lord . . . .
Confession of Sins
Scripture Sentence
Absolution
Decalogue (First Table)
Prayer
Decalogue (Second Table)
(Psalm in Genevan Form)
Prayer for Illumination
Scripture Reading and Sermon
Great Prayer (Intercession) and Paraphrase of Lord's Prayer
Apostles' Creed
Preparation of Bread and Wine
Prayer for Worthy Reception, Concluding with Lord's Prayer
Institution of the Lord's Supper
Exhortation and the Fencing of the Table
Words of Delivery and Communion with Bread and Wine
Psalm
Prayer of Thanksgiving
Nunc Dimittis
Benediction (Aaronic)

The first notable fact concerning Calvin's liturgy is that it is not canonical. Calvin accommodated himself to liturgical practices in Geneva and Strasbourg. While he had strong preferences, the variations he tolerated in this liturgy indicate he did not try to impose any one authoritative pattern for the worship of God. While he wished the Lord's Supper to be celebrated each Sunday, he agreed to less frequent communion in Strasbourg and Geneva. He omitted absolution from the Genevan service, though he recorded in 1561 his desire that the absolution should remain in the service.

> Everyone knows that it is most useful to unite public confession with some sign of promise that raises sinners to a hope of forgiveness and reconciliation. At the beginning (Geneva) I wished to

introduce that practice, but when some were fearful of offense to new converts, I conceded much too easily. Thus it is omitted. Now there is no opportunity to change it, for before the end of the confession a great many begin to rise.[34]

In the *Institutes* Calvin insisted that confession is the proper beginning of any sacred assembly.[35] He also maintained,

It is no common or light solace to have present there the ambassador of Christ, armed with the mandate of reconciliation, by whom it hears proclaimed its absolution. . . . Here the usefulness of the keys is deservedly commended, when this embassy is carried out justly, in due order, and in reverence.[36]

But Calvin was also careful to point out that "absolution is conditional upon the sinner's trust that God is merciful to him, provided he sincerely seek expiation in Christ's sacrifice and be satisfied with the grace offered him."[37] Calvin quite clearly had his preferences, but it is equally clear that he sought to impose no one liturgy on all Christians or that he himself held to one order.

Forms of worship, Calvin wrote Somerset in England, ought to be accommodated to the conditions and the tastes of the people.[38] Calvin's position is admirably summarized in a letter to the church at Wezel about the use of candles in worship.

We do not hold lighted candles in the celebration of the eucharist nor figured bread to be such indifferent things, that we would willingly consent to their introduction, or approve of them, though we object not to accommodate ourselves to the use of them, where they have been already established, when we have no authority to oppose them. If we were called upon to receive such ceremonies, we should hold ourselves bound according to the position in which God hath placed us, to admit of no compromise in resisting their introduction, and in maintaining constantly the purity which the church confided to us already possesses. But should our lot be cast in some place where a different form prevails, there is not one of us who from spite against a candle or a chasuble would consent to separate himself from the body of the church, and so deprive himself of the use of the sacrament. We must be on our guard not to scandalize those who are already subject to such infirmities, which we should certainly do by rejecting them from too frivolous motives. And then it would be for us matter of deep regret, if the French church which might be erected there should be broken up, because we would not accommodate ourselves to some ceremonies that do not affect the substance of the faith. For as we have said, it is perfectly lawful for the children of God to submit to many things of which they do not approve. Now the main point of consideration is, how far such liberty should extend. Upon this head let us lay it down as a settled point, that we ought to make mutual concessions in all ceremonies, that do not involve any prejudice to the confession of our faith, and for this end that the unity of the church be not destroyed by our excessive rigour or moroseness.[39]

A second characteristic of this liturgy is the emphasis on hearing and receiving in faith the word of God in word and sacrament. The centrality of the sermon cannot be disputed.[40] It has been argued that the sermon was the only form in which the Scripture was read in the liturgy. The evidence is not clear that in Calvin's liturgy the Scripture was first read and then explicated in a sermon. Hence it has been contended that the sermon, a commentary on Scripture, was the word of God in the worship service.[41] Calvin referred to the minister as the mouth of God,[42] and the Second Helvetic Confession refers to the sermon as the word of God.[43] Calvin knew that the words of the minister in preaching are never identical with the word of God, but this knowledge was obscured when he spoke of the minister's role in preaching and in the ordering of the church generally. Calvin's exaggerated estimate of the minister should not nullify his estimate of the importance of preaching, certainly in his liturgy. "The Reformation was a great preaching revival, probably the greatest in the history of the Christian church."[44]

The Strasbourg liturgy of 1545 included the Ten Commandments. The reformers had recognized three uses of the law: (1) to convict of sin and to lead to repentance (2) to maintain public order and (3) to guide and encourage the Christian in righteousness. Luther had emphasized the first usage, and in the Lutheran liturgies the law precedes the confession of sin. Calvin claimed that the third use was the principal usage, and in his liturgy the commandments come after confessions and assurance of forgiveness.[45] The liturgical order here declares that the forgiven worshipers still had to deal with the law and that with God's help they can keep it at least in part. The inclusion of law contributes to the character of Calvin's liturgy—as the hearing and obeying of the word of God.[46] In Farel's liturgy the confession comes after the sermon and the law on the grounds one must first hear the word of God to know what to confess, another illustration of variation in worship in the same theological framework.

A third characteristic of the Calvinist worship is the singing of psalms. Calvin did away with the medieval choir and emphasized congregational singing. Today it is difficult to recapture the thrill of worship in the language of the people and the new experience of congregational singing. As has been indicated, Calvin preferred the Psalms. While he himself translated a few Psalms for the 1539 Psalter, he made use of the greater poetical talents of Clement Marot and Theodore Beza.[47] Calvin's first psalter in 1539 had contained nineteen psalms. By 1562 Theodore Beza had completed the Psalter. The Psalms, put in French rhyme by Marot and Beza and set to music by Louis Bourgeois and Claude Goudimel, became one of the great books of the Reformation. It went through many editions and was translated into German, Dutch, Italian, Spanish, Bohemian, Polish, Latin, Hebrew, and English. It was also used by Roman Catholics, Lutherans, and others.

Psalm-singing became a vital part of Reformed piety. French Protestants sang psalms with such vigor as they were led to jail or to the stake that psalm-singing was outlawed and those who persisted had their tongues slit. Psalm 68 was the Huguenot Marseillaise:

> Let God arise, let his enemies be scattered;
> Let those who hate him flee before him,
> As smoke is driven away, so drive them away;
> As wax melts before the fire,
> Let the wicked perish before God!

Some Huguenots sang Psalm 118 as they went to battle.

> This is the day which the Lord has made
> Let us rejoice and be glad in it.
> Save us, we beseech thee, O Lord,
> O, Lord, we beseech thee, give us success!

The present generation of Americans is critical of the use of any Christian hymn as a battle song. This critical stance may be a sign of a protected life in a free society as well as a sign of greater sensitivity to brutality. In any case the following paragraphs from the Calvinist historian Émile Doumergue, however hagiographic, reveal the role of the Psalms in the concrete life of the Huguenots.

> Now, in describing the battle of Coutras (1587) won by Henry of Navarre, the son of Jeanne d' Albret, from the Duke de Joyeuse

and the Catholic army, D'Aubigné expresses himself thus:

"Of the two artilleries, the last to come, that of Huguenots, was the first in position, and commenced to play before nine o'clock. Laverdin, seeing the damage which it did, rode towards his general and cried out, while still some distance off: 'Sir, we are losing by waiting: we must open up.' The response was : 'Monsieur the Marshal speaks the truth.' He returned at a gallop to his place, gave the word and charged.

"On the other side, the King of Navarre having had prayer offered throughout the army, some began to sing the Hundred-and-eighteenth Psalm: *'This is the happy day.'* Many Catholics of the White-Cap cried out loudly enough to be heard: 'S'Death! They are trembling, the poltroons; they are making confession.' Vaux, lieutenant of Bellegarde, who had more frequently rubbed knees with these people and who alone rallied for the combat, said to the Duke: 'Sir, when the Huguenots take this figure, they are ready to lay on with a will.' " And some hours later the victory was theirs.

But this same song, *"This is the happy day"*, has sustained the Calvinists in other combats, more dangerous, more difficult. It is heroic to cast ourselves at a gallop without fear into the midst of the battle. It is more heroic, laid on a bed of agony, to receive, calm and smiling, the assault of the last enemy which man has to conquer on this earth. Such a hero, the author whose narrative we have just read showed himself. His widow relates: "Two hours before his death, he said with a joyful countenance and a mind peaceable and content, *'This is the happy day'.*" There is something more heroic still. Listen! Far from the excitement of the combat, unsustained by the affections and care of friends, face to face with the mob howling with rage and hate, on the scaffold, at the foot of the gallows, here are the martyrs of the eighteenth century,—the Louis Rancs, the François Bénézets, the François Rochettes,—who, with their glorious souls, raise towards the heavens where their Saviour listens to them, the song of triumph: *"This is the happy day!"*[48]

The Psalms spoke to many different human situations. In the preface to his commentary on the Psalms, Calvin calls them an anatomy of the soul.

The favorite psalms [of the sixteenth century Calvinists] were not the same as those twentieth-century congregations might choose. Instead of Psalm 23 or 139 sixteenth-century congregations used by preference such psalms as 46; 68; 76; 124.[49]

Psalm-singing contributed to the shaping of Reformed character and piety, and its influence can hardly be overestimated. The Psalms were the prayers of the people in Calvin's liturgy.[50] Through them the worshipers responded to the word of God and affirmed their trust and gratitude and loyalty to God.

As a fourth characteristic Calvin's liturgy, it must be noted, adds the sacraments to the word.

> The Lord teaches and instructs us by his Word. Secondly, he confirms it by the sacraments. Finally, he illumines our minds by the light of his Holy Spirit and opens our hearts for the Word and sacraments to enter in.[51]

Much has been made of the fact that Calvin's liturgy developed out of the service of the Mass as it was revised by the reformers at Strasbourg and that it is aborted when the Lord's Supper is not observed. Calvin wanted a service that included preaching and the Lord's Supper as well as the sacrament of Baptism. He also wanted to observe this service each Sunday. This was his hope as is witnessed in his insistence in the *Institutes* that the Lord's Supper should be administered "at least once a week."[52] "It became the unvarying rule (Acts 2:42) that no meeting of the church should take place without the Word, prayers, partaking of the supper and almsgiving."[53]

Calvin did, however, agree to a service of preaching without the sacraments. He would never have agreed to the sacraments without the word in preaching and teaching. The spoken words of preaching and teaching were necessary for the intelligibility of the worship and particularly for the intelligibility of the word in the sacraments. The personal and responsible character of worship had to be maintained over against magic, which by-passes personal decision and responsibility.

For Reformed theology the sacraments always take place in the context of preaching and teaching, and their ultimate validity depends upon the work of the Holy Spirit. Calvin emphasized that the bread and the wine became under the power of the Holy Spirit the occasion for the real presence of Jesus Christ and for the communion of the believer with the Risen Lord. The views of Zwingli in his radical break with the medieval mass and in his emphasis upon the sacrament as a pledge by which believers present themselves to the church as disciples and soldiers of Christ have often been contrasted with those of Calvin. Yet Zwingli's understanding of the Lord's Supper was no "mere commemoration." Real commemoration involved the contemplation in faith of the work of Christ and trust in that work. The spiritual presence of Christ was not disputed by Zwingli. There is a difference of emphasis between the more rational Zwingli and the more mystical Calvin, but the difference can be exaggerated or else Calvin and Bullinger, Zwingli's successor in Zurich, could never have agreed on a common Reformed position in the Zurich Consensus (Consensus Tigurinus), 1549.

Calvin's teaching on baptism is similar to his doctrine of the Lord's Supper. He wanted baptism to take place in the presence of the assembly of believers and thus in the context of teaching and prayer. The service of baptism was to be simple and free of all pomp that might dazzle the eye or deaden the mind.

Worship for Calvin was a centered act of the person; that is, it involved every personal capacity of mind, of emotion, of will. Even though he held together the word in preaching and sacraments, his liturgy remained a highly verbal service involving all of a person's intellectual powers. Calvin gave up many aids to worship that had assisted less highly disciplined and committed worshipers. Calvinist worship required a disciplined congregation that could support the dialogue of faith with minimal external props.

## Farel's Liturgy

When John Calvin first arrived at Geneva, worship was conducted according to a liturgy that William Farel had worked out along Zwinglian lines in 1524. The liturgy is essentially a preaching service, and the Lord's Supper is celebrated only occasionally. While Farel did not object to the singing of psalms in the vernacular, his liturgy does not provide for music. Zwingli had substituted antiphonal Biblical and creedal responses as a means of congregation participation. The practice could not sustain itself. The resulting liturgy was a service of the hearing of the word of God, as the title indicates.

*The Manner Observed in Preaching When the People Are Assembled to Hear the Word of God*[54]

Bidding Prayer
Lord's Prayer
Proclamation of the Word
The Law of God
The Confession of Sins
The Apostles' Creed
Intercessions

OUR LORD'S SUPPER

Exhortation
Invitation
Self-examination
Excommunication
Confession—The Lord's Prayer
The Creed
Assurance of Pardon
Words of Institution
Sursum Corda
Communion
Post Communion (Prayer of Thanksgiving)

Preaching services had become popular in the generation before the Reformation particularly under the influence of Johann Ulrich Surgant of Basel whose book on practical theology, *Manuale Curatorum* (1503) emphasized preaching. These preaching services, sometimes called prone, had no fixed order. They fitted into different situations and included concern for the knowledge of the Apostles' Creed, the Ten Commandments and the Lord's Prayer. Farel's service is similar to Zwingli's service in Zurich and the service Oecolampadius established in Basel. It is customary for contemporary critics to note the plainness and drabness of the service. It was plain, but it was also exciting. Today it is difficult to recover the thrill of hearing the word of God in the common language, of listening to that word being systematically expounded, and of holding the bread and wine of the communion in one's own hands. It is also a significant fact that this "preaching service" has been more influential in the subsequent history of the Reformed community than Calvin's service, though Calvin's theology was far more influential than Zwingli's. It has captured the minds and hearts of worshipers in every age, sometimes in remarkable ways.

The distinction between the two types of service represented in Calvin's and Farel's liturgies are interpreted differently. Some (Old) see the various liturgical patterns as part of one movement that reached its fruition in the Geneva liturgy of 1542. Others (Hageman) underscore the fact that Calvin maintained the order for the Lord's Supper when the supper was not celebrated. In all the Reformed services there was a profound insistence on hearing, believing, and obeying the word of God. The persistence of the two emphases today indicates again that there is no one pattern of Reformed worship.

## *The Westminster Directory*

A third decisive influence in the shaping of Reformed worship, in particular Presbyterian worship in America, was the Puritan Revolution and the Westminster Assembly. The Assembly produced a church polity, a confession, catechisms, a psalter, and a directory for worship. While the Assembly was united in its understanding of Reformed theology, it was divided on the matter of worship between the Scottish Presbyterians, the English Presbyterians, and the Independents. The *Directory* is a compromise. It is also replete with ambiguous directives that could be interpreted in different ways.[56] The *Directory*, however, bears the marks of the Puritan movement, and it shaped worship in that direction.

The preface to the *Directory* specifies several concerns of the Assembly in regard to worship. First, the use of a service book, in particular the *Book of Common Prayer* in England, had undercut the significance of preaching "as far inferior to the reading of common prayer."[57] The Assembly intended to emphasize the centrality of preaching. Secondly, the use of service books had been a

> means . . . to make and increase an idle and unedifying ministry, which contented itself with set forms made to their hands by others, without putting forth themselves to exercise the gift of prayer, with which our Lord Jesus Christ pleaseth to furnish all His servants whom he calls to that office.[58]

Moreover, the service book had been used to impose an order of worship on people who in conscience objected to it.

The Assembly replaced the service book that contained the prayers and forms of worship with a directory that served as a guide. The Scots, who had been influenced by the same anti-service book sentiment of the English Puritans, did not even submit their *Book of Common Order* for the Assembly's consideration. Yet the *Directory* suggests an order of worship that is not very different from that of Geneva and of the Scottish *Book of Common Order*.

PUBLIC WORSHIP OF GOD[59]

Prayer
Reading of the Word [ordinarily one chapter of each Testament]
    [An exposition of the reading could follow the complete
    reading but with care not to detract from the sermon.]

Singing of a Psalm
General Prayer [Option open to postpone some parts of prayer
    until after the sermon]
Preaching of the Word
Prayer [Use of Lord's Prayer recommended]
Psalm
Blessing

Baptism and the Lord's Supper, when celebrated, followed
the final hymn. The order for the Lord's Supper is as follows:[60]

Exhortation, Warning, Invitation
Sanctifying and Blessing the Elements:
    Words of Institution
    Prayer of Thanksgiving and Blessing of Bread and Wine
Taking and Giving of Bread and Wine
Reminder of Grace of God in Jesus Christ Held Forth in Sacrament
Thanksgiving
Collection for the Poor

The large place that this liturgy gave to the reading, exposition, and preaching of the word of God is notable. The *Directory*
contains an excellent section on the art of preaching, advocating
the plain style of the Puritans, who insisted on the *communication*
of the message of Scripture. The Scots objected to the homileti-
cal practice of the English Puritans, but no one could doubt the
Puritans' seriousness about preaching or their effectiveness. The
*Directory* summarizes their judgment of the preacher's task and
plain-style method.

But the Servant of Christ, whatever his method be, is to perform
his whole ministry:
    1. Painfully, not doing the work of the Lord negligently.
    2. Plainly, that the meanest may understand; delivering the truth
not in the enticing words of man's wisdom, but in demonstration
of the Spirit and of power, lest the cross of Christ should be made
of none effect; abstaining also from an unprofitable use of unknown
tongues, strange phrases, and cadences of sounds and words; spar-
ingly citing sentences of ecclesiastical or other human writers, ancient or modern, be they never so elegant.
    3. Faithfully, looking at the honour of Christ, the conversion,
edification, and salvation of the people; not at his own gain or glory;
keeping nothing back which may promote those holy ends, giving
to every one his own portion, and bearing indifferent respect unto
all, without neglecting the meanest, or sparing the greatest in their
sins.
    4. Wisely framing all his doctrines, exhortations, and especially
his reproofs, in such a manner as may be most likely to prevail;

showing all due respect to each man's person and place, and not mixing his own passion or bitterness.

5. Gravely, as becometh the Word of God; shunning all such gesture, voice, and expressions, as may occasion the corruptions of men to despise him and his ministry.

6. With loving affection, that the people may see all coming from his godly zeal, and hearty desire to do them good, And,

7. As taught of God, and persuaded in his own heart, that all that he teacheth is the truth of Christ; and walking before his flock, as an example to them in it; earnestly, both in private and public, recommending his labours to the blessing of God, and watchfully looking to himself, and the flock whereof the Lord hath made him overseer: So shall the doctrine of truth be preserved uncorrupt, many souls converted and built up, and himself receive manifold comforts of his labours even in this life, and afterward the crown of glory laid up for him in the world to come.[61]

The Assembly's *Directory,* while not prohibiting the use of traditional forms, did set the practice for the next three centuries of English-speaking Presbyterianism. The Creed, the Gloria Patri, and even the Lord's Prayer were increasingly dropped from worship. The *Directory* presupposed that the minister was a converted man who could and would pray and lead worship out of his Christian experience. For a highly disciplined community and ministry such a practice was very effective. With the waning of discipline a voluntary liturgical order and free prayers became the occasion for much trivia, senseless repetition, and personal idiosyncrasy.

## The American Experience

English-speaking Presbyterians from Britain carried with them the practices of their homeland. The new land with its open frontier would shape these practices in its own way. The frontier was "open." There were few church buildings, and worship was held in improvised settings. A settled and regular ministry was the exception. Settlements were widely scattered, and means of travel were slow. External aids and supports for worship were minimal.

Religious practices were developed to meet the actual needs of the new land.[62] Sacramental seasons, week-ends and Mondays given over to preaching, teaching, congregational meetings, and sacraments became great occasions in rural church life. The camp meeting, the revival, and the protracted meeting all developed as ways of nurturing and particularly evangelizing the nominally Christian or non-Christian population in America. Probably more than at any other time in church history, the regular worship services of the church became the means of bringing non-Christians into the church's membership and life. Worship was directed to this end, and the notion that the Lord's Supper was a "converting ordinance" spread. The Westminster Assembly had rejected this interpretation of the Lord's Supper.[63] The evangelistic development of American church life in general and of worship in particular is understandable in the light of the fact that probably less than ten per cent of the American people had any connection with an organized church in 1800. The fact that many American churches were established by "laity," not by the clergy or by any organized ecclesiastical mission, gave to church life a communal and nonclerical character that is also unique.

The freedom of American Presbyterians to develop their own indigenous church life and patterns of worship was enhanced by the absence of any strictly held directory for life and worship. The *Westminster Directory* had been recommended by the Synod of 1729, but the evidence indicates that it was at best a guide. A new *Directory of Worship* was prepared for the American church (1786–1788) in advance of the first General Assembly which met in 1789. The American document continued the tradition of Westminster but contained sufficient changes to make it indigenous and native. The committee that had been charged with this work was urban, old-school, and formal. The synod revised the work of the committee in the direction of the more open, informal, evangelistic American style.[64] New-school and revivalist Presbyterians continued throughout the following century to exert their influence on worship in this direction. The Puritan influence, as in the South with Thornwell and Girardeau, also continued to flourish.

The worship that was nourished in the American situation lived in part out of its authenticity. It faithfully expressed the devotion of the worshipers, and it was a means of God's grace to them. It also placed very heavy demands on the minister, who, being denied a service book with set forms, had to lead worship out of the depth of his own religious experience and theological competence. Inadequacies either in personal experience or competence quickly came to the surface. As the century passed, the worship that was an authentic product of American church life began to fail.

Some Presbyterians, dissatisfied with their worship, were attracted to episcopal forms. Others began to work for a recovery of the riches of the tradition and for an enrichment of the worshiping life of the church. In 1855 Charles Baird published his *Eutaxia, or the Presbyterian Liturgies: Historical Sketches,* a still useful book that collected the classic Reformed liturgies. Throughout the second half of the century, worship was a subject of debate. Some opposed any changes. Others like Charles Hodge were glad to establish a middle position that held to free and simple American tradition but also made use of classical forms.[65] In 1897 the Church Service Society was organized under the leadership of Louis Benson, the hymnologist, and Henry van Dyke. In 1906 *The Book of Common Worship,* prepared under the chairmanship of Henry van Dyke, was accepted by the General Assembly of the Presbyterian Church, U.S.A. for voluntary use. In 1929 it was endorsed for use in the Presbyterian Church, U.S.

The struggle over worship in nineteenth-century Presbyterianism had centered on the identification of worship with the simplicities of an earlier American situation. In the struggle the proponents of classical liturgies sometimes sought to impose on American worship patterns and forms which had been developed in Europe and which were foreign to American experience. After a liberal theology became common in American churches, contradictions also became apparent between the theology that was believed and the worship that was advocated. Worship sometimes was determined more by aesthetic and psychological considerations than by responsible theological judgment. Because of the social and cultural embarrassment concerning the austerity and trivia of American church worship, the Reformed demands for authenticity, intelligibility, and theological integrity were often forgotten.[66]

Criticism of American patterns of worship became finally too easy. Those patterns had been created by exposure to the realities of American life. In actual fact they were or had been suitable to their situation. The percentage of American people involved in the church and in worship rose from less than ten before 1800 to above fifty per cent by 1950. This is a record scarcely equaled anywhere else in church history. Traditional worship of Presbyterian churches had been an effective means for the proclaiming of the word of God and for the response of the people in devotion and commitment. It needed revision by the second half of the nineteenth century, but it is not yet certain that the revisions have sprung authentically from the depths of the religious life of the congregation or are adequate means of expression of devotion and commitment.

The Americanization of worship was less drastic in those Reformed churches that had roots on the continent and that maintained much of their ethnic and ecclesiastical heritage in the new, English-speaking environment. Among the German Reformed, the Mercersburg movement gave attention not only to a recovery of liturgy but also to a theology of worship with emphasis on the sacraments.[67] Philip Schaff brought his extensive knowledge of Reformed history to this movement. John W. Nevin, a graduate of Princeton, wrote on the sacraments, emphasizing the presence of Christ in the Lord's Supper, an emphasis which had been neglected in the more "Zwinglian" American context that understood the sacrament more as a recollection and memory of what Jesus said and did and a pledge of allegiance to him.

One unique American contribution to worship was the development of the offering as a basic part of worship. From the earliest days there had been the collection as a means of help for the poor. This offering had always persisted in Christian worship, especially as part of the communion service. The new aspect of the offering in American worship grew out of the voluntary character of the church, which placed upon every member the responsibility for buildings, services, missions, and ministry. The American churches were financed neither by the state, nor the nobility, nor the rich, but by the people. The offering therefore became a much more significant personal act, and its integration into the worship of the church after many experimental methods of church finance failed was a significant achievement.[68]

Authentic worship cannot be imposed on worshipers. It always grows out of the depths of experience and commitment and is determined by the disclosure of the mystery toward which it moves. Certainly there is no one pattern of Christian worship or of Reformed worship. Yet there are the decisive marks that are given to Christian worship by the revelation of God in Jesus Christ. And there are the decisive marks of Reformed worship that are formed by its awareness of the Presence of the Lord God, Creator of Heaven and Earth, who calls the people of God into being, gives to them their destiny, and elects them for the working out of the divine purposes in history. All pretense is cleared away, and the believer stands in the presence of God in simplicity, even austerity, to hear and do the will of God.

*Appendix I:*

## REPRESENTATIVE REFORMED LITURGIES AND DIRECTORIES OF THE SIXTEENTH AND SEVENTEENTH CENTURIES

The Zurich Liturgy: Liturgy of the Word, 1525 (Zwingli)
Action or Use of the Lord's Supper, 1525

William Farel: The Manner Observed in Preaching, 1524(?)

Basel Liturgy: Form and Manner of the Lord's Supper, 1525(?) (Oecolampadius)

The Strassburg Liturgy: Psalter, with Complete Church Practice, 1524–1539 (Bucer)

John Calvin: The Form of Church Prayers, 1540, 1542, 1545

John Knox: The Form of Prayers, 1556 (Book of Common Order)

John à Lasco: Whole Form and Method of Church Service in the Strangers Church, 1550 and 1555 (Forma ac Ratio)

Liturgy of the Palatinate, 1563

Liturgy of the Reformed Dutch Church, 1566

The Middleburg Liturgy: A Book of the Form of Common Prayers, 1586

The Westminster Directory, 1644

The Savoy Liturgy, 1661

Texts may be found in Bard Thompson, *Liturgies of the Western Church* (New York: World Publishing Co., 1961); "The Palatinate Liturgy," trans. Bard Thompson, *Theology and Life,* vol. 6, no. 1 (Spring 1963), pp. 49–67.

# VII

# CULTURE
# AND
# THE REFORMED TRADITION

The Reformed tradition, according to the typology of H. Richard Niebuhr, belongs among the converters of culture.[1] Neither rejecting culture nor identifying with culture, it has sought to transform culture. This relationship to culture is based upon the conviction that culture, as part of the creation of God, is good and therefore is convertible. It is also based upon the conviction that culture is fallen or disordered and therefore needs transformation. History provides abundant evidence that the Reformed community has been energetic in the pursuit of the transformation of culture, particularly in the ethical and political areas. The vigorous way in which the Reformed tradition has stimulated political and social change has not, however, been matched by any equal vigor and fruitfulness in the arts and in those concerns of culture that have to do with the physical, the emotional, and the aesthetic. Hence it has been easy to denigrate the Reformed tradition as culturally sterile. No one has put this complaint with greater sharpness than Edwin Muir (1887–1959), Scottish poet and author of a controversial biography of John Knox.

> The Word made flesh here is made word again,
> A word made word in flourish and arrogant crook.
> See there King Calvin with his iron pen,
> And God three angry letters in a book,
> And there the logical hook
> On which the Mystery is impaled and bent
> Into an ideological instrument.
> ............................................................................
> The fleshless word, growing, will bring us down,
> Pagan and Christian man alike will fall,
> The auguries say, the white and black and brown,
> The merry and sad, theorist, lover, all

Invisibly will fall:
Abstract calamity, save for those who can
Build their cold empire on the abstract man.[2]

The relation between the Reformed tradition and culture is complex. Erwin Panofsky, a distinguished historian of art, has rightly warned against thinking of the connection between art and Reformation in terms of straight cause-and-effect relationship.[3] Nevertheless, several factors in the Reformed tradition give some credibility to this complaint. The first is the preoccupation of the tradition with the ethical, the moral, the social, and the political. This preoccupation is rooted in the nature of Reformed tradition and also in the social and political context of its history. The social, political, and religious ordering of human life was the great issue of Calvin's day. Any criticism of Calvin's preoccupation with these issues must take account of this fact. Secondly, Reformed theologians have understood the work of Jesus Christ primarily, if not exclusively, as the redemption of the human race from sin. This was to them the clear purpose of the incarnation.[4] Calvin refused to speculate on whether Christ would have become incarnate if sin had not been a part of human history. He concentrated his attention on Jesus Christ as the redeemer from sin, not the fulfiller of creation. This has been the prevailing emphasis of the Reformed tradition. This particular concentration of theological energy has been both a strength and a weakness. It has emphasized in a powerful way the responsibility of every human being in the presence of God, the conversion of the sinner, and ordering of society according to the will of God. It has also led to a benign neglect of those arts that fulfilled the human spirit and that enhanced creation. Finally, the Reformed tradition has placed great emphasis on an economic ordering of life, on the assignment of life's energies and time to different tasks according to a theologically sound measure. This has meant that little time and energy have been left for many cultural endeavors that have not been rated as important as the political ordering of life.

A fair assessment of the history of the Reformed tradition, however, will reveal far greater cultural vigor than its critics have admitted, even in the area of the arts. This cultural embodiment is worth investigation. No one can know a theology until the embodiment of that theology in human life and community is analyzed, for the pre-eminent embodiment of any theology is not in books but in the lives of Christian people and in the life of the Christian community. In addition, the embodiments of theology in the achievements of culture are also revealing. Stephen Neill once risked the judgment that the finest monuments of Protestantism in culture were to be found in Rembrandt's painting, in Bach's music, in Christopher Wren's St. Paul's Cathedral.[5] Cogent reasons for this judgment can be given though no such listing is definitive. Furthermore, every artist draws on many sources; and no cultural achievement claims the religious as the exclusive source. Christian artists draw on the whole Christian tradition as well as upon the insights of a particular tradition. In addition, the artist may draw upon the whole range of human experience. The theologian of the church is under obligation to test theological statements by the rubrics of a particular community in a way that the artist is not. Any effort to compel cultural life to conform to a particular tradition would stifle freedom and creativity and at best produce propaganda. Hence cultural expressions of the faith are "less pure" than expressions of the faith within the confines of the church's life, such as worship, church polity, and theology. Nevertheless, there are cultural achievements in literature, visual arts, architecture, economics, and political life that do in significant measure embody the Christian faith. These cultural expressions of the faith tell us something about the faith. Grünewald's Isenheim Altarpiece expresses the scandal (1 Corinthians 1:23) of the incarnation, for example, in a way that written and spoken theology cannot duplicate.[6] Hence it is worthwhile to note some of the classic cultural expressions of the Reformed faith. None of them is a "pure" statement of Reformed faith; but all of them embody the Reformed faith and the community life out of which they came, and all of them clarify for us the nature of the faith. Rembrandt's paintings, *Paradise Lost* and *Pilgrim's Progress,* Charenton Church and New England meeting houses, the *Psalter,* schools and colleges established for a literate ministry and citizenry, as well as the influence of Reformed communities upon political and economic life, are in a measure an arbitrary list. Other choices could have been made. Yet this list is adequate to indicate the ways in which the Reformed tradition has significantly informed culture.

## *Visual Arts*

From the beginning the Reformed tradition rejected paintings and sculpture as means of Christian education and as aids to worship. As humanists the reformers had confidence in the power of words, and as observers of history they saw or believed they saw the theological illiteracy and corruption that reliance on images had produced. Images and paintings cannot communicate the faith. Charles Garside summarizes Zwingli's position as follows:

> "If now you show an unbelieving or unlettered child images, then you must teach him with the Word in addition, or he will have looked at the picture in vain" (120,22–25). For if "you were newly come from the unbelievers and knew nothing of Christ and saw Him painted with the apostles at the Last Supper, or on the Cross, then you would learn nothing from this same picture other than to say: 'He who is pictured there was a good-looking man in spite of it all' "(121, 18–22). Zwingli's witticism is a particularly telling index to his contempt for the Gregorian defense of images. One may have images of Christ, but they are powerless; the "story must be learned only from the Word, and from the painting one learns nothing except the form of the body, the movements or the constitution of the body or face" (121, 26–29).[7]

John Calvin did not give much attention to visual arts. He also did not believe that they were effective instruments in communicating the gospel, and he was himself an exceedingly busy person with responsibilities that precluded cultural activities. This inattention to art does not mean that he did not give it a place of value. He did believe that the visual arts were gifts of God and therefore should be used in pure and legitimate ways. Art must not be perverted by misuse or turned to the destruction of the human.[8] As God's gift, art is a source of joy and pleasure. Art that represents events, especially events of some historical importance, has some use "in teaching or admonition," but Calvin was not convinced that art is an effective medium of communication and teaching. He preferred the spoken and written word. In the worship of the church the symbols of bread and wine in the Lord's Supper and of water in baptism were enough. Yet this was a judgment about communication, not art. The content of art is too ambiguous and too subject to personal interpretation. Calvin believed that this judgment was confirmed by the theological illiteracy of his time. If the medieval church had taught and preached more, and if it had depended less upon the "Bible in stone" and upon symbolism, the church would have been better informed. More recently Karl Barth has insisted that "from the viewpoint of Christology there can be no question of using the picture of Christ as a means of instruction."[9]

Calvin not only insisted that art is a gift of God; he also insisted on integrity in any artistic expression. Any representation of the divine in art is wrong not merely because God had forbidden it but also because art could not represent God without defacing his glory. "Only those things are to be sculptured or painted which the eyes are capable of seeing."[10] The material of art is the created world that is accessible to the sense of man. Art must not presume to represent that which is beyond its grasp. In addition, art must be realistic, not in the artistic sense of the word but in the moral sense. It must deal with reality and authentically present it. Calvin's insistence on the integrity of art indicates that he took it very seriously as a human activity by which the real is distinguished from falsehood and from fantasy.

There is little if anything in Calvin to indicate that he could have appreciated modern, abstract art. He was too cautious about flights of unrestrained imagination. He placed too much emphasis upon the concrete, and he was too opposed to ambiguous forms of communication. Words, written and spoken, were for him the clearest and most effective means of communication and of preaching and teaching.

The Reformed tradition has not been, on the whole, productive of great art. This lack of artistic productivity is grounded not so much in any lack of appreciation of art but in the ordering of priorities. Calvin's first concerns on the human level were ethical and political. The work of Christ was conceived primarily as the redemption of sinners and the reordering of a broken society, not as the fulfillment of creation.[11] Ethical, social, and political matters consumed most of the Reformed energies. Yet within the Reformed community there have been significant achievements in art.

Rembrandt van Rijn, who was born on July 15, 1606, in Leiden, embodied the Reformed perspective in his art better than any other great artist. He was born in a Reformed community during a period of considerable theological excitement.[12]

His parents were married in the Reformed Church, and his marriage to Saskia van Uylenburch also took place in a Reformed church. Saskia was from a strict Reformed family; and her brother-in-law was a theologian of some note, Johannes Maccovius. The children of Rembrandt and Saskia were baptized in the Reformed Church. These connections with the Reformed Church have to be noted because of a seventeenth-century report that Rembrandt was a Mennonite. It is apparent that he did have close contacts with the Mennonites. He made paintings and drawings of the Mennonite preacher, Cornelis Claesz Anslo. He appreciated the simplicity of the Mennonites; yet his own style of life, in many ways undisciplined, would not have fitted into a highly disciplined Mennonite community. He also had close associations with the Jewish community as is apparent in his paintings. After Saskia's death, Rembrandt's relation to the church was made difficult by his liaison with Hendrickje Stoffels, who "entered his home about 1645 as a servant girl, to remain as his life companion."[13] Rembrandt was prevented from marrying her by Saskia's will, which left her estate to their son Titus in case Rembrandt remarried. After the birth of a daughter, Cornelia, Rembrandt was called before the church council. He did not appear. Yet he was present as the godfather for the baptism of his granddaughter in 1669. He died on October 4, 1669.

Rembrandt's career began with great promise. His art in the early period, 1631–1642, reflected his confident spirit when he enjoyed wealth, acclaim, and success in every way. Rembrandt's situation radically changed in the 1640s. His work no longer pleased the public, for he painted as he saw and understood, not what was expected. This change in his art had already begun when he painted the "Night Watch" (1642), one of the greatest of all pictures. His commissions began to decrease. His mother died in 1640. Saskia died in 1642, barely thirty years of age. From this point on, Rembrandt was financially insecure, finally declaring bankruptcy in 1656. The personal sorrow and tragedy of these years gave depth to his painting.

Rembrandt was a painter of the Bible. No other great painter embodied so much of the Bible in his art. "Of Biblical subjects there have survived about one hundred and sixty paintings, about eighty etchings, and more than six hundred drawings, which means a total of approximately eight hundred and fifty in this field."[14] W. A. Visser 't Hooft writes that Rembrandt became a servant of the Word of God.

> He was Protestant, because he became more and more deeply absorbed in the biblical testimony, because he interpreted the gospel in the light only of this very gospel, without calling in the assistance of any classical or humanist ideal, and because he did not attempt to force the paradox of the cross into human dimensions.[15]

Rembrandt's paintings have the integrity and the theological authenticity that Calvin insisted upon. In Rembrandt's art the viewer is confronted with the scandal (1 Corinthians 1:23) of Christian faith. The nativity occurs not in a castle but in a barn;[16] the man on the cross is not a Greek god who is asleep but a man who is dead; Mary at the foot of the cross is not a Greek goddess with a tear on her face but a mother who has been bereaved of her beloved son. As in Grünewald's great Isenheim Altarpiece, Rembrandt's art confronts the viewer with the question of faith: can this man be the incarnate God? The paintings of Christ at Emmaus, especially those done in 1648 and 1661, expound the drama of faith and unbelief in the presence of the risen Christ. Seated at the table, one companion has recognized the risen Christ; the other is puzzled; and the waiter is unconcerned or oblivious to the struggle of faith taking place in his presence.[17] Rembrandt's painting of his mother (1631, Rijksmuseum) can be considered an excellent statement of Protestant faith in art. Here he pictured an old woman in deep concentration, studying the Scripture. "The Return of the Prodigal," (Hermitage) painted late in his career, powerfully points to the divine forgiveness in the vivid depiction of a father's forgiving welcome to a returning son. In all of his mature art Rembrandt captures the human question of faith in a very Biblical context.

Rembrandt's portraits also reflect theological commitments that are closely related to the Reformed tradition. Paul Tillich finds in such portraits, as that of Jan Six, strong, lonely, tragic, but unbroken persons, "carrying the marks of their unique histories in every line of their faces, expressing the ideals of personality of a humanistic Protestantism."[18] Wencelius concludes, not wholly in disagreement with Tillich, that the portrait of Jan Six poses very sharply the drama of predestination.[19] The mystery of existence is etched into the face of Jan Six. He is a man with a purpose, a mission, and a destiny.

Rembrandt did not set out to embody Reformed theology in his paintings. If he had, his paintings, drawings, and etchings would have been propaganda. He lived in a culture informed by Reformed theology, and he lived with the Bible. His own life, though in many ways undisciplined, faced the realities of rejection, bereavement, and poverty. As an artist he was a genius. The result is a body of paintings, drawings, and etchings that embody many of the characteristic motifs of Reformed theology and piety.

## *Literature*

The influence of Christian humanism on the origins of the Reformed tradition has already been indicated.[20] From the beginning the Reformers used all the literary skills available in plumbing the meaning of Scripture, and they prized and cultivated the power of words to express and communicate the Christian faith. John Calvin, in using French to write theology, especially his polemical treatises that he wished persons outside scholarly circles to read, contributed significantly to the development of the French language.[21]

In the beginning the primary focus of literary activity in the Reformed community is found in theological writings. All the Reformers were prolific writers of treatises and letters. Calvin himself put into French verse possibly six Psalms,[22] and he wrote at least one poem that has survived.[23] He quickly found that he neither had the time nor perhaps the gifts for poetry, and he gave the task of translating the Psalms into verse over to Marot and Beza. Beyond this there was little encouragement of a Christian literary imagination. In part this may have been due to the pressure of other tasks. Calvin appreciated poetry for its power to uncover human sinfulness and to incite the emotions of the reader or hearer.[24] Yet there is no clear indication that he had much confidence in the power of the Christian imagination to do much in poetry and drama for communicating the Christian faith or for uncovering its deeper meaning.

Two works of the Christian imagination that were produced in a Reformed context and that stand out both for their intrinsic merit and for their embodiment of the faith are John Milton's *Paradise Lost* and John Bunyan's *Pilgrim's Progress.* [25] Milton (1608–1674) was an irregular Calvinist. He has been called the bard of Calvinism unbound, but in his justification of the ways of God with men he belongs to the tradition.[26] He was a Puritan who visited Italy and appropriated the learning of the Renaissance. He lived at the high watermark of English Puritanism; and he was a spokesman for the Puritans during the Commonwealth period, though he broke with the Presbyterians and parodied the Westminster Assembly. He shared the confidence of many Puritans in the power of truth to win the battle if only freedom of speech and printing is allowed. His *Areopagitica* is one of the great monuments in the struggle for freedom of thought, speech, and printing. In his own life he knew tragedy: marital dissension, the failure of the Puritan saints to establish the holy community, and blindness. At the Restoration he barely escaped with his life as he had justified tyrannicide. How could the "saint" make sense of the Puritan failure (historical evil) and of blindness (physical evil)? Once Milton had hoped to write the great English epic of Arthur and his Round Table. Now he chose to write the Christian epic, the drama of creation, the fall, and redemption. This he did with an imagination that indelibly imprinted this drama on English culture for three centuries at least. Today there is still some confusion in popular Christianity between the imagery of Milton and the Bible. Milton did not write systematic theology, and yet he combined the critical powers of reflections and observations with the power of image and metaphor in such a way that the Ninth Book of *Paradise Lost* uncovers the nature of temptation, evil, and human pride in ways that no systematic theology can.

John Bunyan (1628–1688) was different from John Milton. He was a "mechanick preacher," not a connoisseur of Renaissance learning. He lived after the Puritan Revolution in a time when the failure of the Commonwealth had destroyed hope of the holy community in England's "green and pleasant land." Bunyan himself spent time in the Bedford jail for preaching the gospel as he understood it. His vision of the Christian life was not so much participation in the great dramas of human history as it was the pilgrimage of the Christian through this vale of tears toward the celestial city.

Yet Bunyan was no ordinary mechanic preacher of the Baptist church in Bedford. *Pilgrim's Progress* is a work of genius. No one could have been taught to write it in the schools. It is the product of a remarkable Christian imagination and of the wisdom of Christian experience. Behind it lay the "bruised conscience" that knows the terror of life without God, the vision of human existence as it came from God, and the transformation of fallen and disordered lives by the grace of God. *Pilgrim's Progress* is parabolic theology.[27] It tells the story of ordinary human experience in such a way that the reader moves from those experiences that he knows to the grace of God that illumines and transforms those experiences. The Christian imagination that produced *Pilgrim's Progress* and that uncovers the reality of human existence under God produces theology in parable form. This theology is quite as true and quite as useful as the theologies of Calvin and Barth are true and useful in other ways. As a work of Christian imagination, *Pilgrim's Progress* has never been surpassed.

## *Architecture*

Protestantism defined the church primarily as the people of God, not as an institution and certainly not as a building. The church exists where the word of God is rightly preached and heard and the sacraments rightly administered and received. There are no holy places, and God's presence is not tied to any finite and determinate objects, not even to the elements of bread, wine, and water in the sacraments. These theological convictions determined the Reformed understanding of the nature of church buildings, the most immediate involvement of the Reformed community with architecture.

In the beginning Reformed Christians had to reconstruct the arrangement of cathedrals and churches which had come to them from the past. Sometimes the paraphernalia of medieval worship, such as statues and even stained-glass windows, were removed or destroyed with irresponsible enthusiasm.[28] More significantly, the space of the older churches was arranged to accommodate the new understanding of the nature of the church and worship. This meant the closing off of the chancels and arranging seats in such a way that the congregation was gathered around the pulpit and the communion table. It was important for the arrangement to help the worshipers gather as a community, hear the word of God preached, see the actions of the sacraments, and participate in the worship of the church. In Geneva this meant that the congregation was seated from different angles around the pulpit and table.[29] For the Reformed community with its emphasis on the church as the people of God, church buildings became more and more utilitarian. Their primary function was to serve the

needs of the worshiping, believing, obeying congregation. Moreover, the Reformed had no holy places and things, and therefore
the church building could be shut except when it was in use. The
removal or destruction of the symbols of medieval worship does
not mean that the Reformed minimized symbols. They thought
symbols were critically important, and for this reason they
changed the symbols and arrangements of worship. They were
concerned for the arrangement of the congregation in worship
in ways appropriate to their theology and for the centrality of the
pulpit, Bible, and table with a minimum of distractions from this
focus.

Calvin himself had very little to say about church buildings.
His usual emphases on simplicity, integrity, and clarity are appli-
cable to all architecture and to church buildings in particular.
Since God by his word ordains common prayer and worship,
there ought to be church buildings in which common worship can
conveniently take place. False uses of or attitudes toward church
buildings must be avoided.

> We . . . must guard against either taking them to be God's proper
> dwelling places, whence he may more nearly incline his ear to us
> —as they began to be regarded some centuries ago—or feigning for
> them some secret holiness or other, which would render prayer
> more sacred before God. For since we ourselves are God's true
> temples, if we would call upon God in his holy temple we must pray
> within ourselves.[30]

Calvin repeatedly condemns the false confidence of those who
point to temples and outward ceremonies when the true temple
of the Holy Spirit is in the human heart and in the church as the
people of God. Church architecture must be appropriate for its
function as the place where the Christian community gathers as
the people of God to hear the word of God, receive the sacraments, confess the faith, and praise the name of God.

When the early Reformed communities first had the opportunity to build churches, they had limited physical resources. This
historical fact in part determined Reformed church architecture,
but it was possible for the Reformed communities to build
churches that were adequate for their needs in the light of their
theological convictions. The first Reformed churches in France
experimented with square, rectangular, octagonal, oval, and el-
liptical designs. All of these designs permitted "the gathering of

the community by the Word of God around the holy table in the joy of the Resurrection."[31] André Biéler has written:

> With the Reformation, piety, while keeping the mystery of Christ intact, changed its significance. Fear was forsaken for joy. The accent was no longer on the cross and on penitence, but on the resurrection and the new life.[32]

> The rediscovery of the freedom of forgiveness and of the final triumph of the Risen One over the depth of death and pain, which had been foreshadowed and heralded by the Pre-Reformation, led people to abandon the cross as the distinctive symbol of Christianity. On steeples, for example, it was replaced by the cock, herald of a new dawn.[33]

Karl Barth has expressed his theological approval of the intention of these early designs.

1. The principle of a "circular place" ("Zentralraumprinzip") seems to me to be right because it shows that church buildings are designed to be places for preaching of the Word of God and for the prayer of the assembled community. I hope that eventually this idea will prevail.
2. What should be placed at the centre? To my mind, a simple wooden *table,* slightly raised, but distinctly different from an "altar". This seems to me to be the ideal solution. This table, fitted with a removable lectern, should serve *at one and the same time* for pulpit, communion table and "baptismal font". (No matter how it is done, the separation of pulpit, communion table and "baptismal font" can serve only to dissipate attention and create confusion; such separation could not be justified theologically.)[34]

Barth has stated his conviction with his usual vigor, and he is authentically Reformed in his prescription for worship. However, as Barth himself continually affirms, there is no one canonical arrangement or order for worship.

The sanctuary at Charenton, near Paris, became a model for Reformed architecture. It was designed by Salomon de Brosse in 1623 to seat 5,000.

> The Temple de Charenton, a simple rectangle, with two tiers of galleries on all four sides, was inspired by the secular basilica of the Roman Empire . . . . There was no confusion of function. The Temple was designed as a place of preaching, but the idea was carried out with simple dignity; stout Doric columns corrected the horizontal lines of the galleries; the ceiling was in the form of a timber barrel-vault; in front of the canopied pulpit was the "par-

quet," the raised platform with its balustrade for Sacraments and Ordinances. It is not surprising that the Temple de Charenton was admired in its day as a logical model for the Reformed Church, and that its precedent was followed, at home and abroad.[35]

The Charenton church has been described as "well lit, majestic and simple."[36] There was no symbolism beyond the arrangement around pulpit and table and the inscribed texts and the Decalogue on the walls.[37]

The New England meeting house also can be described as a classic statement of Reformed theology in architecture. The Puritan churches were simple with geometrically rational designs.[38] They were particularly suited to the preaching and hearing of the word of God. The windows were of clear glass through which Paul Tillich has said the white light of rationality shone.

> The development of light in the churches is very interesting. Slowly the daylight replaced the light that is broken through stained-glass windows. The daylight is not the outburst of Divine light but rational light by which one can read and the congregation can see one another.[39]

A different theology and churchmanship guided the building of the New England churches than that which influenced the Gothic cathedrals with the mystery of their high ceilings as well as their arrangements for worship and piety. Architecture is determined not only by the accidental facts of history but also by theology. The New England churches do not exhaust the possibilities of Christian imagination in architecture, but they do express certain aspects of Reformed theology with a clarity that justifies their designation as classic examples of the embodiment of Reformed faith and churchmanship in architecture.

## *Music*

Zwingli and Calvin alike took music with utmost seriousness. As a consequence, Zwingli eliminated it from the worship of the church, and Calvin provided strict guidelines for its use in worship. Zwingli was himself accomplished in music and was "one of the most enthusiastic proponents of the domestic cultivation of music."[40] Yet Zwingli, the servant of the word, rather than Zwingli, the musician, eliminated music from worship. He was directed by what for him [were] inescapable facts—namely that God has not commanded a musical worship, and that the principle of freedom from liturgy was proclaimed by Christ. Music, choral or instrumental, no matter how religiously inspired, artistically beautiful, or superlatively performed, must be prohibited from worship because Scripture has made its existence impossible.[41]

Calvin, who lacked Zwingli's musical gifts but who, like Zwingli, appreciated music as a gift of God, knew that music had a "secret and almost incredible power" to move the human heart. "When melody goes with it, every bad word penetrates much more deeply into the heart."[42] Calvin advocated, as has been noted, congregational singing under the guidelines that the music and words of songs should be appropriate to worship and that the music should not obscure the words. As a result, Calvin sponsored the publishing of a psalter that turned the Psalms into verse and set them to music.

The Genevan *Psalter* can serve as a pre-eminent illustration of the embodiment of Reformed theology in music. The origins of the *Psalter* are in the Geneva *Articles* of 1537, which expressed the hope that the singing of the psalms would relieve the coldness of heart of the faithful in their public prayers. After his exile from Geneva to Strasbourg, Calvin immediately set about publishing the first Reformed psalter. Writing in 1909 on the four-hundredth anniversary of Calvin's birth, Émile Doumergue has described the great usefulness of the completed Geneva *Psalter* of 1562.

> It was from the Psalter of 1539 that, little by little, the Psalter of 1562 grew. The same year of its publication saw twenty-five editions of it issued. In four years sixty-two editions followed. The bibliographers tell us of fourteen hundred editions, and translations multiplied themselves as marvelously as editions. The Calvinistic Psalter was translated into English, Dutch, Danish, Polish, Bohemian, Rhaeto-Romanic, Ladin, Italian, Spanish, Portuguese, Gascon, Béarnais, Malay, Tamil, Sesouto, Latin, Hebrew, Slavonian, Zend. In less than two centuries there were issued in Holland alone more than thirty editions, and Germany, the land of the admirable choral, jealous of what it calls "the siren of Calvinism", rivalled Holland.[43]

The Psalms are a very appropriate expression of Reformed faith. They give profound expression to the believer's trust in God and confidence in the divine providence. In a time when the Reformed community was threatened by overwhelming political foes and when it appeared matched against the gods of fortune and historical necessity, the singing of the Psalms was a powerful affirmation of the personal governance of the world by the living God.

Calvin's opposition to instrumental music in worship must be understood in the light of his emphasis on knowledge of the words in singing and in the light of the use of organs for nonliturgical purposes in the sixteenth century.[44] Calvin insisted that music should be appropriate to the words and to worship, but the contention that he opposed four-part singing as such or its use in worship has been refuted by Doumergue.[45] Calvin and Zwingli alike were guided in worship by Biblical and theological principles, not by psychological or aesthetic considerations. Calvin, like Zwingli, appreciated music as the gift of God; but Calvin in particular was too occupied with his work to contribute much to music save in its use in the church. Much attention was given, however, by Calvin and his associates to the production of the *Psalter*. When completed, it served to express and to stimulate Reformed faith and life in a remarkable way. For this reason the *Psalter* is an excellent example of the embodiment of Reformed theology in music.

## *Political Order*

The impact of Calvinist theology on political order is well documented in histories of political theory. According to one judgment, "in the history of political thought in the sixteenth century, there was no agent of more importance than was Jean Calvin."[46] There is no question that Calvin's attention was focused upon the political ordering of life, though his overwhelming concern was church polity, not the state. To a considerable extent Calvin's relationship to the state was accidental. In his concern for freedom for the church he was continuously involved in Geneva with town councils that were friendly but jealous of their authority, and beyond Geneva he had to deal with rulers who were opposed to the Reformed church and who were not likely to be converted. Calvin's primary concern was the church, not the ordering of the state; but he also believed that the state was ordained of God to serve the divine purpose. In this sense the state was a primary concern of Calvin. Nevertheless, his most significant influence in political theory grows out of his theology and his churchmanship, not out of any endeavor to work out the problems of political order as such.

Calvin's thought about political order has been subjected to a wide range of interpretations.[47] The center of the debate about his political theory is focused in the question: did Calvinism contribute to the development of political democracy or did it not? The ambiguity rests in part in the semantic differences in the use of the word "democracy," in the difference between the context today in which the question is asked and the situation in the sixteenth century, and in the lack of sharp focus in Calvin's writings, especially concerning questions that were not an issue for him.

In a well-known passage in the *Institutes,* Calvin admits there is no simple answer as to the best form of government, but he commits himself to a government by the aristocracy (that is, government by the best,[48] as Calvin uses the word "aristocracy" in the Aristotelian sense) or government by a combination of aristocracy and democracy. He opposed tyranny and disorder and sought to balance liberty and order.

> If you compare the forms of government among themselves apart from the circumstances, it is not easy to distinguish which one of them excels in usefulness, for they contend on such equal terms. The fall from kingdom to tyranny is easy; but it is not much more difficult to fall from the rule of the best men to the faction of a few; yet it is easiest of all to fall from popular rule to sedition. For if the three forms of government which the philosophers discuss be considered in themselves, I will not deny that aristocracy, or a system compounded of aristocracy and democracy, far excels all others: not indeed of itself, but because it is very rare for kings so to control themselves that their will never disagrees with what is just and right; or for them to have been endowed with such great keenness and prudence, that each knows how much is enough. Therefore, men's fault or failing causes it to be safer and more bearable for a number to exercise government, so that they may help one another, teach and admonish one another; and, if one asserts himself unfairly, there may be a number of censors and masters to restrain his willfulness.[49]

The problem of interpreting Calvin's thought in political matters also arises from the difficulty in correlating the numerous statements in his writings that urge obedience to the state and the statements that insist not only upon the right but the duty of resistance. "The first duty of subjects towards magistrates is to think most honorably of their office."[50] A positive attitude toward the state as an ordinance of God is a part of Christian piety. Obedience to the state is a Christian duty. "The magistrate cannot be resisted without God being resisted at the same time."[51] Furthermore, obedience is required to unjust rulers and to unjust laws. Calvin was no exponent of popular revolution or of what is today called participatory democracy.

There are limits, however, to toleration of the corruption of the magistrate. First of all, the magistrate is accountable to God, who is the ruler of men and nations. "Let the princes hear and be afraid."[52] Furthermore, Calvin allowed orderly opposition to the rulers through the lower magistrates. The lower or minor magistrates are appointed protectors of the people by God's ordinance, and they should lead in resisting the injustice of the ruler. This doctrine of the lower magistrates, which Calvin based on the role of the ephors in the time of the Spartan kings and other ancient examples, was widely used by Calvin's followers in advocating opposition to the rulers.

Calvin is clear that no person should disobey God in order to obey the ruler. The problem is that in this instance he limits disobedience to a narrower range of actions than seems justified by his own exposition of the law of God. When obedience to God is at stake, Calvin is very emphatic on the Christian's duty to resist. In a sermon on Daniel 6, Calvin writes:

> If, as St. Paul says, it be necessary for us to obey princes and our superiors who are established over us and yet see that they burden us in the flesh, that they use tyranny and cruelty against us, yet when they rise up against God, it is necessary that they be put down, and that one consider them no more than a pair of old shoes. Why? For there is the foundation which is quite ruined as to-day. If one regards the fashion of ruling this world, one will find great excess on the part of the princes—that they burden their subjects, that they are transported by ambition and greed so that they no longer know what they are—they are so intoxicated, so bewitched that it seems to them the world was created only for them; they abuse men without any humanity, but in all of that it is necessary for the subjects to humble themselves and that they know that it is for their sins they endure this, that they pray to God to give them patience and to enable them, moreover, to perform their duty. But when princes forbid that God be served and honored, when they command that one pollute himself in idolatry, when they will that one consent to all the abominations which are contrary to the service of God and yield himself to them, oh, they are not worthy to be called princes nor to be given authority.[53]

In a commentary lecture on Daniel 6:22, he writes:

> The fear of God ought to precede, that kings may obtain their authority. For if any one begins his reverence of an earthly prince by rejecting that of God, he will act preposterously, since this is a complete perversion of the order of nature. Then let God be feared in the first place, and earthly princes will obtain their authority, if only God shines forth. . . . For earthly princes lay aside all their power when they rise up against God, and are unworthy of being reckoned in the number of man-kind. We ought rather utterly to defy [*conspuere in ipsorum capita*, lit., "to spit on their heads"] than to obey them whenever they are so restive and wish to spoil God of his rights, and, as it were, to seize upon his throne and draw him down from heaven.[54]

Calvin also insisted upon freedom for the church to determine her own affairs. Most of his ministry in Geneva was concentrated in the struggle for freedom of the church to determine her own worship and discipline, especially admission to the Lord's Table. For this freedom he accepted dismissal from Geneva in 1538, and for it he risked his career and possibly his life during the period from 1541 to 1555. Yet Calvin never gave up the idea of the *Corpus Christianum* (the Christian Society, in which church and state alike work under Christian commitments), and he allowed the magistrate more power in maintaining the discipline and well-being of the church than his own doctrine would admit. Calvin was not entirely clear as to proper functions of church and state, and he was continually under the pressure of a city government jealous for its authority. He could not have imagined a voluntary church in a secular and pluralistic society, and in his perspective he would not have approved of it, as his theological descendants in another historical situation have approved. It is important to note, however, that in his lectures on Amos 7 he expressly disapproved of the church state arrangement in Germany and England, especially under Henry VIII, as giving too much authority to the rulers. In the affairs of the church, as has been indicated, he advocated a government that combined aristocracy (the best) and democracy.[55]

Calvin's greatest contribution to political theory is not to be found in any specific proposals but in his theology. The insistence upon the lordship of God before whom all human beings are equal and the insistence on the sinfulness of all people when translated into political actions were powerful incentives for a political order of checks and balances. In addition, the doctrines of creation and of predestination which rooted human existence in the will of God and dignified the concrete, historical lives of ordinary people with the purposes of God likewise shaped the political order. The real political significance of Reformed theology must be found in the worship and faith commitments of the church.

Calvin's political theory was developed by a number of writers who were influenced by him: Ponet, John Knox, Buchanan, Hotman, Beza, Mornay, Althusius, among others.[56] Most of these writers were set over against their rulers, and they developed what Calvin had said about resistance, some even to the point of tyrannicide. Minority status no doubt contributed to the development of Calvin's radical principle of resistance to rulers rather than the conservative principle of obedience.

John Knox, more impetuous than Calvin, did not hesitate to speak out against rulers in the name of a higher allegiance to God. Knox himself has given us the record of his interviews with Mary, Queen of Scots, but even if his answers were bolder in the writing than in the saying, they nevertheless indicate how Knox thought about the Christian and the political order.

> "What have ye to do," said she, "with my marriage? Or what are ye within this Commonwealth?"
>
> "A subject born within the same," said he, "Madam. And albeit I neither be Earl, Lord, nor Baron within it, yet has God made me (how abject that ever I be in your eyes), a profitable member within the same: Yea, Madam, to me it appertains no less to forewarn of such things as may hurt it, if I foresee them, than it does to any of the Nobility; for both my vocation and conscience crave plainness of me. And therefore, Madam, to yourself I say that which I speak in public place: Whensoever that the Nobility of this Realm shall consent that ye be subject to an unfaithful husband, they do as much as in them lieth to renounce Christ, to banish his truth from them, to betray the freedom of this Realm, and perchance shall in the end do small comfort to yourself."[57]

The Reformed community in the sixteenth and seventeenth centuries, especially its Calvinist branch, did not set out to establish either a democratic society or religious toleration. Yet it can be argued that the Reformed community and even Calvinism as it took shape in English Puritanism contributed significantly to liberal political democracy, to religious liberty, and to the denominational pattern of church life. This contribution is first to be found in its theology.

Puritanism contributed powerful forces to the ultimate development of religious liberty. Profoundly swayed by his belief in the direct guidance of God in his life; stubbornly devoted to that most powerful dissolvent of religious tyranny—the right of private judgment; and jealous of the interference of the secular power in his personal beliefs and worship, and in his purpose to erect a Kingdom of God upon earth, the Puritan remained untouched by the steady erosion of the government policy of comprehensive uniformity which operated so successfully in other sections of English religious life. By successfully maintaining his peculiarity he made necessary, in the end, some compromise which would ensure the right of his position in the religious life of the nation.[58]

The Calvinist emphasis on the lordship of God, on the sinfulness of all men in their best as well as their worst deeds, and on the necessity of justification by grace through faith for all men were doctrines that supported democratic patterns of life. As Reinhold Niebuhr has put it, "Man's capacity for justice makes democracy possible; but man's inclination to injustice makes democracy necessary."[59]

The historical fact of diversity in the Christian community and of the refusal of the various communities to collapse in seventeenth-century England also compelled doctrine and theory to conform to reality in the acceptance of religious liberty and the denominational pattern of church life. Furthermore, in Reformed churches, especially in the Congregational but also in the Presbyterian, churchmen were learning the meaning of democratic and representative government in church affairs. Democratic life in the church preceded democratic life in the state.

Calvin could not have imagined, much less advocated, a voluntary church in a free, pluralistic, and secular society; but basic emphases in his theology contributed both to denominational patterns of church life and religious freedom, however little he envisioned or intended either.[60]

## Economic Order

Karl Marx insisted that a person's economic status and the way he makes his livelihood determine his religious convictions. Over against Marx, the German sociologist Max Weber (1864–1920) concluded that religion shapes economic life and, more particularly, that Reformed theology and ethics have been an important ingredient in the development of capitalism in northern Europe and America. His well-known study *The Protestant*

*Ethic and the Spirit of Capitalism* (1904–1905) has linked Calvinism with capitalism both in popular thought and in learned discussions.[61] Weber did not intend to substitute a one-sided, spiritualistic, causal interpretation for a one-sided, materialistic interpretation. He knew that influences flow both ways, but he did insist that the association between Reformed theology and ethics with capitalism was more than a historical accident. Reformed theology and ethics were an ingredient but certainly not the only one in the development of a capitalistic society.

Weber's thesis has been widely debated.[62] Many have found fault not only with his understanding of the relation of Calvinism to capitalism but also with his understanding of the nature of Calvinism itself. It should be noted that Weber insisted that Calvinism was only one factor in the development of capitalism and that the relation was not inevitable or necessary. In addition, Weber's understanding of Reformed theology does not necessarily depend upon his documentation of it in the writings of Benjamin Franklin and Richard Baxter.

Weber's argument was based upon his understanding that the doctrine of predestination invigorates life, adding to its zest and drive, and that Calvin understood the Christian life in terms of an intramundane (within the world) asceticism with every person's living the disciplined life associated with the monk and the monastery. Calvin also placed great emphasis upon a well-ordered, simple life and upon hard work.[63] His whole theology insisted that life must be lived for the glory of God and is not fulfilled when one's own physical needs have been supplied. Moreover, Calvin was world-affirming, positive in his attitude toward historical developments, and ready to use reason to order life. All of these thrusts of Reformed theology and ethics inevitably influenced and shaped economic life. They supported the "rationalization," "bureaucratization," and "laitization" of society, all important factors in the development of a capitalist society. They do not inevitably issue in capitalism as it has developed, but there is a convincing amount of evidence that Reformed theology and ethics have been an important ingredient in shaping the lives of the persons and communities that have been identified with the development of capitalism.

The issue of the relation of Reformed theology to capitalism is confused by the emotions that capitalism elicits and by the excesses of the system. The influence of the Reformed theology and ethics may also be seen in the simpler development of Presbyterian (Scotch-Irish) cultures in the piedmont areas of the southern United States. The Scotch-Irish who settled the piedmont district of South Carolina were desperately poor, so poor that their poverty was confused with ignorance and immorality by an Episcopal priest from plantation society in the Deep South.[64] They slept on dirt floors in one-room shacks; yet they set about on their own to build churches and schools. They developed a culture with a high sense of personal honesty and of responsibility for every person's taking care of himself and his own. They helped their neighbors, but they did not want charity. Even the aristocracy, when it developed, cherished simplicity and disavowed the pompous, the conspicuous, and the contrived. This plain but remarkable cultural achievement came about in spite of original poverty and in spite of the devastation of the Civil War. The indispensable factor in this achievement was the heritage of the Reformation and of Puritanism.

The achievement of the Presbyterian Scotch-Irish is flawed by blindness concerning the evils of slavery and racial segregation. This blind spot ought not to be allowed to obscure the real achievement. The Scotch-Irish Presbyterians in piedmont Carolina owned very few slaves, but they were caught up in the approval of the system, especially after 1830. Over against the approval of the system, the courageous action of the Presbyterian Covenanters from South Carolina, who migrated to the Mid-West in protest against slavery, should be noted as an example of those who on religious grounds withstood the pressure of the times. The interaction of Reformed theology with slavery in the southern states and with apartheid in South Africa involves many issues that are difficult to unravel.[65] In neither case are the issues as simple as external critics easily affirm. In each instance, however, these cultural involvements of the Reformed community illustrate the insidious way in which economic interests corrupt theology and the ease with which faith becomes an ideology.

## *Learning*

Karl Holl, a distinguished Luther scholar, has written that the religious point of origin gave Protestantism an inevitable concern for culture.

> For it was indeed not an enthusiastic movement expecting its assurance of God through a direct bestowal of the spirit. Instead, by referring the individual to the Bible, a not inconsequential measure of knowledge, of examining something historically given, was included in the religious experience itself. And further, how should one be in a position to exercise the rights of the universal priesthood, i.e., to maintain his independent judgment in the highest ethical and religious questions, if he was not educated for this purpose? Not only was the education of the will necessary for this end, but also a universal education of the intellect.[66]

Consequently, from 1523 Luther promoted schools. Literacy is an optional concern for some forms of piety, but for Protestants it is a virtual necessity.

John Calvin emphasized the importance of learning not merely in order to study the Bible but also in order to study God's created order. The study of the liberal arts was for him an act of Christian obedience. One of the most significant of Calvin's achievements in Geneva was the establishment of the Academy in 1559, an institution which attracted students from all of Europe. Its charter clearly states that the work of the Academy is a Christian concern.

Wherever Reformed communities came into existence, schools were established hard by the churches. The notable declaration of the New England Puritans in the establishment of Harvard is a monument of the tradition.

> After God had carried us safe to New England, and we had builded our houses, provided necessaries for our livelihood, reared convenient places for Gods worship, and settled the civil government, One of the next things we longed for, and looked after was to advance learning and perpetuate it to posterity, dreading to leave an illiterate ministry to the churches when our present ministers shall lie in the dust. And as we were thinking and consulting how to effect this great work, it pleased God to stir up the heart of one Mr. Harvard (a godly gentleman and a lover of learning, there living amongst us). . . .[67]

In the period prior to the Civil War, Presbyterians built forty-nine colleges, Congregationalists twenty-one, German Reformed four, Dutch Reformed one.[68] This record of college-building is all the more notable in the light of the minimal financial resources that were available. Liberal arts colleges to train churchmen and citizens have been a noble and notable embodiment of the Reformed tradition.

Recent studies have indicated the significance of Christian faith, especially the doctrines of God and creation, for the development of modern science.[69] It is also worthy of note that the Reformed tradition has been open to and supportive of scientific development. Calvin feared that preoccupation with things of earth would detract from the Kingdom of God, but he appreciated the work of astronomers and students of the natural order.[70] Puritans were prominent among the founders of the influential Royal Society in seventeenth-century London.[71] It is a historical fact that the scientific revolution occurred in western culture which had been shaped chiefly by the Christian tradition and the legacy from classical thought. Highly committed members of the Reformed tradition, Calvinists and Puritans alike, participated in the scientific achievements of the seventeenth and eighteenth centuries; and they did so in fulfillment of their Christian vocation. Reformed theology discouraged excessive curiosity and speculation, but on the pragmatic level it has consistently sponsored and encouraged learning.

* * * *

The great Reformed theologians and churchmen did not originally set out to enrich culture. Their work was the interpretation and application of the word of God and leadership in the life of the church. Yet in performing these functions with integrity and competence, they mightily shaped culture. The particular cultural expressions of Reformed faith and practice listed in this chapter are illustrations of a pervasive influence that also included home and family life, community life, and forms of personal piety. Karl Marx rightly emphasized the role of "interests," particularly economic interests, in shaping culture as well as theology. Yet as Weber, Troeltsch, and Holl argued at the beginning of this century religion, and, in particular, Protestantism, also shaped culture. Indeed, many of the most precious qualities of social, political, and cultural life in the United States are inconceivable apart from the heritage of the Protestant Reformation and of the Reformed tradition, including, in particular, English Puritanism.

# VIII

## PROSPECTS

In 1933 Alfred North Whitehead wrote that until then it had been assumed that "each generation will substantially live amid the conditions governing the lives of its fathers" and that the traditions of the fathers would be passed on. "We are living," he concluded, "in the first period of human history for which the assumption is false."[1] This judgment has been substantiated and is even more descriptive of the situation now than when it was first written. The velocity of change has accelerated so greatly that individual persons and society are threatened with disorientation.[2] Furthermore, the character of the change raises additional questions for the Christian community. Society is increasingly secular, and there is a growing disparity between Christian experience and human experience in a secular society.[3] Therefore, any study of the history of the Christian tradition and of the Reformed tradition in particular must conclude by asking about the future.

Every age is tempted to exaggerate its uniqueness. This is no doubt true of the present age. Certainly the church has lived through the death and birth of cultures. Karl Barth has warned that the great problem of the church is heresy, the corruption of its message, not paganism and doubt.[4] Actually Barth has insisted that Christian faith may have been more difficult for enlightenment man than for contemporary man.[5] In any case the persistence of religion and the rise of unusual forms of religion, especially in the counter culture, are evidence that modern people are not as modern or secular as the pronouncements of the 1950s or 1960s indicated.[6] In addition, students of society find evidence that secularism is reversible.[7] Nevertheless, when the exaggerated notions of modernity have been dispelled, it remains quite clear the changes are sufficient to challenge any tradition and to make it wise to look at specific problems.

## *The Freedom of God*

Any discussion of the future of the Reformed tradition ought to begin with the freedom of God, for the tradition itself has made this doctrine a cardinal affirmation of its faith. God is not bound to any tradition, and God does not guarantee the future of any who justify themselves by an appeal to their heritage. John the Baptist once expressed this truth with penetrating clarity to a people with a great tradition. " 'Do not presume to say to yourselves, "We have Abraham as our father"; for I tell you, God is able from these stones to raise up children to Abraham.' " (Matthew 3:9) From the perspective of the Reformed tradition the proper stance toward the future is not a Promethean effort to guarantee it but trust in God and loyalty to his cause in all the earth. The future is in God's hands, not in man's.

On the historical level no one can guarantee the future, at least the long-run future. Too many ingredients go into the shaping of the future for human efforts to control it. There is the givenness of physical and historic environments that have defied the best-laid plans of human beings and their organizations. There is also the biochemical and genetical make-up of human beings, as well as the mystery of human freedom. The control of the future is beyond the power of human beings partly because of the complexity of the human situation that defies mastery and partly because of an element of unpredictability in nature and the mystery of human freedom.

A church historian once observed that no decree of a council ever destroyed a powerful heresy,[8] and it may be asserted that no true doctrine was ever established by a council. The future of a tradition likewise cannot be programmed, guaranteed, or scheduled by human wisdom or work. The best of plans for the future are flawed by human sin and ignorance. The best techniques and skills of psychology and group dynamics, like mechanical respirators maintaining biological life, can sustain the appearance of spiritual life only for a brief time. Vital traditions grow out of the interaction of the Holy Spirit and the human spirit in the life of the Christian community. The future is first of all God's gift, and it is the object of prayer and hope. The freedom of God is a warning against the arrogance of the conservative and of the liberal, indeed against all human arrogance.

The freedom of God is not an excuse for human indolence. Every faithful act of religious devotion and responsible commitment is important in the ongoing of history. The freedom of God, however, warns against too high an opinion of human plans and intentions for the future. It may be that God in his freedom will establish his people where there have been little claiming of his promises, little prayer, and little obedience. Those outside the camp (Hebrews 13:12–13) may fare better than those who have been unfaithful to a great tradition. No one can presume on the election of God. Human hopes and plans for the future must be offered to God with great humility and with prayer. Yet it is the faith of the Reformed community, confirmed in experience, that hitherto the Lord has helped his people. Here they raise their Ebenezer (1 Samuel 7:12). Their hope in the face of an uncertain future is in the God of Abraham, Isaac, and Jacob; of Peter, John, and Paul; of Augustine, Calvin, Jeanne d'Albret and John Wither-spoon; in the God of the tradition that has been bequeathed from the past. The ancient wisdom "Let us now praise famous men, and our fathers in their generations" (Ecclesiasticus 44:1) is an appropriate Reformed practice, but it is not canonical Scripture. It must be balanced by the freedom of God, which is attested in Scripture and which is able "from these stones to raise up children to Abraham." (Matthew 3:9)

## The Reality of the Power and Presence of God

The vitality and drive of the Reformed tradition has been rooted in a vivid awareness of God's presence as power, energy, intentionality. One of the characteristics of contemporary life has been the eclipse of the divine presence. The radical change that has occurred in culture and in the church can be documented by a comparison of the sermons preached before Parliament by members of the Westminster Assembly (1643–1647) and sermons preached in American churches during the Vietnam War. The Puritans related the course of the Civil War, military victory or defeat in particular, to the purposive action of God in human history. It is not likely that many American sermons directly related the course of events in Vietnam to the purposive action of God. Contemporary people are even more reluctant to affirm the purposive action of God in nature. Many live their lives with no conscious reference to God. The consequence is a culture opaque to the divine presence.

The revival of religion even in strange forms is a sufficient reminder that the advocates of a religionless Christianity and of a human maturity that has no need for God were overconfident about the secularity of the modern person. The advocates of a death-of-God theology were also unaware of a mystery that encompasses existence and that has made its presence felt in many ways among the most modern of people even on university campuses.[9] Yet it is not easy for modern people to experience the purposive action of God in nature and in history or to conceptualize what is meant by an act of God. Hence for some sophisticated theologians religion has become a dialogue of God and the soul with scant attention to either nature or history. The Reformed community can be satisfied with this reduction of Christian faith only at the peril of losing its character. In fact, the Reformed tradition cannot be conceived apart from this vivid awareness of God and of his purposive action in nature and in history.

One of the most important theological tasks today for the Christian community as a whole and for the Reformed community in particular is a conceptualization of an "act of God" in such a way as to do justice to the tradition and to the facts of contemporary experience. The conceptual tools that were adequate for Calvin in the sixteenth century are not adequate for people whose culture has been shaped by the scientific revolution and achievements of the past four centuries. Theological work can clarify faith and contribute to the strengthening of faith. Apart from this theological work, no sustained revival of faith is likely.

The presence of God, however, is no human achievement. It is always God's gift. Even on the human level the experience of anything in nature or history as the purposive action of God and the vivid awareness of his presence are dependent more on the piety, devotion, and worship of the community in which the believer participates than on theological work, as indispensable as the latter may be. While there are works of learning and piety that make it more likely that people today shall experience the presence and power of God, this presence is finally a mystery and a gracious gift.

## The Bible as the Word of God

Next to a vivid awareness of God as energy, will, and intention, the Reformed community has been shaped by an awareness of the Bible as the word of God and as the norm of Christian faith and life. This awareness has likewise been susceptible to erosion by the temptations of a secular society. The application of the methods of historical-critical study has illuminated the meaning of the Christian Scriptures and has been a means of deepening faith, but at the same time it has enhanced the possibility that the Bible can be regarded as just another book which grew out of a particular human situation. Even within the Christian community where the Bible is taken seriously, there is a disjuncture between the use of the Bible in devotions and the use of it in study, and sometimes the substitution of the latter for the former.[10] Yet the Christian life in the contemporary world depends upon the integration of the study of the Bible and the devotional use of the Bible: the Bible as a historical achievement and the Bible as the word of God.

The problem of the Bible that has now become acute was resolved by John Calvin through his doctrine of the indissoluble union between word and Spirit.[11] The conviction that the Bible is the word of God does not grow out of the authority of the church or out of any of the humanly discernible qualities that may be found in its pages. No achievement of scholarship can establish that the Bible is anything more than another human book with all the relativities of human frailty, time, and space. The experience of the Bible as the word of God depends finally upon the "witness of the Holy Spirit."[12] Here again it is apparent that a revival of the Reformed tradition cannot be programmed or commanded. It depends upon a gift of grace and upon that mysterious interaction of the spirit of God and the human spirit in the reading of the Scripture.

The serious study of the Bible with the use of the best intellectual equipment available must be carried on, for God has commanded his people to love him with their minds. Moreover, this, too, is a clear and indispensable part of the Reformed tradition. Yet the recovery of the experience of the Bible as the word of God is a gift of God's Spirit and is ordinarily related on the human level to participation in a community of worship, of prayer, and of obedience.

### The Emphasis on the Word: Spoken and Written

The Reformed tradition has been a very verbal religion with great confidence in spoken and written words to communicate thought, emotion, and intention. Critics of contemporary culture have warned of the declining power of words and have emphasized the effectiveness of new forms of communication in television, in the arts, and in personal relationships.[13] If these critics are correct in their assessment, the Reformed tradition is bereft of a traditional power.

There is not yet convincing evidence that words, either written or spoken, have lost their power. Language still ranks as one of the highest and most significant human achievements. It may be supplemented, but it cannot be supplanted without impoverishing the human spirit.[14] Unfortunately prophecies such as the prediction of the demise of spoken and written words are self-fulfilling. There are indications that increasing numbers of persons who could have achieved real competence in speaking, writing, and reading have failed to do so. This does constitute a problem and a challenge to Protestant and Reformed Christian communities.

Thus far in Christian history, spoken and written words have been indispensable in the communication of the faith. Christian communities that have minimized the importance of preaching and reading have produced a different form of piety and different styles of life.[15] Value judgments as to which is the higher form of Christian piety are self-serving and inconclusive. There is no one pattern of Christian piety. However, it is clear that the Reformed tradition with its emphasis on words has produced a Christian pattern of life that has expressed Christian faith in ways which have liberated the highest powers of human personality: reason in the service of God, the capacity to think and act for oneself, the critical discernment to distinguish reality from fantasy, the capacity for self-transcendence and self-criticism. Christians who minimize words in the conceptualization and communication of the faith and in the worship of the church must also choose the consequences for piety.

The focus of the Reformed emphasis on the word is preaching. Critics of preaching have announced its declining importance.[16] The predictions have not come true, but in this area also, predictions of the demise encourage the decline of preaching skills. This has been a great loss, for it is a significant fact that millions of Americans each week leave their work, their rest, their recreation, to worship God and to hear a sermon, not infrequently a poor sermon. This is a phenomenon without parallel in our society. It can be duplicated neither by sports, entertainment, politics, nor business. On the strictly human level, it is an opportunity in the struggle for the loyalties of people that other missionary groups would give anything to have. The only possible rival to preaching is television that does not require a communal gathering. The Christian community forfeits its own greatest opportunity when it minimizes the significance of preaching.

The effectiveness of preaching is difficult to measure. Yet it is a documentable fact that over a period of years the quality of preaching determines in significant measure the quality of a local congregation's life.[17]

Preaching is a unique act, *sui generis*. It ought not to be identified with a lecture, a discussion, or a meditation. In preaching, an ordinary human being, called, trained, and certified by the church, stands over against the people of God in the name of God and proclaims the word of God. The critic may reject preaching as fantasy or presumption, but its uniqueness cannot be denied. It makes sense only in the context of the church's faith and worship. It is responsible only when done under the strictest standards of competence to interpret the word of God, of personal integrity, and of faith commitment. It is easily corrupted by lack of intellectual and personal integrity.

The strength of the Reformed tradition has inhered in no small measure in its skill in the use of words. This emphasis has appealed to the unique human capacities for reason, for language, for self-transcendence. The need to supplement this emphasis can never justify acquiescence in the decline of skills in the use of language. There is adequate evidence of unrivaled opportunity that preaching provides both in the life of the church and in culture and of the power of words to shape human life.

## *The Vision of the Christian Community*

The association of the Reformed tradition with a vision of the holy community has been clearly indicated in this survey. There have been exceptions as in the case of *Pilgrim's Progress* following the failure of the Puritan commonwealth in the 1640s and 1650s and as in the case of some communities under the domination of totalitarian states in the twentieth century.[18] Historical developments now make this vision in its older form obsolete. The emergence of a secular and pluralistic society, the greater awareness of the historical relativity of all human achievement and of the persistence of sin in the life of the redeemed, undercut both the possibility and desirability of such a community. A religiously homogeneous society is less and less a likely possibility, at least in societies where the Reformed faith has been traditionally strong.[19] The damage that has been done by religious coercion in the past and by political coercion in the twentieth century is sufficient warning against the achievement of religious purposes at the expense of the human conscience and freedom. It is to be hoped that any future pattern of society will do justice to the needs of human freedom and of human conscience even though this hope is far from a certainty of fulfillment, as restrictions on freedom in the new nations as well as the old nations indicate. The heritage of freedom of religion and of speech in the United States is a most precious possession that has been rarely if ever duplicated elsewhere in history.

The basic incompatibility between the Reformed tradition and any understanding of the Christian life in terms of personal piety alone and of the Christian community in isolation from the larger community makes it imperative that the vision of the holy community and the Christian commonwealth be recovered in a way that is appropriate to the new situation. It is still possible that a Reformed community that lives with integrity in the larger community will shape the larger community without compromising its own integrity and without doing an injustice to the freedom and the conscience of all people. In its best moments the Reformed community has been willing to depend upon the power of the preached word and the testimony of the Christian community's life to create a godly public opinion and to shape the future. The opportunity for this witness is open in a free and pluralistic society. It is not too much to hope that in a free and pluralistic society the holy community may continue as a vision and in some measure exist as a fact.

## The Possibility of Discipline

A life rationally ordered by moral and theological commitments has been a mark of the Reformed tradition from the beginning. The doctrine of delayed satisfaction provided the rationale for denying momentary desires for the sake of the fulfillment of greater and more important long-range goals. The Protestant doctrine of the priesthood of all believers encouraged the development of the capacity to think for oneself and to act for oneself. The image of the Christian as one who lived life in obedience before God and who assumed responsibility for oneself before God long motivated the Reformed Christian.

Many factors in contemporary culture conspire to undercut personal responsibility and personal discipline. A new naturalism has emphasized spontaneity partly in reaction to overly rationalized and disciplined lives that quenched all spontaneity and naturalness.[20] Preoccupation with the self and with self-consciousness, with human potential and human actualization, has undercut a life disciplined by anything more than its own fulfillment. Techniques of group dynamics make it much easier to manipulate people today than previously, and communities have new ways of destroying privacy and individuality. The pervasiveness of mass media in society makes possible mass-produced personalities in ways that were formerly impossible.

The possibility of the kind of personal discipline that has led in the past to great achievement in science, in industry, in the church, as well as in personal life, is now very much a matter of personal choice. The pressures and sanctions that supported this discipline in the past have fallen away, especially during the economic affluence and relative peace that have characterized the period between the Second World War and the end of the Vietnam War. It may be that a changed cultural and political situation may once again make discipline a desired virtue. In any case, for the present discipline is a matter of freedom, and without it the Reformed way of being a Christian is not possible.

## The Simple Life

Simplicity has been a hallmark of the Reformed life-style. It received notable emphasis in the writings and life of John Calvin. It has been a major concern of writings on polity and ecclesiology which protested pomp and ostentation in the affairs of the church. It was a characteristic of the Scotch Irish settlers in America who made plainness and authenticity distinctive marks of their life-style. Opposition to the pretentious, the artificial, the contrived, the pompous has been pervasive of the manner of life of the Reformed.

Contemporary life with its affluence in areas where the Reformed tradition has thrived and with its techniques for creating artificial desires and pretentious life-styles constitutes a threat to this traditional emphasis. Yet the ethical problems of contemporary life created by hunger, poverty, and the diminishing supply of natural resources call for restraint in personal desires and moderation in expectations for the self. Learning to live simply is an imperative of the culture as well as the Reformed tradition. Yet it is no easy achievement for either the rich or the poor.

Simplicity of life is integrally related to integrity of life. Jesus said, "Let what you say be simply 'Yes' or 'No'; anything more than this comes from evil." (Matthew 5:37) What is true of language is true of the whole range of human existence. The Christian's manner of living avoids the contrivances and the pretenses that cover the real, and cleaves to the authenticity, the plainness, and the honesty that reveal the real. The pretentious, the pompous not only waste energy in a world in which energy is in limited supply; they also obscure reality. In the world of the affluent, and in a world in which the techniques for the cultivation of the artificial are so advanced, the achievement of a simple manner of life and churchmanship will not be easy. Yet it is possible.

\* \* \* \* \*

The cross of Jesus Christ is sufficient evidence that Christian faith and devotion do not guarantee success in history. Augustine wrote his *City of God* to declare that human security is to be found in no human enterprise but in the City of God which can be identified with neither church nor state. The Reformed tradition has placed its confidence in the sovereignty of the Creator of heaven and earth. The future does not depend upon the Reformed tradition.

Yet it has also been an article of faith that God is working his purposes out in history and that what happens in history is important for eternity that fulfills as well as judges history. Within this context it is proper and necessary to be concerned about the future of the tradition. The questionableness of the Reformed tradition's future is identical with the questionableness of the Christian community's future. The great question for all Christians is the disparity between the Christian faith as it has been "believed, taught, and confessed" and life as it is experienced today. This is the crucial issue now as it has been the crucial issue in other times of great social change. In this survey six particular characteristics or emphases of the Reformed tradition's way of being the Christian community have been singled out as points of especial tension or erosion. These points of tension are not wholly attributable to flaws in the tradition. In part, they indicate the need for adjustment, for creativity. In part, they represent the strength of the tradition over against weaknesses of the culture. In each case, however, imagination is required for the authentic living out or representation of the tradition in a new cultural situation.

The crisis of faith in the present time cannot be answered by a servile repetition of the faith and practice of the past. The best service that can be rendered the universal church and the Reformed community is to bring to the task today the same intellectual labor, the same moral integrity, and the same vision and imagination that have served the tradition in the past. Constructive solutions are more likely to come from an assimilation of the past in the present task than from a rejection or a sterile repetition of its wisdom. Many problems are susceptible to human wisdom and planning, to theological work, and to the skill of churchmanship. On the historical, human level the future of the Reformed tradition, indeed the Christian tradition, is wholly a human work and depends upon human fidelity and zeal. Yet, finally, the health of the tradition depends upon the conversion of believers and the power of the Holy Spirit in the life of the church. This conversion and power are gifts of the Holy Spirit for which we must pray.

The future can be faced without fanaticism, without ingratitude, and without presumption. Fanaticism takes the future into its own hands because it despairs of God. Ingratitude discards the wisdom of the tradition because it cannot be simply repeated. Presumption forfeits personal responsibility because it forgets that God elects to service and to the fulfillment of his purposes. Faith serves God and trusts God for the future.

The Scots Confession of 1560 concludes with a prayer that is strange in content and idiom to Protestant communities in the last quarter of the twentieth century. The idiom has changed, but the substance of the prayer is integral to the Reformed vision and is an appropriate conclusion for this introduction to the Reformed tradition.

Arise, O Lord, and let Thine enemies be confounded; let them flee from Thy presence that hate Thy godly name. Give Thy servants strength to speak Thy word with boldness, and let all nations cleave to the true knowledge of Thee. Amen.

# Notes

## I. TRADITIONING THE FAITH

1. Philip Schaff, *The Creeds of Christendom, with a History and Critical Notes*, 3 vols., 6th ed. (Grand Rapids: Baker House, 1969), copyright 1877 by Harper & Brothers, copyright 1905, 1919 David S. Schaff. Reprinted by arrangement with Harper & Row, 1: 28.

2. Albert C. Outler, *The Christian Tradition and the Unity We Seek* (New York: Oxford University Press, 1957), p. 110. Used by permission.

3. Emil Brunner, *The Misunderstanding of the Church,* trans. Harold Knight (Philadelphia: Westminster Press, 1953), p. 35.

4. Norman Pittenger, *The Word Incarnate: A Study of the Doctrine of the Person of Christ* (New York: Harper & Row, 1959), pp. 57–58.

5. Émile Bréhier, *The History of Philosophy: Vol. I: The Hellenic Age,* trans. Joseph Thomas (Chicago: University of Chicago Press, 1963), ©1963 by The University of Chicago, 1:32.

6. Outler, *The Christian Tradition,* p. 111.

7. Karl Barth, *Church Dogmatics,* 4 vols (Edinburgh: T.&T. Clark, 1936–69), 1,2:609. Used by permission.

8. *Ibid.,* 613.

9. Quoted by Jacques de Senarclens in "Karl Barth and the Reformed Tradition," *Reformed World,* 30, 206 from interview in *Réalité* (February 1963), p. 25.

10. Quoted by Roland H. Bainton in *Women of the Reformation: In France and England* (Minneapolis: Augsburg Publishing House, 1973), p. 61.

11. See Martin Luther's "Treatise on Good Works," "To the Christian Nobility of the German Nation," "The Babylonian Captivity of the Church," "The Freedom of a Christian."

12. Charles N. Cochrane, *Christianity and Classical Culture: A Study of Thought and Action from Augustus to Augustine* (New York: Oxford University Press, 1957), pp. 235 ff., 402, 456 ff.

13. Cf. Martin E. Marty, *Second Chance for American Protestants* (New York: Harper & Row, 1963), pp. 13–54.

14. Franklin Le Van Baumer, *Religion and the Rise of Scepticism* (New York: Harcourt, Brace & World, Inc., 1960).

15. Cf. Winthrop S. Hudson, "Denominationalism as a Basis for Ecumenicity: A Seventeenth Century Conception," *Church History* (March 1955), pp. 32–50.

16. W. K. Jordan, *The Development of Religious Toleration in England* (Cambridge: Harvard University Press, 1932–40).

Roland Bainton, *The Travail of Religious Liberty: Nine Biographical Studies* (Philadelphia: Westminster Press, 1951).

17. H. Richard Niebuhr, *The Meaning of Revelation* (New York: The Macmillan Company, 1946), pp. 43 ff. Copyright, 1941, by the Macmillan Company. Used with permission.

18. From A HISTORY OF ISRAEL, by John Bright. © MCMLIX, W.L. Jenkins. © MCMLXXII, The Westminster Press. Used by permission. P. 146.

19. H. Richard Niebuhr, *The Meaning of Revelation*, pp. 115–116.

20. "The search in common memory for the great principles which lie back of accustomed ways and of which these are perversions as well as illustrations can be a very radical and pregnant thing." H. Richard Niebuhr, *The Meaning of Revelation*, pp. 5–6. Cf. Michael Hill, *The Religious Order* (New York: Crane, Russak & Co., Inc., 1973), pp. 85 ff. Advocates of theological change in the Presbyterian Church not infrequently appealed to Calvin. Advocates of liturgical change also appealed to tradition. Tradition does not necessarily support any change, but its utility in assuming an open future against the tyranny of the moment has been amply demonstrated.

21. 1955 is a convenient date to mark the end of dominant influence of theologies associated with Karl Barth and the emergence of many new theological interests.

22. Schubert Ogden in a lecture at Union Theological Seminary in Virginia.

## II. THE REFORMED CHURCHES

1. Schaff, *Creeds of Christendom*, The Scotch Confession of 1560, Article 5, 3: 442–443.

2. *Ibid.*, 1: 358 (note).

3. R. Newton Flew and Rupert E. Davies, eds., *The Catholicity of Protestantism* (London: Lutterworth Press, 1950), pp. 13–14.

4. Roland H. Bainton, *Here I Stand: A Life of Martin Luther* (New York: Abingdon-Cokesbury Press, 1950).

5. E. G. Rupp, "The Reformation in Zürich, Strassburg, & Geneva" in *The Reformation*, vol. 2 of *The New Cambridge Modern History*, G. R. Elton, ed. (Cambridge: The University Press, 1958), pp. 96–119.

James Isaac Good, *History of the Swiss Reformed Church since the Reformation* (Philadelphia: Publication and Sunday School Board of the Reformed Church in the United States, 1913).

6. Cf. John T. McNeill, *The History and the Character of Calvinism* (New York: Oxford University Press, 1954), pp. 3 ff.

Oskar Farner, *Zwingli the Reformer: His Life and Work*, trans. D. G. Sear (New York: Philosophical Library, 1952).

Jacques Courvoisier, *Zwingli, a Reformed Theologian* (Richmond: John Knox Press, 1963).

7. G. W. Bromiley, ed., *Zwingli and Bullinger*, Vol. XXIV of The Library of Christian Classics (Philadelphia: Westminster Press, 1953), pp. 90–91.

8. For discussion of the name "Reformed," see Heinrich Heppe, *Ursprung und Geschichte der Bezeichnungen "reformirte" und "lutherische" Kirche* (Gotha: Verlag von Friedrich Andreas Perthes, 1859); Schaff, *The Creeds of Christendom*, 1:358–359 (note); M. Eugene Osterhaven, *The Spirit of the Reformed Tradition* (Grand Rapids: Eerdmans Publishing Co., 1971), Appendix: "The Name 'Reformed,'" pp. 171–178.

9. For text of "A Most Christian Letter" by Cornelisz Hoen which Rode introduced to the Swiss theologians see Heiko Augustinus Obermann: *Forerunners of the Reformation, the Shape of Late Medieval Thought* (London: Lutterworth Press, 1967), 268–276.

10. Williston Walker, *John Calvin, the Organiser of Reformed Protestantism (1509–1564)* (New York: G. P. Putnam's Sons, 1906) is old but still an admirable biography, especially the Schocken Books edition with bibliographical essay by John T. McNeill. Other useful biographies: Jean Cadier, *The Man God Mastered, a Brief Biography of John Calvin*, trans. O. R. Johnston (Grand Rapids: Eerdmans

Publishing Co., 1960); T. H. L. Parker, *Portrait of Calvin* (Philadelphia: Westminster Press, 1955); François Wendel, *Calvin: The Origins and Development of His Religious Thought,* trans. Philip Mairet (New York: Harper & Row, 1963).

11. Cf. McNeill, *The History and Character of Calvinism,* pp. 237 ff. for discussion of French Reformed community.

Also, Émile G. Léonard, *A History of Protestantism,* trans. from the French by Joyce M. H. Reid, 2 vols. (London: Nelson, 1965). See especially Vol. 2.

12. Maurice G. Hansen, *The Reformed Church in the Netherlands, Traced from A. D. 1340 to A. D. 1840 in Short Historical Sketches* (New York: Board of Publications of Reformed Church in America, 1884).

Douglas Nobbs, *Theocracy and Toleration: A Study of the Disputes in Dutch Calvinism from 1600 to 1650* (Cambridge, England: The University Press, 1938).

13. McNeill, *The History and Character of Calvinism,* p. 260.

14. See page 114.

15. The moderate statement of Dort must be evaluated in the light of the vigorous statement of a doctrine of limited atonement as in *The Doctrine of Absolute Predestination:*

"As God doth not will that each individual of mankind should be saved, so neither did He will that Christ should properly and immediately die for each individual of mankind, whence it follows that, though the blood of Christ, from its own intrinsic dignity, was sufficient for the redemption of all men, yet, in consequence of His Father's appointment, He shed it intentionally, and therefore effectually and immediately, for the elect only."

Girolamo Zanchi, *The Doctrine of Absolute Predestination Stated and Asserted: With a Preliminary Discourse on the Divine Attributes,* (London: Grace Union, 1930), p. 53.

16. Peter Y. DeYoung, *Crisis in the Reformed Churches: Essays in Commemoration of the Great Synod of Dort, 1618–1619* (Grand Rapids: Reformed Fellowships, 1968).

Nobbs, *Theocracy and Toleration.*

Carl Bangs, *Arminius, A Study in the Dutch Reformation* (Nashville: Abingdon Press, 1971).

17. James I. Good, *The Origin of the Reformed Church in Germany* (Reading: D. Miller, 1887).

18. Imre Revesz, *History of the Hungarian Reformed Church,* trans. George A. F. Knight (Washington: The Hungarian Reformed Federation of America, 1956).

Good summaries of the origin of Reformed churches in Poland and Bohemia may be found in Harold J. Grimm, *The Reformation Era, 1500–1650* (New York: The Macmillan Co., 1954) and in such older histories of Presbyterianism as R. C. Reed, *History of the Presbyterian Churches of the World* (Philadelphia: The Westminster Press, 1905). Also, McNeill, *The History and Character of Calvinism.*

19. J. H. S. Burleigh, *A Church History of Scotland* (London: Oxford University Press, 1960) is the best general history.

Gordon Donaldson, *The Scottish Reformation* (Cambridge, England: Cambridge University Press, 1960) is based on extensive research, but Donaldson writes as a strong advocate of episcopacy. Cf. review by Professor Alec Cheyne of the University of Edinburgh, *Scottish Journal of Theology,* vol. 16, no. 1 (March 1963), pp. 78–88.

20. Cf. James Hastings Nichols, *Corporate Worship in the Reformed Tradition* (Philadelphia: The Westminster Press, 1968), pp. 60–67; Bard Thompson, *Liturgies of the Western Church* (New York: The World Publishing Co., 1962), p. 229.

21. Schaff, *Creeds of Christendom,* 1: 620–621 3: 486–516.

22. John M. Barkley, *A Short History of the Presbyterian Church in Ireland* (Belfast: Publications Board, Presbyterian Church in Ireland, 1959).

23. James G. Leyburn, *The Scotch-Irish: A Social History* (Chapel Hill: The University of North Carolina Press, 1962), pp. 157 ff. As to the number of immigrants, Professor Leyburn concludes:

"Using the lowest figure suggested (6.7 per cent), this would give a Scotch-Irish total of 212,554. Using the figure of 14.3 per cent, the total would be 453,655. Using the highest figure suggested (16.6 per cent), the total would be 528,731. It would be safe to say only that considerably more than a quarter of a million Americans in 1790 had Scotch-Irish ancestry. Certainly this element, next to the English, was the largest nationality group in the country, with the Germans next. (The Census Bureau's 1909 figure for German names in 1790 was 5.6 per cent; the Council of Learned Societies' figure for them was 8.7 per cent.)" (P. 183)

24. Louis B. Wright, *Religion and Empire: The Alliance between Piety and Commerce in English Expansion, 1558–1625* (Chapel Hill: The University of North Carolina Press, 1943), p. 45.

25. *Ibid.*, p. 53.

26. *Ibid.*, p. 165.

27. Sydney E. Ahlstrom, *A Religious History of the American People* (New Haven: Yale University Press, 1972), p. 124.

28. *Ibid.*, p. 1079.

29. Ralph Barton Perry, *Puritanism and Democracy* (New York: The Vanguard Press, 1944), p. 81.

30. Ahlstrom, *op. cit.*, p. 1079.

31. R. Pierce Beaver, "The Geneva Mission to Brazil" in John H. Bratt, ed., *The Heritage of John Calvin* (Grand Rapids: Eerdmans, 1973), pp. 55 ff.

32. David Duncan Wallace, *The History of South Carolina* (New York: The American Historical Society, Inc., 1934), pp. 35 ff.

33. Williston Walker, *A History of the Congregational Churches in the United States* (New York: The Christian Literature Co., 1894).

34. Robert G. Torbet, *A History of the Baptists* (Philadelphia: The Judson Press, 1950), pp. 272 ff., 441 ff. Cf. Kenneth H. Good *Are Baptists Calvinist?* (Oberlin, Ohio: Regular Baptist Heritage Fellowship, 1975).

35. Herman Harmelink III, *Ecumenism and the Reformed Church* (Grand Rapids: Eerdmans, 1968).

D. H. Kromminga, *The Christian Reformed Tradition* (Grand Rapids: Eerdmans, 1943).

Howard G. Hageman, *Our Reformed Church* (New York: Board of Christian Education, 1963).

Willard Dayton Brown, *A History of the Reformed Church in America* (New York: Board of Publication and Bible School Work, 1928).

Gerald F. DeJong, *The Dutch in America, 1609–1974* (Boston: Twayne Publishers, 1975), especially pages 194–206.

36. Leonard J. Trinterud, *The Forming of an American Tradition: A Re-examination of Colonial Presbyterianism* (Philadelphia: Westminster Press, 1949) is the best account of early Presbyterianism in the United States. Leyburn, *The Scotch-Irish: A Social History.*

Duane Meyer, *The Highland Scots of North Carolina 1732–1776* (Chapel Hill: University of North Carolina Press, 1961).

37. Ian Charles Cargill Graham, *Colonists from Scotland: Emigration to North America, 1707–1783* (New York: Cornell University Press for the American Historical Association, 1956), pp. 188–189.

38. Trinterud, *op. cit.*, p. 22.

39. James I. Good, *History of the Reformed Church in the United States, 1725–1792* (Reading: Daniel Miller, 1899).

James I. Good, *History of the Reformed Church in the U.S. in the Nineteenth Century* (New York: The Board of Publication of the Reformed Church in America, 1911).

David Dunn *et al.*, *A History of the Evangelical and Reformed Church* (Philadelphia: The Christian Education Press, 1961).

40. John S. Moir, *Enduring Witness, a History of the Presbyterian Church in Canada* (Printed and bound in Canada by the Bryant Press Limited, n.d.).

41. John W. de Gruchy, "Afrikaans and English Speaking Churches: Some Reflections," *Reformed World*, vol. 33, no. 1 (March 1974), pp. 17–23.

42. Gustav Warneck, *Outline of a History of Protestant Missions from the Reformation to the Present Time*, 3rd English edition, being authorized translation from the 8th German edition, George Robson, ed. (New York: Fleming Revell, 1906).

43. John Calvin, *Commentaries on the Epistles to Timothy, Titus, & Philemon*, trans. Rev. William Pringle (Grand Rapids: Eerdmans, 1948), 1 Tim. 2: 4, pp. 54–55.

44. Beaver, "The Geneva Mission to Brazil."

45. *Ibid.*, p. 64.

46. Robert M. Kingdon, *Geneva and the Coming Wars of Religion in France, 1555–1563* (Geneva: E. Droz, 1956).

47. *Ibid.*, p. 129.

48. Kenneth Scott Latourette, *A History of the Expansion of Christianity*, 7 vols. (New York: Harper & Brothers, 1939), 3: 50–51.

49. D. T. Niles, *Buddhism and the Claims of Christ* (Richmond: John Knox Press, 1967).

Kazōh Kitamori, *Theology of the Pain of God* (Richmond: John Knox Press, 1965).

50. Jules Bonnet, ed., *Letters of John Calvin* (Philadelphia: Presbyterian Board of Publication, 1858) 2:348 (Letters to Cranmer, April 1552).

51. From CALVIN: INSTITUTES OF THE CHRISTIAN RELIGION, Volume XX, XXI, LCC. Edited by John T. McNeill and translated by Ford Lewis Battles. Published in the U.S.A. by The Westminster Press. Copyright © MCMLX, by W. L. Jenkins. Used by permission. XXI: 1025–1028 (IV, i, 12–13). (All references unless otherwise noted are to this Library of Christian Classics edition, hereafter *LCC*.

52. *Ibid.*, XX: 845 (III, xix, 13); XXI: 1046 (IV, ii, 5).

53. Marcel Pradervand, *A Century of Service, A History of the World Alliance of Reformed Churches, 1875–1975* (Grand Rapids: Eerdmans, 1976).

54. For a helpful treatment of the Reformed involvement in ecumenicity see John T. McNeill and James Hastings Nichols, *Ecumenical Testimony, The Concern for Christian Unity Within the Reformed and Presbyterian Churches* (Philadelphia: The Westminster Press, 1974).

For a criticism of the ecumenical movement by a Reformed theologian see Ian Henderson, *Power Without Glory: A Study in Ecumenical Politics* (Richmond: John Knox Press, 1969).

## III. THE ETHOS OF THE REFORMED TRADITION

1. Roger Hazelton, *A Theological Approach to Art* (Nashville, Tennessee: Abingdon Press, 1967).

2. Thomas Aquinas, *Summa Contra Gentiles*, trans. Vernon J. Bourke (New York: Doubleday, 1956), 3:37, 125.

3. H. Richard Niebuhr, *The Kingdom of God in America* (New York: Harper & Row, 1937; Harper Torchbook, 1959) pp. 20–21.

4. Ernst Troeltsch, *The Social Teaching of the Christian Churches*, trans. Olive Wyon (New York: The Macmillan Co., 1931), 2:589.

5. *Ibid.*, p. 583.

6. Nicolas Berdyaev, *The Destiny of Man* (New York: Charles Scribner's Sons, 1937), p. 146.

7. Karl Barth, *The Faith of the Church, A Commentary on the Apostles' Creed according to Calvin's Catechism*, Jean-Louis Leuba, ed., trans. Gabriel Vahanian (New York: Meridian Books, Inc., 1958), p. 137. Used by permission of New American Library, Inc.

8. *Letters of John Calvin*, 1:280–281 (Letter to Farel, August 1541).

9. *The Works of President Edwards*, 4 vols. (New York: Robert Carter & Brothers, 1879), 1:16, 17.

10. "Prayer for our Country" in *The Book of Common Prayer* (Greenwich: Seabury Press, 1952), p. 36.

11. Alexander Schweizer, *Die Glaubenslehre der Evangelisch-reformierten Kirche dargestellt und aus den Quellen belegt* (Zurich: Orell, Füssli und Comp. 1844–1847), 1:45.

12. John H. Leith, "John Calvin's Polemic against Idolatry," in *Soli Deo Gloria*, ed. J. McDowell Richards (Richmond: John Knox Press, 1968), pp. 111 ff.

13. *LCC*, XX:100 (I, xi, 1).

14. H. Richard Niebuhr, *The Kingdom of God in America*, p. 69.

15. Lord Eustace Percy, *John Knox* (London: Hodder & Stoughton, 1937).

16. Paul Lehmann, *Ethics in a Christian Context* (New York: Harper & Row, 1963), p. 85.

17. Christopher Dawson, *The Judgment of the Nations* (New York: Sheed & Ward, 1942), pp. 44–46.

18. David Laing, ed., *The Works of John Knox* (Edinburgh: Johnstone and Hunter, 1855), 4:240. (Spelling changed by author.)
Cf. Duncan Shaw, ed. *John Knox: A Quatercentenary Reappraisal* (Edinburgh: St. Andrew Press, 1975), p. 26.

19. Perry Miller, *Errand into the Wilderness* (Cambridge: Belknap Press of Harvard University Press, 1956), p. 11.

20. H. Richard Niebuhr, *The Kingdom of God in America*.

21. Michael Walzer, *The Revolution of the Saints: A Study in the Origins of Radical Politics* (Cambridge: University of Harvard Press, 1966), pp. 1, 2, 3. But see Walzer's critique of Calvinism, especially its repressiveness, *ibid.*, pp. 302 ff.

22. W. Fred Graham, *The Constructive Revolutionary: John Calvin & His Socio-Economic Impact* (Richmond: John Knox Press, 1971), p. 198.

23. Roland H. Bainton, *The Reformation of the Sixteenth Century* (Boston: Beacon Press, 1952), pp. 116–118.
Also, cf. McNeill, *The History and Character of Calvinism*, pp. 436–437: "This is a piety not much identified with peculiar words and rites of worship. It is characterized by a combination of God-consciousness with an urgent sense of missions. . . . The Calvinist may not know how it happens; he may be a very simple-minded theologian; but he is conscious that God commands his will and deed as well as his thought and prayer. This is what makes him a reformer and a dangerous character to encounter on moral and political issues. He is a man with a mission to bring to realization the will of God in human society."

24. Cf. the excellent study "Sphere-Sovereignty in Calvin and the Calvinist Tradition" by Gordon Spykman in *Exploring the Heritage of John Calvin*, David E. Holwerda, ed. (Grand Rapids: Baker Book House, 1976), pp. 163–208.

25. "Preliminary Principles," Chapter 1 of "The Form of Government, United Presbyterian Church in the United States of America," *The Constitution of the Presbyterian Church in the United States of America* (Philadelphia: Office of the General Assembly by the Board of Christian Education, 1954).

26. Reinhold Niebuhr, *The Nature and Destiny of Man* (New York: Charles Scribner's Sons, 1943), 2: 200.

27. Westminster Larger Catechism, Question 77, *The Constitution of the Presbyterian Church in the United States of America*, pp. 131–290.

28. *LCC*, XX: 360–361 (II, vii, 12).

29. Robert Kingdon has argued that the Calvinist concern with morals was assimilated into the tradition more through the attempt to *enforce* morality than through theology. Kingdon's point is well taken though he underestimates the significance of theology. "The Control of Morals in Calvin's Geneva" in *The Social History of the Reformation*, Lawrence P. Buck and Jonathan W. Zophy (Columbus: Ohio State University Press, 1972), pp. 3–16.

30. Cf. Josef Bohatec, *Budé und Calvin* (Fraz: Bohlaus, 1950).

31. *LCC*, XX: 53 (I, v, 2).

32. From CALVIN: THEOLOGICAL TREATISES, Volume XII, LCC. Translated with introductions and notes by J. K. S. Reid. Published in the U.S.A. by The Westminster Press, 1954. Used by permission. "Draft Ecclesiastical Ordinances: September & October (1541)," pp. 62, 63.

33. *Ibid.*

34. *Letters of John Calvin*, 2:191 (Letter to the Protector Somerset, October 22, 1548).

35. *LCC*, XXI: 896 (III, xx, 33).

36. Nichols, *Corporate Worship in the Reformed Tradition*, p. 29.

37. *Letters of John Calvin*, 2:190 (Somerset).

38. Texts of 1,460 sermons are now available. Records in Geneva indicate that the texts of more than 1,000 sermons have been lost. Hence, 3,000 sermons seems a fair estimate, considering Calvin's ministry in Strasbourg and the possibility of unrecorded sermons.
    Cf. Bernard Gabnebin, "L'histoire des manuscrits de sermons de Calvin," *Supplementa Calviniana*, ed. Erwin Mulhaupt (Neukirchen Kreis Moers: Neukirchener Verlag, 1961), 2:xxviii.

39. John H. Leith, ed., *Creeds of the Churches: A Reader in Christian Doctrine from the Bible to the Present*, rev. ed. (Richmond: John Knox Press, 1973), The Second Helvetic Confession, Chapter 1, p. 132.

40. Thomas Harding, ed., *The Decades of Henry Bullinger*, trans. H. I. for the Parker Society (Cambridge, England: The University Press, 1849), 1: 84–85.

41. *Corpus Reformatorum: Ioannis Calvini Opera Quae Supersunt Omnia*, Guilielmus Baum, Eduardus Cunitz, and Eduardus Reuss, eds. (Brunsvigae: C. A. Schwetschke et Filium, 1863–1897), Sermon on Deuteronomy, 25: 713. References to this work are hereafter cited by *CR*, followed by volume and column numbers. Translations are usually from the Edinburgh Calvin Translation Society and *Library of Christian Classics* editions of Calvin's works.

42. *LCC*, XXI: 1284 (IV, xiv, 8).

43. John F. Wilson, *Pulpit in Parliament, Puritanism During the English Civil Wars 1640–1648* (Princeton: Princeton University Press, 1969), pp. 138, 142.

44. Reinhold Niebuhr, *Leaves from the Notebook of a Tamed Cynic* (Hamden, Connecticut: The Shoestring Press, 1956), p. 9.

45. Jean-Daniel Benoit, *Calvin, Directeur d'Âmes* (Strasbourg: Editions Oberlin, 1944), p. 11.

46. *Ibid.*, p. 11.

47. *LCC*, XXI: 1229–1242 (IV, xii, 1–15).
    Cf. "Draft Ecclesiastical Ordinances: September & October 1541, *LCC*, XXII: 70.

48. John T. McNeill, *Modern Christian Movements* (Philadelphia: The Westminster Press, 1954), p. 47.

49. Troeltsch, *The Social Teachings of the Christian Churches*, p. 611.

50. *LCC,* XXI: 876 (III, xx, 19).

51. *LCC,* XXI: 1319 (IV, xv, 19); XXI: 1294 (IV, xiv, 18); XXI: 1191–93 (IV, x, 14).

52. John Calvin, Preface of *Commentaries on the Epistle of Paul the Apostle to the Romans,* trans. and ed. by Rev. John Owen (Grand Rapids: Eerdmans, 1955), pp. xxiii, xxvi.

53. John Calvin, *Commentary on the Epistles of Paul the Apostle to the Corinthians,* trans. and ed. by Rev. John Pringle (Grand Rapids: Eerdmans, 1948), vol. 1, 1 Cor. 1:17, p. 77.

Cf. Francis M. Higman, *The Style of John Calvin in His French Polemical Treatises* (London: Oxford University Press, 1967), pp. 153 ff.

## IV. THEOLOGY AND THE REFORMED TRADITION

1. Augustine, "On Predestination of the Saints," chap. 5; "On the Profit of Believing," "On the Freedom of the Will," 2:6.

2. Edward Schillebeeckx, *Revelation and Theology,* trans. N. D. Smith, 2 vols. (New York: Sheed and Ward, 1967), 1:95.

3. Barth, *Church Dogmatics,* 3,2:122.

4. For the distinction between problem and mystery, see Gabriel Marcel, *Being and Having,* trans. Katharine Farrer (Boston: Beacon Press, 1951), p. 117–118.

Also cf. Milton Karl Munitz, *The Mystery of Existence* (New York: Appleton-Century-Crofts, 1965), p. 33 ff.

Reinhold Niebuhr, *Discerning the Signs of the Times: Sermons for Today and Tomorrow* (New York: Charles Scribner's Sons, 1946), pp. 152-173.

5. Cf. Reinhold Niebuhr, *Nature and Destiny of Man* (New York: Charles Scribner's Sons, 1941), 1:125 ff.

Gordon Kaufman, *God the Problem* (Cambridge: Harvard University Press, 1972), pp. 45 ff.

6. Theodosius Dobzhansky, *Genetic Diversity and Human Equality* (New York: Basic Books, Inc., 1973), pp. 115–116.

7. Albert C. Outler, "Revelation and Reflection: A Comment in Favor of Apophatic Theology," *Perkins Journal,* vol. 26, no. 2, pp. 14–20. Outler defines theology as "sustained human reflection on the interplay between the self-disclosure of the divine mystery and our reactions to it." (p. 17)

8. H. Richard Niebuhr, *The Meaning of Revelation* (New York: The Macmillan Co., 1946), pp. 109 ff.

9. Albert C. Outler in class lecture.

10. H. Richard Niebuhr, "Faith in Gods and in God," *Radical Monotheism and Western Culture* (New York: Harper & Brothers, 1960), p. 121.

11. Karl Marx and Friedrich Engels, *Basic Writings on Politics and Philosophy,* ed. Lewis S. Feuer (New York: Doubleday & Co., 1959), pp. 262-263.

12. Sigmund Freud, *Totem and Taboo,* trans. James Strachey (London: Routledge & Kegan Paul, 1950), p. 145.

Sigmund Freud, *The Future of an Illusion,* trans. W. D. Robson-Scott (New York: Liveright Publishing Corp., 1955) pp. 36 ff., 56 ff.

13. For a perceptive discussion of the contextual character of theology by a theologian who maintains the priority and initiative of revelation, see Paul Lehmann, "On Doing Theology: A Contextual Possibility" in *Prospect for Theology, Essays in Honour of H. H. Farmer,* F. G. Healey, ed. (Welwyn, England: Nisbet, 1966), pp. 137–166.

14. Paul Tillich, *The Future of Religions* (New York: Harper & Row, 1966), pp. 31, 80-94.

15. Barth was engaged principally with revelation and the history of doctrine.

Reinhold Niebuhr took revelation and the history of doctrine seriously, but he also gave attention to experience and the social sciences. Tillich intended for his theology to be an explication of Scripture, and he took the history of doctrines seriously. He is distinguished by the attention he gave to psychotherapy and the arts. Schleiermacher was, of course, pre-eminently a theologian of Christian experience.

16. Lehmann, "On Doing Theology: A Contextual Possibility," in *Prospect for Theology,* ed. F. G. Healey, pp.134–135.

17. Joseph Sittler, *Essays on Nature and Grace* (Philadelphia: Fortress Press, 1972), p. 20.

18. H. Richard Niebuhr, "The Doctrine of the Trinity and the Unity of the Church," *Theology Today,* 3 (October 1946), 371–384.

19. Émile Doumergue, *Jean Calvin, Les hommes et les choses de son temps,* Vol. IV: *La pensée religieuse de Calvin* (Lausanne: Georges Bridel & Cie Éditeurs, 1910), p. 428.

20. I. John Hesselink, "The Charismatic Movement and the Reformed Tradition," *Reformed Review,* 28, no. 3, (Spring 1975), 147–156, clearly presents the emphasis on the Holy Spirit in Reformed theology.

21. H. Richard Niebuhr, *Radical Monotheism and Western Culture,* pp. 16 ff.

22. H. Richard Niebuhr, "Faith in Gods and in God," *ibid.,* p. 122.

23. Copyright 1932 Christian Century Foundation. Reprinted by permission from the April 6, 1932 issue of *The Christian Century.* p. 447.

24. In this section the author has made use of material that he published in an article entitled "John Calvin—Theologian of the Bible" in *Interpretation,* vol. 25, no. 3 (July 1971). See also the author's article "Theology and the Bible" in *Interpretation,* vol. 30, no. 3 (July 1976), pp. 227–241.

25. *CR,* 20: 299.

26. Gilbert Rist; "Modernité de la méthode théologique de Calvin," *Revue de théologie et de philosophie,* 18 (1968); 1, 20.

27. The prefaces are printed in the English translation of the *Institutes.*

28. *LCC, XX:* 124 (I, xiii, 3).

29. *LCC, XX:* 53 (I, v, 2).

30. Léon Wencelius, *L'esthétique de Calvin* (Paris: Société d'Édition "Les Belles Lettres," n.d.).

31. "Preface to the Institutes," 1559 ed., XX: 4.

32. E.g., James Mackinnon, *Calvin and the Reformation* (New York: Longmans, Green & Co., 1936) and E. Choisy, *La théocratie à Genève au temps de Calvin* (Geneva: J. G. Fliek, 1897).

33. *LCC, XX:* 719–720 (III, xxi, 1).

34. See the author's dissertation, "John Calvin's Doctrine of the Christian Life" (Yale University, 1949), pp. 171 ff.

35. *Ibid.,* pp. 190 ff.

36. *LCC, XXI:* 960–961 (III, xxiii, 12).

37. "The Eternal Predestination of God," *CR* 8:260.

38. "Antidote to the Council of Trent," *CR* 7:479.

39. Francis Thompson, *The Poems of Francis Thompson* (London: Hollis and Carter, Ltd., 1947), pp. 101, 104–106.

40. See E. David Willis, *Calvin's Catholic Christology* (Leiden: E. J. Brill, 1966), for a discussion of the so-called *extra calvinisticum.*

41. Thomas Aquinas, *Summa Theologica,* trans. Fathers of the English Dominican Province (London: Burns Oates & Washborne Ltd, 1920) pt. 1, q.1, art. 4, p. 6.

42. "Reply to Sadolet," *CR* 5: 396–397; *LCC* 22:233.

43. *LCC, XX:* 160 (I, xiv, 1).

44. *LCC, XX:* 469 (II, xii, 5).

45. Bohatec, *Budé und Calvin.*

Quirinus Breen, *John Calvin, A Study in French Humanism* (Grand Rapids: Eerdmans, 1931).

Humanistic sources of Calvin's thought ought not to be emphasized at the expense of other sources, such as the theologians of the Ancient Church and his dialogue with the scholastic theologians.

46. *LCC, XX:* 95 (I, ix, 3).

Cf. Bohatec, *Budé und Calvin,* pp. 119 ff.

47. Lucien Joseph Richard, *The Spirituality of John Calvin* (Atlanta: John Knox Press, 1974), pp. 91ff.

48. Cf. Thomas à Kempis, *Imitation of Christ,* trans. Ronald Knox and Michael Oakley (London: Burns & Oate, 1959).

49. Barth, *Church Dogmatics,* 4, 3, 2: p. 882.

50. Jaroslav Pelikan, *Development of Christian Doctrine: Some Historical Prolegomena* (New Haven: Yale University Press, 1969).

John Henry Newman, *An Essay on the Development of Christian Doctrine* (New York: Doubleday, Image Books, 1960).

Owen Chadwick, *From Bossuet to Newman: The Idea of Doctrinal Development* (Cambridge, England: The University Press, 1957).

Robert Rainy, *The Delivery and Development of Christian Doctrine* (Edinburgh: T. & T. Clark, 1874), pp. 175 ff.

William Cunningham, *Discussions on Church Principles* (Edinburgh: T. & T. Clark, 1863), pp. 35-77.

Rainy and Cunningham represent cautious Reformed replies to Newman.

George A. Lindbeck, "The Problem of Doctrinal Development and Contemporary Protestant Theology" in *Man as Man and Believer,* Edward Schillebeeckx & Boniface Williams, Concilium, Theology in the Age of Renewal, vol. 21 (Paramus: Paulist/Newman, 1966).

51. Cf. Pelikan, *Development of Christian Doctrine,* pp. 91, 99, 114.

52. Jaroslav Pelikan, *The Light of the World: A Basic Image in Early Christian Thought* (New York: Harper & Brothers, 1962), pp. 53-72.

53. William Cunningham, a conservative Calvinist, allowed only a subjective development of doctrine. "There is a subjective development of Christian doctrine both in individuals and in churches, whereby men grow in the knowledge of God's revealed will, and whereby theological science is extended and improved. But the result of this development is merely to enable individuals and churches to understand more fully and accurately, and to realize more thoroughly, *what is actually contained in, or deducible from, the statements of the written word, and can be shown to be so.* This, however, is essentially different from, nay, it is in a certain sense the reverse of, an objective development, which changes and enlarges or diminishes the external revelation, the standard or system of faith." *Discussions on Church Principles,* p. 56.

54. Karl Rahner, *Theological Investigations* (Baltimore: Helicon Press, 1961) 1:63 ff.

55. Schubert Ogden in a class lecture.

56. In this section the author is indebted to the work of his teacher, Professor Albert C. Outler.

57. Roland H. Bainton, "Interpretations of the Reformation," *The American Historical Review* 66 (October 1960), 74–84. (Also reprinted in *The Reformation, Material or Spiritual,* ed. Lewis W. Spitz [Boston: D. C. Heath, 1962]).

58. E.g., Kilian McDonnell, *John Calvin, The Church, and the Eucharist* (Princeton: Princeton University Press, 1967), p. 156.

59. Barth, *Church Dogmatics,* 2, 2:127 ff.

60. Perry Miller, "The Marrow of Puritan Divinity" in *Errand into the Wilderness* (Cambridge: Harvard University Press, 1956), pp. 48-98.

61. Van Austin Harvey, *The Historian and the Believer* (New York: The Macmillan Co., 1966), pp. 102 ff.

For a good, brief review of this period, see H. G. Wood, *Belief and Unbelief Since 1850* (Cambridge, England: The University Press, 1955).

62. René Descartes, *Discourse on Method,* trans. John Veitch (London: J. M. Dent & Sons Ltd, 1949), pt. 2, pp. 11–18.

63. John W. Beardslee III, ed. and trans., *Reformed Dogmatics* (New York: Oxford University Press, 1965), p. 12.

64. Blaise Pascal, *Pensées,* trans. W. F. Trother (New York: Random House, Modern Library, 1941), Fragment 205, p. 74.

65. Sigmund Freud, *General Introduction to Psychoanalysis,* rev. ed. (New York: Simon & Schuster, 1969).

66. Freud, *Totem and Taboo,* p. 145.

Freud, *Future of an Illusion,* pp. 52 ff.

67. Cf. Stewart G. Cole, *The History of Fundamentalism* (New York: Richard R. Smith, 1931).

Norman F. Furniss, *The Fundamentalist Controversy, 1918-1931* (New Haven: Yale University Press, 1954).

Ernest R. Sandeen, *The Roots of Fundamentalism: British and American Millenarianism, 1800–1930* (Chicago: University of Chicago Press, 1970).

Henry P. van Dusen, *The Vindication of Liberal Theology: A Tract for the Times* (New York: Charles Scribner's Sons, 1963).

Kenneth Cauthen, *The Impact of American Religious Liberalism* (New York: Harper & Row, 1962).

David E. Roberts and Henry Pitney van Dusen, *Liberal Theology: An Appraisal* (New York: Charles Scribner's Sons, 1942).

68. Cf. Charles Howard Hopkins, *The Rise of the Social Gospel in American Protestantism, 1865–1915* (New Haven: Yale University Press, 1940).

69. Competent introductions to this period: William Hordern, *A Layman's Guide to Protestant Theology,* rev. ed. (New York: The Macmillan Co., 1970).

Daniel Day Williams, *What Present-Day Theologians Are Thinking,* 3rd. ed. rev. (New York: Harper & Row, 1967).

Heinz Zahrnt, *The Question of God: Protestant Theology in the Twentieth Century,* trans. R. A. Wilson (London: Collins, 1969).

70. Langdon Gilkey, *Naming the Whirlwind: The Renewal of God-Language* (New York: The Bobbs-Merrill Co., 1969), p. 6.

William Hordern, *op. cit.*

Daniel Day Williams, *op. cit.*

Heinz Zahrnt, *op. cit.*

71. Quirinus Breen, "St. Thomas and Calvin as Theologians: A Comparison," *The Heritage of John Calvin,* ed. John H. Bratt (Grand Rapids: Eerdmans, 1973), pp. 23–39.

E. David Willis, "Rhetoric and Responsibility in Calvin's Theology," *The Context of Contemporary Theology: Essays in Honor of Paul Lehmann,* ed. Alexander J. McKelway and E. David Willis (Atlanta: John Knox Press, 1974), pp. 43–63.

72. William Ames, *The Marrow of Theology,* trans. & ed. John D. Eusden (Philadelphia: Pilgrim Press, 1968), p.3.

Matthew Nethenus, Hugo Visscher, and Karl Reuter, *William Ames,* trans. Douglas Horton (Cambridge: Harvard Divinity School Library, 1965).

73. John Walter Beardslee, "Theological Development at Geneva under Fran-

cis and Jean-Alphonse Turretin, 1648–1737" (Ph. D. dissertation, Yale University, 1957).

John W. Beardslee, *Reformed Dogmatics: J. Wollebius, G. Voetius, and F. Turretin* (New York: Oxford University Press, 1965).

74. A. A. Hodge, *The Life of Charles Hodge, D. D. LL. D.* (New York: Charles Scribner's Sons, 1880).

Useful dissertations on Hodge's theology have been written by Penrose St. Amant, "The Rise and Early Development of the Princeton School of Theology" (University of Edinburgh, 1958), and John Oliver Nelson, "The Rise of the Princeton Theology" (Yale University, 1935).

75. Charles Hodge, *Systematic Theology* (New York: Charles Scribner and Company, 1872), 1:19.

Lefferts Augustine Loetscher, *The Broadening Church: A Study of Theological Issues in the Presbyterian Church Since 1869* (Philadelphia: University of Pennsylvania Press, 1954).

76. A. A. Hodge, *The Life of Charles Hodge, D. D. LL. D.* (New York: Charles Scribner's Sons, 1880), p. 161.

77. *Presbyterian Review*, 1845, p. 190. (Probably by Charles Hodge but it is an unsigned review.)

78. Nelson, "The Rise of the Princeton Theology," p. 141.

79. Cauthen, *The Impact of American Religious Liberalism*, p. 41 ff.

80. *Ibid.*, pp. 5 ff. van Dusen, *The Vindication of Liberal Theology.*

81. William Adams Brown, *Christian Theology in Outline* (New York: Charles Scribner's Sons, 1906), p. viii.

82. Arnold B. Come, *An Introduction to Barth's Dogmatics for Preachers* (Philadelphia: Westminster Press, 1963).

Hans Urs von Balthasar, *The Theology of Karl Barth*, trans. John Drury (Garden City: Doubleday & Co., 1972).

Thomas F. Torrance, *Karl Barth: An Introduction to His Early Theology, 1910–1931* (London: SCM Press, Ltd, 1962).

83. Barth, *Church Dogmatics*, 1, 1:26–47.

84. *Ibid.*, 1,1:16.

85. *Ibid.*, 4,3,2:879.

86. Good introductions to the work of Reinhold Niebuhr and H. Richard Niebuhr:

June Bingham, *Courage to Change: An Introduction to the Life and Thought of Reinhold Niebuhr* (New York: Charles Scribner's Sons, 1961).

Ronald H. Stone, *Reinhold Niebuhr: Prophet to Politicians* (Nashville, Tennessee: Abingdon, 1972).

Nathan A. Scott, ed., *The Legacy of Reinhold Niebuhr* (Chicago: University of Chicago Press, 1975).

John D. Godsey, *The Promise of H. Richard Niebuhr* (Philadelphia: J. B. Lippincott Co., 1970).

James W. Fowler, *To See the Kingdom: The Theological Vision of H. Richard Niebuhr* (Nashville: Abingdon, 1974.)

87. Schaff, *The Creeds of Christendom*, vols. 1 & 3.

Arthur C. Cochrane, *Reformed Confessions of the 16th Century* (Philadelphia: Westminster Press, 1966).

Paul Jacobs, *Theologie Reformierter Bekenntnisschriften im Grundzügen* (Neukirchen: Neukirchener Verlag, 1959).

88. I. John Hesselink, "Contemporary Protestant Dutch Theology," *Reformed Review*, vol. 26, no. 2 (Winter 1973), pp. 67–89. An excellent review of a Reformed theological tradition that receives inadequate treatment in this book.

## V. POLITY AND THE REFORMED TRADITION

1. E.g., "The Book of Discipline of the Elizabethan Presbyterians" in Charles Augustus Briggs, *American Presbyterianism* (New York: Charles Scribner's Sons, 1885).

2. Benjamin Charles Milner, Jr., *Calvin's Doctrine of the Chruch* (Leiden: E. J. Brill, 1970), p. 195.

3. David Little, *Religion, Order, and Law: A Study in Pre-Revolutionary England* (New York: Harper and Row Publishers, 1969), p. 68.

4. Schaff, *Creeds of Christendom*, The Belgic Confession, Article 29, 3: 419.

5. *LCC*, XXI: 1023 (IV, i, 9). Cf. Barth, *Church Dogmatics*, 4,1: 650–651: "The Church *is* when it takes place that God lets certain men live as His servants, His friends, His children, the witnesses of the reconciliation of the world with Himself as it has taken place in Jesus Christ, the preachers of the victory which has been won in Him over sin and suffering and death, the heralds of His future revelation in which the glory of the Creator will be declared to all creation as that of His love and faithfulness and mercy. The Church *is* when it happens to these men in common that they may receive the verdict on the whole world of men which has been pronounced in the resurrection of Jesus Christ from the dead."

6. *LCC*, XXI: 1022 (IV, i, 8).

7. Leith, *Creeds of the Churches*, p. 147.

8. James Stevenson McEwen, *The Faith of John Knox* (London: Lutterworth, 1961), pp. 59–60.

9. Barth, *Church Dogmatics*, 4,1:661

10. *LCC*, XXI: 1014 (IV, i, 2).

11. Barth, *Church Dogmatics*, 4,1: 656–657.

12. From CYRIL OF JERUSALEM AND NEMESIUS OF EMESA, Volume IV, LCC. Translated and edited by W. Telfer. Published in the U.S.A. by the Westminster Press. Used by permission. P. 186.

13. *LCC*, XX: 1014 (IV, i, 2).

14. Karl Barth, *The Faith of the Church*, p. 139.

15. Graydon F. Snyder, ed. *The Shepherd of Hermas*, Vol. 6 in *The Apostolic Fathers: A New Translation and Commentary*, Robert M. Grant, ed. (New York: Thomas Nelson, 1964), Mandate IV, pp. 67–73.
This was also the position of the Novatianists in the third century.

16. This was the position advocated by the Donatists in the fourth century. See Augustine, "The Seven Books of Augustine, Bishop of Hippo, On Baptism, Against the Donatists," in *Nicene and Post-Nicene Fathers of the Christian Church*, Philip Schaff, ed., (Grand Rapids: Eerdmans, 1956), IV: 411–514.

17. *Ibid.*

18. Barth, *The Faith of the Church*, pp. 137–138.

19. Kenneth Kirk, ed., *The Apostolic Ministry: Essays on the History and the Doctrine of Episcopacy* (London: Hodder & Stoughton, 1946), pp. 530–532.

20. *LCC*, XXI: 1042–45 (IV, ii, 2–3). See also *Letters of John Calvin*, 3: 99–109 (Letter to the King of Poland, Dec. 5, 1554).

21. T. W. Manson, *The Church's Ministry* (London: Hodder & Stoughton, 1948), pp. 21–22.

22. *LCC*, XXI: 1134 (IV, vii, 15).

23. *LCC*, XXII: 62.

24. *LCC*, XXII: 63.

25. *CR*, 15: 713.

26. Ian Brevard, "The Presbyterian Eldership Yesterday & Today," *Colloquium*, (May 1967) pp. 127–143. Professor Brevard claims that all Reformed

churches that looked to Geneva for leadership except the Reformed Church in Hungary had congregational senates.

27. *LCC,* XXI: 1232–33 (IV, xii, 5).

28. Cf. *LCC,* XXII: 69.

29. Robert M. Kingdon, "Social Welfare in Calvin's Geneva," *The American Historical Review,* vol. 76, no. 1 (February 1971), pp. 50–69. Careful research balances Calvin's contribution with that of the city.

Cf. R. W. Henderson, "Sixteenth Century Community Benevolence: An Attempt to Resacralize the Secular," *Church History,* vol. 38, no. 4 (December 1969), pp. 421–428.

On the development of the office of deacon, see Ernest Trice Thompson, *Presbyterians in the South,* 3 vols. (Richmond: John Knox Press, 1963–1973), 1: 520 ff.; 2: 418 ff.

30. *CR,* 16: 498.

Doumergue, *Jean Calvin Vol. V: La pensée ecclesiastique et la pensée politique de Calvin,* p. 679.

31. From "Presbyterianism" in *Encyclopaedia Britannica,* 14th edition (1967), 18: 467.

32. Robert M. Kingdon, *Geneva and the Consolidation of the French Protestant Movement, 1564–1572* (Madison: University of Wisconsin Press, 1967), pp.37 ff.

G. D. Henderson, *Presbyterianism* (Aberdeen, Scotland: The University Press, 1954), pp. 92–111.

Janet G. Macgregor, *The Scottish Presbyterian Polity: A Study of Its Origins in the Sixteenth Century* (Edinburgh: Oliver and Boyd, 1926), pp. 131–137.

33. G. D. Henderson, *op. cit.,* pp. 94 ff.

34. Charles Hodge, *Discussions in Church Polity* (New York: Charles Scribner's Sons, 1878), p. 119. For Hodge's difference with Thornwell, see p. 127.

35. John B. Adger & John L. Girardeau, eds., *The Collected Writings of James Henley Thornwell* (Richmond: Presbyterian Committee of Publication, 1873) vol. 4: 134–135.

36. *Ibid.,* pp. 134–139. Cf. pp. 234–235.

37. For Thornwell's emphasis on Scripture, see 4: 21, 167, 218.

For the conflicts between Thornwell and Hodge over church boards, see 4: 224. Cf. Thompson, *Presbyterians in the South,* 2: 414 ff.

For Thornwell on the ruling elder, see *Collected Writings,* 4: 115ff. Also, Thompson, *op. cit.,* 2: 417 ff.

For Hodge on eldership, see *Discussions in Church Polity,* pp. 262 ff.

For discussions of the nature of the eldership and its role in the history of Presbyterian polity, see Robert W. Henderson, "Concerning the Eldership, Part I," *Reformed World,* vol. 32, no. 8 (December 1973), pp. 363–373; Ian Brevard, "The Presbyterian Eldership Yesterday and Today," *Colloquium* (May 1967).

Robert W. Henderson, *A Profile of the Eldership 1974: A Preliminary Report* (World Alliance of Reformed Churches, 1975).

For a perceptive discussion of conflicting views of the eldership see also Eugene Heideman, *Reformed Bishops and Catholic Elders* (Michigan: Eerdmans, 1970), p. 124.

38. James Moffatt, *The Presbyterian Churches* (Toronto: Methuen Publications, A Division of The Carlswell Company, 1928), pp. 1–2.

39. G. D. Henderson, *Why We Are Presbyterians* (Edinburgh: Church of Scotland Publications, n.d.), pp. 82–83.

40. *LCC,* XXI: 1053 (IV, iii, 1).

41. *LCC,* XXI: 1110 (IV, vi, 9).

42. *LCC,* XXII: 58 (Footnote 1).

248    An Introduction to the Reformed Tradition

43. Schaff, *Creeds of Christendom,* Gallican Confession, Article 29, 3: 376.
44. *LCC,* XXI: 1205 (IV, x, 27).
45. *LCC,* XXI: 1206 (IV, x, 28).
46. *LCC,* XXI: 1207–08 (IV, x, 30). Cf. XXI: 1209 (IV, x, 32).
47. Doumergue, *Jean Calvin Vol. V: La pensée ecclesiastique . . .,* pp. 48–52.
48. Walter Travers, *A Full and Plaine Declaration of Ecclesiastical Discipline out of the Word of God and of the Declining of the Church of England from the Same,* 1617 ed., p. 6.
49. Briggs, "Book of Discipline," Appendix, p. ii. Cf. *Collected Writings of Thornwell,* 4: 218.
50. John Calvin, *Commentary: Acts of the Apostles,* Henry Beveridge, ed. (Grand Rapids: Eerdmans, 1949), p. 44.
51. *Ibid.*
52. *Collected Writings of Thornwell,* 4: 101.
53. Leith, *Creeds of the Churches,* Second Helvetic Confession, chapter 18, pp. 157–58.
54. Schaff, *Creeds of Christendom,* Gallican Confession, Article 30, 3: 377.
55. *Ibid.,* Belgic Confession, Article 31, 3: 422.
56. *LCC,* XXI: 1060 (IV, iii, 8).
57. *LCC,* XXI: 1072 (IV, iv, 4).
58. *LCC,* XXI: 1065, 1066 (IV, iii, 15).
59. *LCC,* XXI: 1064–66 (IV, iii, 13–15); XXI: 1080 (IV, iv, 12).
60. Moffatt, *The Presbyterian Churches,* pp. 26–27, 78.
61. Heideman, *Reformed Bishops and Catholic Elders,* p. 124.
   See articles on the importance of the deacon by John L. Girardeau in *Southern Presbyterian Review,* Vols. XXX, XXXI, XXXII.
62. Norman Sykes, *Old Priest and New Presbyter* (Cambridge, England: The University Press, 1956), especially chapters 4 and 5.
63. Kenneth Kirk, ed., *The Apostolic Ministry: Essays on the History and Doctrine of Episcopacy* (London: Hodder & Stoughton, 1947), p. 8.
64. *LCC,* XXI: 1069–70 (IV, iv, 2,4).
65. *LCC,* XXI: 1071–72 (IV, iv, 4).
66. *LCC,* XXI: 1071–72 (IV, iv, 4 [Footnote 12]).
   John T. McNeill, "The Doctrine of the Ministry in Reformed Theology," *Church History,* vol. 12, no. 2 (June 1943), pp. 77–97.
   Cf. Jacques Pannier, *Calvin et l'éspiscopat* (Strasbourg and Paris: Librairie Istra, 1927).
   J. L. Ainslie, *The Doctrines of Ministerial Order in the Reformed Churches of the 16th and 17th Centuries* (Edinburgh: T. & T. Clark, 1940).
67. Cf. Alexandre Ganoczy, *Calvin, théologien de l'église et du ministère* (Paris: Les Editions du Cerf, 1964), p. 429.
68. John Calvin, *Calvin Commentaries: The Epistles of Paul the Apostle to the Galatians, Ephesians, Philippians and Colossians,* David W. Torrance and Thomas F. Torrance, eds., trans. T. H. L. Parker (Grand Rapids: Eerdmans, 1966), p. 227.
69. *Letters of John Calvin.* 2: 345–348 (Letter to Cranmer, April 1552).
70. *Ibid.,* 2: 182–198 (Letter to Somerset, October 22, 1548). Bullinger and Reformed leaders in Zurich also were positive in their attitude toward English episcopacy.
71. *Ibid.,* 3: 99–109 (Letter to Sigismund, King of Poland, December 5, 1554).
72. Letter of Theodore Beza to Whitgift, Archbishop of Canterbury, March 1591. Quoted by John T. McNeill, "The Doctrine of the Ministry in Reformed Theology," p. 85.
73. Kingdon, *Geneva and the Consolidation of the French Protestant Movement, 1564–1572.*

74. R. Newton Flew, ed., *The Nature of the Church* (London: SCM Press, 1952), pp. 183–184.

75. *Ibid.*, pp. 169–185.

76. Charles W. Kegley, ed., *The Theology of Emil Brunner* in The Library of Living Theology, Vol. III (New York: The Macmillan Company, 1962), p. 347.

77. Emil Brunner, "Reply to Interpretation and Criticism," in *The Theology of Emil Brunner*, p. 347.

Cf. Emil Brunner, *Dogmatics*, Vol. 3: *The Christian Doctrine of the Church, Faith, and the Consummation*, trans. David Cairns (Philadelphia: The Westminster Press, 1960), pp. 128–129.

78. Barth, *Church Dogmatics*, 4, 2: 718.

## VI. LITURGY AND THE REFORMED TRADITION

1. Karl Barth, "Introduction," *The Essence of Christianity* by Ludwig Feuerbach, trans. George Eliot (New York: Harper Torchbooks, 1957), p. xiv.

2. St. Augustine, *City of God*, David Knowles, ed., trans. Henry Bettenson (Middlesex, England: Penguin Press, 1972), pp. 593–594.

3. "Form of Administering Baptism" in *Tracts and Treatises on the Doctrine and Worship of the Church*, Thomas F. Torrance, ed., trans. Henry Beveridge (Grand Rapids: Eerdmans, 1958), 2:118.

4. *LCC*, XXI: 892–93 (III, xx, 29); XX: 398–401 (II, vii, 33–34).

5. *LCC*, XXI: 1420 (IV, xii, 43).

6. *LCC*, XXI: 1208 (IV, x, 30).

7. Joannis Calvini, *Opera Selecta*, Petrus Barth, Guilelmus Baum, and Dora Scheuner, eds. (Munich: Chr. Kaiser, 1952), 2: 15.

English text of "Preface" in *Source Readings in Music History*, Oliver Strunk, ed. (New York: W. W. Norton Co., Inc., 1950), pp. 345–348.

8. *LCC*, XXI: 896 (III, xx, 33).

9. *Opera Selecta*, 2: 16–17; *LCC*, XXI: 894 (III, xx, 32).

10. Calvin, *Commentary on Corinthians*, 1 Cor. 2:3–7, 1: 98–104.

11. *LCC*, XXI: 1278–80 (IV, xiv, 3–4)

12. *LCC*, XX: 53 (I, v, 2).

13. *Opera Selecta*, 2:15.

14. "Form of Administering Baptism."

15. *LCC*, XXI: 1319 (IV, xv, 19).

16. *LCC*, XXI: 1421 (IV, xvii, 43).

17. *LCC*, XXI: 1193 (IV, x, 14).

18. *LCC*, XXI: 893 (III, xx, 30).

19. Charles Garside, Jr., *Zwingli and the Arts* (New Haven: Yale University Press, 1966), pp. 26 ff.

20. *Opera Selecta*, 2: 16–17.

21. *Ibid.*, 2: 17.

22. *Ibid.*, 2: 17.

23. Barth, *Church Dogmatics*, 4,2:640.

24. *Ibid.*, 4,2:697.

25. *Ibid.*, 4,3,2:869.

26. *Ibid.*, 4,2:700.

27. *Ibid.*, p. 709.

28. *Ibid.*, 4, 3, 2:884.

29. *Ibid.*, 4, 3,2:866–867. Cf. Bard Thompson, *Liturgies of the Western Church* (New York: The World Publishing Co., 1961).

30. Barth, *Church Dogmatics*, 4, 4:105.

31. *Ibid.*, 4,4:130.

32. *Opera Selecta*, 2:18 ff.; Thompson, *op. cit.*, pp. 197 ff. for English translation.

33. Thompson, pp. 197 ff.

34. *CR,* 10:213.

35. *LCC,* XX: 635–36 (III, iv, 11).

36. *LCC,* XX: 638 (III, iv, 14).

37. *LCC,* XX: 649 (III, iv, 22).

38. *Letters of John Calvin,* 2: 182–198 (Letter to Somerset, October 22, 1548).

39. *Ibid.,* 3:30–31 (Letter to the Brethren of Wezel, March 13, 1554).

40. Cf. James Hastings Nichols, *Corporate Worship in the Reformed Tradition* (Philadelphia: Westminster, 1968), pp. 29–33.

41. Dietrich Ritschl, *A Theology of Proclamation* (Richmond: John Knox Press, 1960), pp. 88 ff.

42. *Opera Selecta,* 2: 16–17.

43. Leith, *Creeds of the Churches,* Second Helvetic Confession, Chapter 1, p. 132.

44. Nichols, *Corporate Worship in the Reformed Tradition,* p. 29.

45. *LCC,* XX: 360 (II, vii, 12).

46. Bard Thompson, *Liturgies of the Western Church,* p. 191.

47. Richard R. Terry, ed., *Calvin's First Psalter (1539)* (London: Ernest Benn, Ltd., 1932).

Pierre Pidoux, *Le Psaultier Huguenot du XVIᵉ Siecle, Melodies et Documents* (Basel: Edition Baereneiter, 1962), vols. 1 and 2.

Millar Patrick, *Four Centuries of Scottish Psalmody* (New York: Oxford University Press, 1949).

Charles Garside, Jr., *The Origins of Calvin's Theology of Music:* 1536–1543 (Philadelphia: The American Philosophical Society, 1979).

48. Émile Doumergue, "Music in the Work of Calvin," *The Princeton Theological Review,* vol. 7, no. 4 (October 1909), pp. 529–552.

Cf. Émile Doumergue, *L'art et le sentiment dans l'oeuvre de Calvin* (Geneva: Slatkine Reprints, 1970, reprint of the Geneva edition of 1902).

Cf. W. Stanford Reid, "The Battle Hymns of the Lord, Calvinist Psalmody of the Sixteenth Century" in *Sixteenth Century Essays and Studies,* vol. 2, Carl S. Meyer, ed. (St. Louis: The Foundation for Reformation Research, 1971).

49. Nichols, *Corporate Worship in the Reformed Tradition,* p. 38.

50. *LCC,* XXI: 894–896 (III, xx, 31–32). Cf. Preface to Geneva Psalter.

51. *LCC,* XXI: 1284 (IV, xii, 8).

Dietrich Ritschl argues that the phrase "word and sacraments" has no Biblical support. There is one life-giving word in sacrament and sermon. (*A Theology of Proclamation,* p. 115.)

52. *LCC,* XXI: 1421 (IV, xiv, 8).

53. *LCC,* XXI: 1422 (IV, xvii, 44).

54. Thompson, *Liturgies of the Western Church,* pp. 216–224.

55. Howard Hageman, *Pulpit and Table* (Richmond: John Knox Press, 1962) is an excellent summary of the two ways. Hageman discusses this theme more specifically in a study, "The Liturgical Origins of the Reformed Churches," published in *The Heritage of John Calvin,* edited by John H. Bratt (Grand Rapids: Eerdmans, 1973). Also, see highly competent summary in Nichols, *Corporate Worship in the Reformed Tradition,* chapters 3 and 4.

56. For the text and explanatory notes, see Thomas Leishman, ed., *The Westminster Directory* (Edinburgh: W. Blackwood & Sons, Ltd., 1901), p. xiii. (A copy of the Directory without notes can be found in Thompson, *Liturgies of the Western Church,* pp. 345–353.

57. *Ibid.,* p. 11.

58. *Ibid.,* p. 12.

59. Thompson, *Liturgies of the Western Church,* pp. 356–368.

60. *Ibid.*, pp. 368–370.

61. *Ibid.*, p. 396.

62. Julius Melton, *Presbyterian Worship in America, Changing Patterns Since 1787* (Richmond: John Knox Press, 1967) has a competent review of the history.

63. Leishman, *The Westminster Directory*, p. 117.

64. Cf. Melton, *op. cit.*, pp. 17 ff. and Leonard J. Trinterud, *The Forming of an American Tradition: A Re-examination of Colonial Presbyterianism* (Philadelphia: Westminster Press, 1949), pp. 304–305.

65. Julius Melton, *op. cit.*, p. 75.

66. Leonard J. Trinterud, "The Problem of Liturgical Reform, in The American Scene." (Mimeographed.) This is a provocative discussion of the issue.

67. James Hastings Nichols, ed., *The Mercersburg Theology* (New York: Oxford University Press, 1966). James Hastings Nichols, *Romanticism in America Today* (Chicago: University of Chicago Press, 1961).

68. Cf. Ernest Trice Thompson, *Presbyterians in the South*, 3 vols., 1:519 ff.; 2:420 ff. Also, for a record of financial experimentation in a particular church, see John H. Leith, *Greenville Presbyterian Church, The Story of a People* (Richmond: Privately Published, 1973), pp. 54–55.

## VII. CULTURE AND THE REFORMED TRADITION

1. H. Richard Niebuhr, *Christ and Culture* (New York: Harper & Brothers, 1951), p. 217.

2. Edwin Muir, *Collected Poems* (New York: Oxford University Press, 1965), p. 228. First called to my attention by John M. Walker, Jr., of Roanoke Rapids, North Carolina.

Cf. Émile Doumergue, *L'art et le sentiment dans l'oeuvre de Calvin*, pp. 7 ff.

3. See excellent article by Erwin Panofsky "Comments on Art and Reformation" in *Symbols in Transformation Iconographic Themes at the Time of the Reformation*, An Exhibition of Prints in memory of Erwin Panofsky (Princeton: The Art Museum, Princeton University, 1969), pp. 9 ff. See also Samuel Laeuchli, *Religion and Art in Conflict* (Philadelphia: Fortress Press, 1980).

4. Cf. W. Norman Pittenger, *The Word Incarnate: A Study of the Doctrine of the Person of Christ* (New York: Harper and Brothers, 1959), pp. 252 ff.

5. Stephen Neill, *The Christian Society* (New York: Harper & Brothers, 1952), p. 159.

6. Jane Dillenberger, *Style and Content in Christian Art* (Nashville: Abingdon Press, 1965), pp. 143–149.

Paul Tillich, "Existentialist Aspects of Modern Art," *Christianity and the Existentialists*, Carl Michalson, ed. (New York: Charles Scribner's Sons, 1956), p. 143.

7. Garside, *Zwingli and the Arts*, pp. 172–173. The Zwingli references are from Huldrych Zwingli's *Sämtliche Werke* (Berlin-Zurich: C. A. Schwetschke and Sohn 1905), Vol. 2. Page and line numbers are indicated. Cf. Second Helvetic Confession, chapter 4.

8. *LCC*, XX: 112 (I, xi, 12).

9. *LCC*, XX: 105–107 (I, xi, 5–7); Karl Barth, *Church Dogmatics*, 4/2 p. 103.

10. *LCC*, XX: 112 (I, xi, 12).

11. *LCC*, XX: 464–503 (II, xii–xv).

12. W. A. Visser 't Hooft, *Rembrandt and the Gospel* (London: SCM Press, 1957), pp. 60–70. Visser 't Hooft carefully outlines Rembrandt's relation to the Reformed community. Cf. Jakob Rosenberg, *Rembrandt: Life and Work*, 3rd ed. (London: Phaidon, 1968), pp. 179 ff.

13. Jakob Rosenberg, *op. cit.*, p. 28.

14. *Ibid.*, p. 169.

15. Visser 't Hooft, *op. cit.*, p. 116.

16. Dutch artists Pieter Brueghel the Elder (1525–1569) and Vermeer of Delft (1632–1675), as well as Rembrandt, rejoiced in ordinary human beings and ordinary things. See for example Vermeer's "The Cook" (Rijks Museum). This capacity to appreciate the ordinary owes much to the Bible and the Christian tradition. Erich Auerbach points out that in the story of Christ there is a "ruthless mixture of everyday reality and the highest and most sublime tragedy." (p. 490) "It [the story of Christ] takes place entirely among everyday men and women of the common people; anything of the sort could be thought of in antique terms only as farce or comedy." (p. 37) *Mimesis: the Representation of Reality in Western Literature* (Garden City: Doubleday & Co., Inc., 1957). See also Karl Holl, *The Cultural Significance of the Reformation,* trans. Karl and Barbara Hertz and John H. Lichtblau (New York: Meridian Books, Inc., 1959), pp. 148–149.

17. This drama of faith was first called to the attention of the author by Professor Roland Frye of the University of Pennsylvania.

18. Paul Tillich, "The World Situation," in Henry P. van Dusen, ed., *The Christian Answer* (New York: Charles Scribner's Sons, 1945), p. 10.

19. Léon Wencelius, *Calvin et Rembrandt* (Paris: Société d' Édition "Les Belles Lettres," n.d.), pp. 85–86.

20. Page 34.

21. Jacques Pannier, *Calvin Écrivain, Sa place et son rôle dans l'Histoire de la Langue et de la Littérature française* (Paris: Librairie Fischbacher, 1930).

22. Doumergue, *Jean Calvin,* Vol. II: *Les premiers essais,* p. 509.

23. Paul Henry, *The Life and Times of John Calvin,* trans. Henry Stebbing, vol. 1 (New York: Robert Carter & Brothers, 1851), p. 241.

*Opera Selecta,* 1:496–498.

24. Léon Wencelius, *L'esthetique de Calvin* (Paris: Société d'Edition "Les Belles Lettres," n.d.), p. 374.

25. On Milton see Roland Mushat Frye, *God, Man, and Satan: Patterns of Christian Life and Thought in "Paradise Lost," "Pilgrim's Progress," and the Great Theologians* (Princeton: Princeton University Press, 1960); Gordon Rupp, *Six Makers of English Religion 1500–1700* (London: Hodder and Stoughton, 1957); Roland H. Bainton, *The Travail of Religious Liberty: Nine Biographical Studies* (Philadelphia: Westminster Press, 1951).

On Bunyan see Frye, *op. cit.;* Rupp, *op. cit.* Roger Sharrock, *John Bunyan* (London: Hutchinson's University Library, 1954).

26. Joseph Moody McDill, *Milton and the Pattern of Calvinism* (Folcroft, Pa.: Folcroft Press, 1969).

27. On parabolic theology see Sallie TeSelle, *Speaking in Parables: A Study in Metaphor and Theology* (Philadelphia: Fortress Press, 1975).

28. Cf. Erwin Panofsky, "Comments on Art and Reformation."

29. From ARCHITECTURE IN WORSHIP, by André Biéler. The Westminster Press. ©Translation, 1965, Oliver and Boyd Ltd. Used by permission. P. 57.

Cf. comment on importance of symbolism for the Reformed community in Donald J. Bruggink and Carl Droppers, *Christ and Architecture: Building Presbyterian/Reformed Churches* (Grand Rapids: Eerdmans, 1965), p. 82.

30. *LCC,* XXI:893 (III, xx, 30).

31. Biéler, *op. cit.,* p. 62.

32. *Ibid.*

33. *Ibid.*

34. *Ibid.*, p. 92. Cf. Leith, *Creeds of the Churches,* Second Helvetic Confession, Chapters 22, 28, pp. 176–179.

35. Andrew Landale Drummond, *The Church Architecture of Protestantism*

(Edinburgh: T. & T. Clark, 1934), p. 33. Cf. André Biéler, *op. cit.*, p. 64.

36. Biéler, *op. cit.*, p. 64.

37. Drummond, *op. cit.*, p. 33.

38. These churches from the perspective of André Biéler and in contrast to the circular design have a tendency to become "lecture halls."

39. "Theology and Architecture" in *Architectural Forum* (December 1955), p. 134.

Cf. Patrils Reuterswärd, "What Color Is Divine Light" in *Light*, ed. by Thomas B. Hess and John Ashbery (New York: Collier, 1969), pp. 101–124.

40. Garside, *Zwingli and the Arts*, p. 182.

41. *Ibid.*, p. 47.

42. "Preface to the *Psalter* (1543)"; *Opera Selecta*, 2:17.

43. Doumergue, "Music in the Work of Calvin."

44. Percy A. Scholes, *The Puritans and Music in England and New England* (London: Oxford University Press, 1934), pp. 332–344.

45. Doumergue, *Jean Calvin*, Vol. 2: *Les premiers essais*, pp. 519–522.

46. J. W. Allen, *A History of Political Thought in the Sixteenth Century*, 2nd ed. (London: Methuen & Co., Ltd, 1941), p. 49.

47. Robert M. Kingdon and Robert D. Linder, eds., *Calvin and Calvinism, Sources of Democracy?* (Lexington: D. C. Heath & Co., 1970). An excellent anthology with competent introductions.

Cf. George L. Hunt, ed., *Calvinism and the Political Order* (Philadelphia: Westminster Press, 1965).

48. Kingdon and Linder, *op. cit.*, p. 25.

49. *LCC*, XXI:1493–94 (IV, xx, 8).

50. *LCC*, XXI:1509 (IV, xx, 22).

51. *LCC*, XXI:1511 (IV, xx, 23).

52. *LCC*, XXI:1518 (IV, xx, 31).

53. Sermon on Daniel, *CR* XLI:415–416.

54. John Calvin, *Commentaries on the Book of the Prophet Daniel*, ed. and trans. by Thomas Myers (Grand Rapids: Eerdmans, 1948), vol. 1; 6:22, pp. 378–382.

55. For an account of Calvin's struggle for a free church in Geneva, see a biography, especially the old but excellent work, Williston Walker, *John Calvin: The Organiser of Reformed Protestantism 1509–1564* (New York: G. P. Putnam's Sons, 1906).

Edwin Sandys (1561–1629), who found in Geneva the model of political order and who greatly influenced the establishment of democratic institutions in Virginia, is a good illustration of Calvinist influence on American institutions. See George MacLaren Brydon, *Virginia's Mother Church and the Political Conditions Under Which It Grew* (Richmond: Virginia Historical Society, 1947–52), pp. 71–73.

56. For an excellent review, see "The Political Theories of Calvinists Before the Puritan Exodus to America," in *Collected Papers of Herbert D. Foster* (Privately Printed, 1929), pp. 77–105.

57. *John Knox's History of the Reformation in Scotland*, ed. William Croft Dickinson, vol. 2 (New York: Philosophical Library, 1950), p. 83.

Hugh Watt, *John Knox in Controversy* (London: Thomas Nelson and Sons, Ltd., 1950), pp. 69–106.

Cf. Duncan Shaw, ed. *John Knox, A Quartercentenary Reappraisal* (Edinburgh: St. Andrew Press, 1975), p. 27.

58. W. K. Jordan, *The Development of Religious Toleration in England* (Cambridge: Harvard University Press, 1932–1940).

59. Reinhold Niebuhr, *The Children of Light and the Children of Darkness: A Vindication of Democracy and a Critique of Its Traditional Defence* (New York: Charles Scribner's Sons, 1944), p. xi.

## 254 AN INTRODUCTION TO THE REFORMED TRADITION

60. For a review of interaction of theology and politics especially in the nineteenth century, see James Hastings Nichols, *Democracy and the Churches* (Philadelphia: Westminster Press, 1951).

61. Max Weber, *The Protestant Ethic and the Spirit of Capitalism,* trans. Talcott Parsons (New York: Charles Scribner's Sons, 1958).

62. For a good review of the debate see *Protestantism and Capitalism: The Weber Thesis and Its Critics,* ed. Robert W. Green (Boston: D.C. Heath and Company, 1959).

André Biéler, *La pensée économique et sociale de Calvin* (Geneva: Librairie de l'Université, 1959), pp. 477–514.

David Little, *Religion, Order, and Law: A Study in Pre-Revolutionary England* (New York: Harper & Row, 1969).

Gerhard E. Lenski, *The Religious Factor: a Sociological Study of Religion's Impact on Politics, Economics, and Family Life* (Garden City, N. Y.: Doubleday, 1961).

63. For Calvin's emphasis upon work, see *CR* 23:72; 28:189, 379, 380; 52:163, typical of many references to work.

64. Richard J. Hooker, ed., *The Carolina Backcountry on the Eve of the Revolution: The Journal and Other Writings of Charles Woodmason, Anglican Itinerant* (Chapel Hill: Published for Institute of Early American History and Culture at Williamsburg, Va. by University of North, Carolina Press, 1953).

65. For Presbyterian attitudes toward slavery, see *The Collected Writings of James Henley Thornwell,* ed. John B. Adger and John L. Girardeau, vol. IV (Richmond, Va.: Presbyterian Committee of Publications, 1873), pp. 379–436.

Robert Manson Myers, ed. *Children of Pride: A True Story of Georgia & the Civil War* (New Haven: Yale University Press, 1972).

Maurice W. Armstrong, Lefferts A. Loetscher, and Charles A. Anderson, *The Presbyterian Enterprise: Sources of American Presbyterian History* (Philadelphia: Westminster Press, 1956), pp. 199–221.

Also see the recent study by Eugene D. Genovese, *Roll, Jordan, Roll: The World the Slaves Made* (New York: Pantheon Books, 1974).

66. Karl Holl, *The Cultural Significance of the Reformation,* pp. 109–110. Used by permission of The New American Library, Inc.

67. Robert Mather, "New England's First Fruits" in *The American Puritans: Their Prose and Poetry,* ed. Perry Miller (Garden City: Doubleday & Co., Inc., 1956), p. 323.

68. Donald G. Tewksbury, *The Founding of American Colleges and Universities Before the Civil War* (New York: Bureau of Publications, Columbia University, 1932), p. 90.

69. Alfred North Whitehead, *Science and the Modern World* (New York: Mentor Books, 1953), p. 13.

R. Hooykass, *Religion and the Rise of Modern Science* (Edinburgh: Scottish Academic Press, 1972), pp. 9–26.

70. John Calvin, *Commentaries on The First Book of Moses Called Genesis,* John King, trans. and ed. (Grand Rapids: Eerdmans, 1948), vol. 1, 1:16, pp. 86–87. Cf. A. Lecerf, "De l'impulsion donnée par le Calvinisme a l'étude des sciences physiques et naturelles," *Bulletin de la Société de l'Histoire du Protestantisme français,* LXXXIV (1935): 192–201.

Hooykass, pp. 105 ff.

Edward Rosen, "Calvin's Attitude toward Copernicus," *Journal of the History of Ideas* 21 (July-Sept. 1960), 431–41.

Edward Rosen, "A Reply to Dr. Ratner: Calvin's Attitude toward Copernicus," *Journal of the History of Ideas* 22 (July-Sept. 1961): 386–88.

John Dillenberger, *Protestant Thought and Natural Science* (Garden City: Doubleday & Co., Inc., 1960), pp. 28 ff.
71. Alfred Rupert Hall, *The Scientific Revolution 1500–1800* (Boston: The Beacon Press, 1956), pp. 192–193.
Dillenberger, *op. cit.,* pp. 104 ff.
Hooykass, *op. cit.,* pp. 135 ff.
For a more modest estimate of the Puritan contribution to science, see Richard L. Greaves, "Puritanism and Science: The Anatomy of a Controversy," *Journal of the History of Ideas,* vol. 30, no. 3 (July-Sept. 1969), pp. 345–368.

## VIII. PROSPECTS

1. Alfred North Whitehead, *Adventures of Ideas* (New York: New American Library, 1955), p. 99.
2. Alvin Toffler, *Future Shock* (New York: Bantam Books, 1971), pp. 19 ff.
3. Leslie Dewart, *The Future of Belief: Theism in a World Come of Age* (New York: Herder & Herder, 1966), pp. 7 ff.
4. Barth, *Church Dogmatics,* 1, 1, 36.
5. *Ibid.,* 1, 1, 29.
6. Theodore Roszak, *The Making of a Counter Culture* (Garden City: Doubleday & Co., 1969) pp. 205 ff.
7. Peter Berger, *Pyramids of Sacrifice* (New York: Basic Books, Inc., 1974), pp. 22–23.
Peter Berger et al. *The Homeless Mind; Modernization and Consciousness* (New York: Random House, 1973), pp. 201 ff. Jacques Ellul, *The New Demons* (New York: Seabury, 1975), p. 219.
8. For an excellent discussion of interaction of community and doctrine see Albert C. Outler, *The Christian Tradition and the Unity We Seek,* especially chapter three.
9. Reinhold Niebuhr, "Faith as the Sense of Meaning in Human Existence," *Faith and Politics,* ed. Ronald H. Stone (New York: George Braziller, 1968), pp. 3 ff.
10. Cf. David H. Kelsey, *The Uses of Scripture in Recent Theology* (Philadelphia: Fortress Press, 1975), pp. 183 ff.
11. *LCC,* XX:74–81 (I, vii).
12. *LCC,* XX:78–80 (I, vii, 4–5).
13. Cf. Herbert Marshall McLuhan, *Understanding Media: The Extensions of Man* (New York: McGraw Hill, 1964), pp. 77–88.
14. Mario Andrew Pei, *The Story of Language,* rev. ed. (Philadelphia: J. B. Lippincott, 1965), pp. 199–291.
Rollo May, *Man's Search for Himself* (New York: W. W. Norton & Co., 1953), pp. 64 ff.
15. E.g., Eastern Orthodoxy. Father Florovsky once chided the writer for making literacy an aid to Christian piety.
16. Theodore Wedel, "Is Preaching Outmoded?" in *Religion in Life* vol. 24, no. 4 (Autumn 1965), pp. 534–547.
Cf. Don Browning, "Should Preaching Be Abolished?" in *Encounter* (Winter 1974), pp. 1–7.
17. In the recent exodus of congregations from the Presbyterian Church, U. S., the leadership of the ministers was almost always a key factor, and preaching was an important element in this leadership. More significantly, in this writer's experience and observation, responsible preaching has always shaped a congregation's life, especially over a period of years.
18. Cf. Charles C. West, *Communism and the Theologians: Study of an Encounter* (Philadelphia: Westminster Press, 1958), pp. 282–283.

19. Berger et al., *The Homeless Mind, Modernization and Consciousness,* pp. 79 ff.

20. Daniel Yankelovich, "The New Naturalism," *Saturday Review* (April 1, 1972), 32–37.

# Subject Index

# Name Index

Abraham, 26, 27, 223, 224
Adger, John B., 173
Ahlstrom, Sydney, 45
d'Albret, Jeanne, 22, 185, 224
Alexander, Archibald, 229
Althusius, 216
Ames, William, 128, 138
Amos, 26
Amyraut, 106, 119, 140
Anselm, 21
Anslo, Cornelius Claesz, 203
Aquinas, Thomas, 21, 109
d'Armagnac, Cardinal, 22
Arminius, Jacob, 38, 106, 119, 140
Athanasius, 21
Augustine, 21, 26, 89, 110, 174, 224, 231
Aycock, Martha, 9

Baillie, Donald, 141
Baillie, John, 141
Bainton, Roland, 8, 22, 77, 116
Baird, Charles, 194
Barth, Karl, 8, 9, 21–22, 27, 72, 84, 90, 96, 106, 111, 112, 117, 125, 126, 131–132, 139, 143, 149, 151, 169–171, 177–180, 209, 222
Barth, Petrus, 172
Baum, Guilelmus, 172
Bavinck, Herman, 138
Baxter, Richard, 218
Benoit, Jean-Daniel, 85
Benson, Louis, 194
Berdyaev, Nicholas, 72
Berkhof, Louis, 138
Berkouwer, Gerrit Cornelis, 138
Beza, Theodore, 36, 38, 140, 167, 185, 205, 216
Biéler, André, 208
Blaikie, William Garden, 54
Blake, Eugene Carson, 55
Bocskay, Stephen, 40

Bodin, Jean, 77
Bonhoeffer, Dietrich, 126
Bonaventura, 21
Bouquin, Pierre, 39
Bourgeois, Louis, 36, 185
Brainerd, David, 52
Bréhier, Émile, 19
de Brès, Guy, 38
Bright, John, 9, 27, 143
Briggs, Charles A., 143
de Brosse, Salomon, 209
Brown, William Adams, 130–131, 139
Browne, Robert, 168
Brunner, Emil, 9, 17, 84, 139, 169
Bucer, Martin, 39, 41, 140
Buchanan, George, 216
Bullinger, Henrich, 36, 83, 138
Bultmann, Rudolf, 126
Bunyan, John, 25, 206–207
Bushnell, Horace, 141

Calhoun, Robert L., 141
Calvin, John, 8, 20, 21, 24, 26, 34, 35, 36, 37, 38, 39, 40, 41, 51, 53, 54, 71, 72, 73, 74, 75, 76, 77, 78, 79, 80, 81, 82, 83, 84, 85, 86, 87, 96, 98–112, 114, 115, 116, 117, 127–128, 130, 138, 145, 146, 148, 150, 151, 152–155, 157, 158–160, 161, 162, 163, 164, 165–167, 170, 175–177, 180, 181–188, 189, 197, 199, 201–202, 205, 208, 210, 211, 212–217, 221, 224, 225, 226, 230
Cameron, James K., 172
Campbell, John McLeod, 141
Cappel, Louis, 119
Carey, William, 52
Cartwright, Thomas, 42
Casimer, John, 40
Cavert, Samuel McCrea, 55
Chandieu, 168
Chartier, Guillaume, 51
Cheyne, Alec C., 9